THE AMBITIONS OF

Understanding the World in Anc

This book explores the origins and growth of systematic inquiry in Greece, China and Mesopotamia. Professor Lloyd examines which factors stimulated or inhibited this development, and whose interests were served. Who set the agenda? What was the role of the state in sponsoring, supporting or blocking research in areas such as historiography, natural philosophy, medical research, astronomy, technology, pure and applied mathematics and the rise of technical terminology in all those fields? How was each of those fields defined and developed in different ancient societies? How did truly innovative thinkers persuade their own contemporaries to accept their work? Three of the main themes elaborated are, first, the different routes those developments took in China, Greece and Mesopotamia; second, the unexpected result of many research efforts; and third, the tensions between state control and individual innovation, and the different ways they were resolved – problems that remain in scientific research today.

G. E. R. LLOYD is Emeritus Professor of Ancient Historian and Science at the University of Cambridge, where he was also Master of Darwin College from 1989 to 2000. His previous books include *Adversaries and Authorities* (1996) and *Methods and Problems in Greek Science* (1991).

IDEAS IN CONTEXT

Edited by Quentin Skinner *(General Editor)*, Lorraine Daston,
Dorothy Ross and James Tully

The books in this series will discuss the emergence of intellectual traditions and of related new disciplines. The procedures, aims and vocabularies that were generated will be set in the context of the alternatives available within the contemporary frameworks of ideas and institutions. Through detailed studies of the evolution of such traditions, and their modification by different audiences, it is hoped that a new picture will form of the development of ideas in their concrete contexts. By this means, artificial distinctions between the history of philosophy, of the various sciences, of society and politics, and of literature may be seen to dissolve.

The series is published with the support of the Exxon Foundation.

A list of books in the series will be found at the end of the volume.

THE AMBITIONS OF CURIOSITY

Understanding the World in Ancient Greece and China

G. E. R. LLOYD

CAMBRIDGE UNIVERSITY PRESS

PUBLISHED BY THE PRESS SYNDICATE OF THE UNIVERSITY OF CAMBRIDGE
The Pitt Building, Trumpington Street, Cambridge, United Kingdom

CAMBRIDGE UNIVERSITY PRESS
The Edinburgh Building, Cambridge CB2 2RU, UK
40 West 20th Street, New York, NY 10011-4211, USA
477 Williamstown Road, Port Melbourne, VIC 3207, Australia
Ruiz de Alarcón 13, 28014 Madrid, Spain
Dock House, The Waterfront, Cape Town 8001, South Africa

http://www.cambridge.org

First published 2002

Printed in the United Kingdom at the University Press, Cambridge

Typeface Baskerville Monotype 11 / 12.5 pt   *System* LATEX 2$_\varepsilon$ [TB]

A catalogue record for this book is available from the British Library

Library of Congress Cataloguing in Publication data

Lloyd, G. E. R. (Geoffrey Ernest Richard), 1933–
The ambitions of curiosity: understanding the world in ancient
Greece and China / G. E. R. Lloyd.
p.   cm. (Ideas in context)
Includes bibliographical references and index.
ISBN 0 521 81542-8 – ISBN 0 521 89461-1 (pbk.)
1. Science, Ancient.   2. Science – Greece.   3. Science – China.
I. Title.   II. Series.
Q124.95. L58 2002
509.3 – dc21   2002025663

ISBN 0 521 81542 8 hardback
ISBN 0 521 89461 1 paperback

Contents

Figures and table

FIGURES

viii

TABLE

Preface

In the Michaelmas Term 2000 I had the honour to be invited to give the Isaiah Berlin lectures at Oxford. This was an assignment that any historian of ideas would find daunting, for all who met Berlin were in awe of the range of his learning, the sharpness of his wit, the elegance and panache of his writing. The experience of giving the lectures celebrating his memory was both intimidating and exhilarating. My very mixed audience was attentive and offered many perceptive comments, though I was a little taken aback, given Berlin's own famous quick-fire delivery, to be asked to speak more slowly.

This book is an expanded version of those lectures and remains close to their original plan. The unifying theme is provided not so much by a concept as by a problem, the growth of systematic inquiry. It obviously will not do to assume that every society has always valued research as in itself a good thing. So just how it gets to be initiated, in what subject areas, by whom, and why, with what aims and ambitions, pose important, if very general, issues that few scholars have had the courage or foolhardiness to broach. What did the investigators hope to find? Did they know what they were looking for? One of the themes of these studies is the openendedness of research and indeed its risky nature. The question this raises is how, when the results of inquiry challenged deep-seated convictions, they came nevertheless to be accepted, or at least not rejected out of hand, by those in authority – and others – in the societies in question. What indeed is the role of the state or other institutional authorities in sponsoring, sustaining or blocking research?

These are problems that remain directly relevant to the modern world. But to study the very beginnings of systematic inquiry we need to go back to antiquity, where indeed we can investigate them in a wide range of fields, not just in what corresponds to philosophy and science, but also in history, technology, language. Greece, China, Mesopotamia, Egypt,

India, all provide opportunities for our investigation, but I concentrate here mainly on the first two of these, a choice that reflects my own competence as much as it does the need to impose some limits on the scope of the discussion. Even so, with such a broad canvas, it is clearly impractical to attempt to cover more than a very small proportion of the ideas and data that can be brought to bear to illustrate the issues. So my aim is not to be comprehensive, but rather to propose arguments, leaving their further elaboration, documentation and testing for other occasions.

To present those arguments as crisply as possible, I have retained something of the style and format of the lectures. While I draw on materials from many different cultures and periods, I endeavour to provide, throughout, the basic information to be intelligible to the non-specialist. The ambitiousness of the project is apparent: in that respect it vies with the ambitions of those I make the object of my study. I am aware of the corresponding danger of seeming merely superficial. That is, however, an inescapable risk in any bid to open up new lines of comparative inquiry on topics of such general significance.

It is a pleasure to acknowledge the help I have received from many scholars who have given me the benefit of their views both on detailed points and on the overall strategy of my arguments. I would have made far more mistakes in my discussion of Mesopotamian astronomy but for the guidance of Francesca Rochberg and David Brown, not that they can be held responsible for how I have used their advice. My studies in Chinese science have everywhere benefited from my close collaboration with Nathan Sivin. We were putting the final touches to our joint work, *The Way and the Word*, as I was writing up these lectures, and its availability now allows me to refer to its more detailed discussion on many particular points. My Hellenist colleagues who have helped me are too numerous to mention, but among those who gave exceptionally useful criticisms and comments were, from my Oxford audience, Myles Burnyeat, David Charles, Sally Humphreys, Oswyn Murray. To these should be added others who gave generously of their advice on other occasions when I have presented one or more of these lectures, or material from them, at other universities, over the last two years, especially at Princeton, Madrid, Chicago and Beijing. I should like to express my thanks, both for their hospitality and for their constructive comments, to Willard Peterson, to Luis Vega, to Ian and Janel Mueller, to Liu Dun and to all their colleagues.

Finally it remains to record a special debt of gratitude to my hosts at Oxford, to the Committee in charge of the Berlin lectures for inviting me in the first place, to the Acting President of Corpus Christi College, Dr Christopher Taylor, and to all the Fellows of that College, for welcoming myself and my wife so warmly, and to Lady Berlin and to all those who made our stay such an enjoyable one.

Notes on editions

CHINESE

With some exceptions to be mentioned, ancient Chinese texts are cited according to standard editions, for example those of the Harvard-Yenching Institute series (HY) or the University of Hong Kong Institute of Chinese Studies series (ICS).

Chunqiu fanlu (春秋繁露) in the edition of Lai Yanyuan, Taibei, 1984.
Daodejing (道德經) in the ICS edition (Philosophical Works 24) 1996.
Erya (爾雅) in the ICS edition (Classical Works 16) 1995.
Guanzi (管子) in the Zhao Yongxian edition, reprinted in the *Sibu beiyao* series, Shanghai, 1936.
Hanfeizi (韓非子) in the edition of Chen Qiyou, Shanghai, 1958.
Hanshu (漢書) in the edition of Yan Shigu, *Zhonghua shuju*, Beijing, 1962, cited by *juan*, page and where necessary column number.
Hou Hanshu (後漢書) in the *Zhonghua shuju* edition, Beijing, 1965.
Huainanzi (淮南子) in the edition of Liu Wendian, Shanghai, 1923.
Huangdi neijing (黃帝內經). The *lingshu* (靈樞) and *suwen* (素問) recensions according to the edition of Ren Yingqiu, Beijing, 1986.
Jiuzhang suanshu (九章算書) in the edition of Qian Baocong, *suanjing shishu*, Beijing, 1963, cited by page number.
Liji (禮記) in the ICS edition (1992).
Lüshi chunqiu (呂氏春秋) in the edition of Chen Qiyou, Shanghai, 1984, cited by *juan* and *pian* number, followed by the page where necessary.
Lunheng (論衡) in the edition of Liu Pansui, Beijing, 1957.
Lunyu (論語) in the ICS edition (Classical Works 14) 1995.
Mengzi (Mencius) (孟子) in the HY series, Supplement 17, Beijing, 1941.
Mozi (墨子) in the edition of Zhang Chunyi, 1931.
Shiji (史記) in the *Zhonghua shuju* edition, Beijing, 1959, cited by *juan*, page and where necessary column number.

Shijing (詩經) in the ICS edition (Classical Works 10) 1995.

Sun Bin (孫臏) in the edition and translation in Lau and Ames (*Sun Pin: The Art of Warfare*) New York, 1996.

Sunzi (孫子) in the edition and translation in Ames (*Sun -tzu: The Art of Warfare*) New York, 1993.

Xunzi (荀子) in the HY series, Supplement 22, Beijing, 1950, cited by *pian* and line number.

Yantielun (鹽鐵論) in the ICS edition (Philosophical Works 14) 1994.

Yijing (易經) in the ICS edition (Classical Works 8) 1995.

Zhoubi suanjing (周髀算經) in the edition of Qian Baocong, *Suanjing shishu*, Beijing, 1963, cited by page number.

Zhouli (周禮) in the ICS edition (Classical Works 4) 1993.

Zhuangzi (莊子) in the HY series, Supplement 20, Beijing, 1947.

Zuozhuan (左傳) in the edition by Yang Bojun, 4 vols., Beijing, 1981, cited by Duke, year and where necessary page number.

GREEK AND LATIN

I cite the major Greek and Latin authors by standard editions, for example, the fragments of the Presocratic philosophers according to the edition of H. Diels, revised by W. Kranz, *Die Fragmente der Vorsokratiker*, 6th edn, Berlin, 1952, the works of Plato according to Burnet's Oxford text, the treatises of Aristotle according to Bekker's Berlin edition. The works of Euclid are cited by the edition of J. L. Heiberg *et al.*, revised by E. S. Stamatis, those of Archimedes by Heiberg's edition, revised by Stamatis (referred to as HS with the volume number). Ptolemy's *Syntaxis* is cited by the edition of J. L. Heiberg, his *Tetrabiblos* by that of Hübner, and his *Harmonics* by the edition of I. Düring (Göteborg, 1930).

Greek and Latin medical texts are cited, for preference, according to the *Corpus Medicorum Graecorum* and *Corpus Medicorum Latinorum* editions (referred to as *CMG* and *CML* respectively). For Hippocratic treatises not included in *CMG* I use E. Littré, *Oeuvres complètes d'Hippocrate*, 10 vols., Paris, 1839–61, cited as L followed by the volume number and page. For Galen's works not included in *CMG*, I use the Teubner editions (Helmreich, Marquardt and others) or failing them, the edition of C. G. Kühn, Leipzig 1821–33, cited as K followed by the volume number and page.

Abbreviations for Greek works are those in the *Greek-English Lexicon* of H. G. Liddell and R. Scott, revised by H. S. Jones, with Supplement (Oxford, 1968). Thus Simplicius, *In Ph.*, refers to Simplicius' work

In Aristotelem Physica Commentaria, ed. H. Diels (*Commentaria in Aristotelem Graeca*, vols. IX and X), Berlin, 1882–95.

MODERN

All modern works are cited by author's name and year of publication. Full details are to be found in the bibliography on pp. 154–69.

With the exception of 'Confucius' and 'Mencius', all Chinese names and words are transliterated according to the Pinyin convention. This is done throughout, including in the quotations from authors who use other systems.

CHAPTER ONE

Histories, annals, myths

Aristotle said that all humans naturally desire knowledge.[1] But not all humans seem to register any particularly urgent need to expand knowledge or to test it, being often quite content, rather, with what passes as received wisdom or with what they are told to believe. Certainly not all have the same explicit or implicit ideas about what counts as knowledge and why, by what criteria, nor as to how to set about increasing it, if indeed they have the ambition to do so.

My target, in this book, is, precisely, what happened when individuals or groups came to have some such ambition, what factors then stimulated or inhibited systematic inquiry.[2] That is to formulate the question in very general terms, but there are, I believe, advantages in focussing on systematic inquiry as such, whatever the fields inquired into and with whatever success. We might be tempted to think of the fields in question as history, or natural philosophy, or medical research, or astronomy or astrology or technology or pure or applied mathematics.[3] But the premature use of those categories of ours is liable to prejudice *our* inquiry. The original investigators did not have *those* categories when they started out, nor even, often, when they finished. Instead of judging their inquiries from the point of view of where we might think they should be headed – 'science', for instance, in a word – we should assess them in the light of their original aims, ambitions, needs, in the contexts of the problems as they saw them.

The undertaking of systematic inquiry reflects one or more very basic human desires (Aristotle was right, for sure, thus far), to understand, to foresee, to explain, to control, the world, or other people. It also

[1] Aristotle, *Metaphysics* 980a21.
[2] I attempt no definition of what I mean by 'systematic', but what I have in mind will become clear as we proceed.
[3] This list is, of course, far from exhaustive: anthropology, psychology, geography are among other modern categories that have investigable equivalents in ancient societies.

requires a particular aim or concern with particular questions. But what do those concerns relate to? Whose interests are served? Who is charged with the investigating, and under what conditions, with what degrees of freedom or constraint? Who sets the agenda, and with what expectations concerning its implementation?

To answer those questions takes one to central issues to do with the values and belief systems of the societies or groups concerned. If inquiry is a response to a particular set of concerns, how far does it serve merely to confirm the positions of those who set the agenda? Under what conditions, and within what limits, can it lead to assumptions being revised? Inquiry may indeed be undertaken in order to legitimate the *status quo*. But the sponsorship of inquiry carries with it an element of risk, at least of unpredictability, insofar as its findings are not known in advance of the inquiry itself being conducted. One of the recurrent themes of these studies will be the unexpected nature of the results of investigations.

A second recurrent theme relates to the tension between what we may take as universal human cognitive ambitions (to understand, explain and so on) and their society-specific manifestations. The focus of my inquiry is on ancient civilisations, for that is where we can best study the inauguration of systematic inquiries. Although it is clearly beyond any single individual's competence to deal with the entire gamut of ancient societies – and for my part I shall concentrate here on Greece and China and to a lesser extent Mesopotamia – I would still insist on the need for a comparative approach, and that for two related reasons. First we need to be careful not to assume that the experience of any one ancient society provides the pattern for them all, let alone that there was any inevitability about the way in which the developments *must* have occurred. Secondly in order, precisely, to identify which features are general, which society-specific.

Among the questions I shall raise are: what techniques of prediction were developed, with what aims in view and with what results? How and in what respects were numbers seen as the key to understanding phenomena and systems accordingly elaborated in order to explore such a possibility? How far was systematic inquiry directed to the development of devices of practical utility, and stimulated by a sense of their desirability? To what extent did inquiry depend on developments in language – on the construction of a technical vocabulary – and lead in its turn to self-conscious reflections on language use? My final chapter will take stock of the different types of institutional framework within which systematic inquiry could and did develop, and the effects of those institutions on the investigators concerned and on the nature of the work they did.

But to start our inquiry into inquiry, where better to begin than with history itself, both in the modern sense of historiography, and in the earlier, more general one, of research, still traceable in our term 'natural history'? Evidently in relation to ancient civilisations we cannot assume there will be a category that corresponds to historiography as such. In practice, as we shall see, the relationship between what we might call historical writings and other disciplines, in Greece and China, exhibits certain differences that have an important bearing on what those writings were for.

But we must first pay attention to the even greater variety of ways in which the past is represented and used as a resource for understanding the present or as a guide for future action. It may or may not be the case that the past is thought of as a seamless whole, continuous with the present. Was past time like the present, inhabited by people like us? Or rather a time of gods or heroes, or in other ways importantly different from today's time? Does time, in any case, always run in the same direction? Many societies have contemplated reversals of time, or cycles that repeat themselves in general or even in every particular, as is reported for Eudemus in Greece, according to Simplicius (*In Ph.* 732.26). In India the sense of the immensity of the Kalpa cycle serves to underline the illusory nature of the present.[4] In many societies the calendar is divided into stretches of sacred and profane time that are experienced as qualitatively different.[5]

Whatever the perception of the flow of time may be, what the past is used for, and the ways in which it is recorded and accessed, may differ profoundly. Whatever myths may say about distant times, they are likely to have messages also for present conduct, laying down rules, explicitly or implicitly, about how things are and must be, and about the dire consequences of deviant behaviour. Those rules themselves, and the myths that convey them, may not be thought to have origins: or they may be thought to have come into being with the present dispensation, the way the world is now. But that does not diminish, but enhances, their authority, their power to express values, constrain, justify, legitimate.[6] Of course the relationship between myth and ritual, the role of myth as

[4] See Thapar 1996.

[5] Leach 1961 provides a good summary of this theme, elaborated earlier by Durkheim among others. The theme of the contrast between the 'time of the gods' and the 'time of humans' in Greek thought was the subject of a classic study by Vidal-Naquet, 1986 ch. 2 (the original French publication dates from 1960).

[6] Jewish accounts of the past, so it has been argued, provide a striking example of the use of such material to legitimate, in this case, the status of the Jews as the elect of god. See, for example, Murray 2000, and cf. Cartledge 1995 on the Greeks.

charter, the very question of how the category of myth is to be defined and whether there *is* a valid category to be used as a tool of analysis, are all hotly debated issues in modern scholarship. But it is enough, for my purposes, that sacred tales about the past often act as guides and constraints for present behaviour and understanding. The potential for change, once the past is scrutinised and researched, is obvious, although that scrutiny may merely serve to confirm what had been believed all along.

How those stories are transmitted raises, to be sure, a further fundamental issue. Once committed to a form of writing, their status changes, though that may be in a variety of far from straightforward ways. We do not need to agree with all of Goody's theses from his seminal work on literacy and orality to appreciate the force of some of the basic points that have emerged.[7] First it is clear that the contrast between literacy and orality is far from being an all-or-nothing affair. Some forms of graphic representation are found in societies that have no standard script. Degrees of fluency in reading and writing exhibit, importantly, wide fluctuations.

Secondly, each oral performance of a myth is a *re*telling, a *re*creation, and that is significant for what counts as the *same* myth. The *Myth of the Bagre*, which Goody transcribed among the LoDagaa, is, according to the LoDagaa themselves, always the same: it never varies. Yet it does. Some of his later transcriptions even contain references to Goody himself, sitting in the background with his tape-recorder.[8]

Nor, thirdly, should we assume that once a written version of a myth exists, that will spell the immediate demise of any version that does not conform to it. The Japanese *Heike Monogatari* shows that that does not always happen, for even after it was written down, two traditions, one to be read, one for oral performance, coexisted for more than 150 years.[9]

That takes me to a fourth, fundamental, point, the question of the nature of the criticisms to which an account, once written, is subject. Clearly if the written version is deemed to be the canonical one, that allows the possibility of checking an oral performance that relies purely on memory. But, as Goody recognises, other modes of criticism, including of the substance of an oral performance, are well attested in oral cultures.[10] Moreover while the existence of written versions opens up one avenue

[7] Goody's own position has evolved: compare Goody and Watt 1962–3 with Goody 1977, 1986, 1987 and 1997. Among the more prominent other contributors to the debate have been Havelock 1963, Vansina 1965 and 1985, Scribner and Cole 1981, Gentili and Paioni 1985, Detienne 1988, Kullmann and Althoff 1993, Street 1997 and Bottéro, Herrenschmidt and Vernant 1996.
[8] See Goody 1972 and Goody and Gandah 1981.   [9] See Butler 1966.
[10] See, for example, Phillips 1981 on Sijobang.

for criticism, it may close others off. Jonathan Parry has urged this point against Goody in relation to the status achieved by *sacred* texts in certain societies.[11] Holy scripture may invite ruminative reflection, meditation, learned commentary, yet be anything but open to sceptical, critical evaluation.

The main topic for our analysis may now be broached. Both China and Greece produced in some abundance, from around the fifth century BCE onwards, what we may provisionally call historical records, accounts that set out and comment on past events. The questions for us are: how was such writing used? On what basis were these accounts compiled? Who did the compiling? By what criteria was their work assessed? My aim is to investigate how the past came to be perceived as an important area of research and how that related to other inquiries.

We may begin with China. While much remains disputed about the earliest beginnings, a clear sequence of development can be traced, through extant texts of the Warring States period (i.e. before the unification in 221), culminating in the work most would identify as the first sustained Chinese general history, namely the *Shiji*. This was started by Sima Tan in the second century BCE and largely brought to completion by 90 BCE by his son, Sima Qian, about whom more in due course. But the *Shiji* drew on, even if it went beyond, earlier models, notably the tradition of the writing of annals, best exemplified, in early extant texts, by the *Chunqiu*, the *Spring and Autumn Annals*, together with the commentaries on them, such as the *Zuozhuan*. The *Spring and Autumn Annals* covers the reigns of the twelve Dukes of the state of Lu, from 722 to 491 BCE, and was often ascribed to Confucius himself (traditionally dated to 551–479), indeed was so already by Mencius in the fourth century.[12] But we have to be careful, since it is entirely uncertain what text Mencius read. As for the *Zuozhuan*, whether its original form was as a commentary is unclear, as also is its date: the compilation as we now have it is more likely to date to the very end of the fourth century BCE rather than to any earlier period.[13]

---

[11] Parry 1985. The point that literacy may not liberate, but foreclose liberation, was already made by Lévi-Strauss (1973, p. 299: 'the primary function of written communication is to facilitate slavery').

[12] Mencius III B 9.

[13] The date of the *Zuozhuan* is disputed. See, for example, Egan 1977, A. Cheng 1993, Brooks 1994 and Sivin 1995b IV 3. The value of this text as a historical source for the period it covers between the late eighth and the mid-fourth centuries BCE is also a matter of controversy. Brooks and Brooks 1998, p. 8, take a highly sceptical line. Pines 1997 is more optimistic about it containing reliable reports of the events it records. See Lloyd and Sivin 2002, p. 305 .

Both these texts purport to contain the records of events. In the *Spring and Autumn Annals*, these are set out season by season (hence the name), though this is done in the barest outline, with no connecting narrative. Births, marriages, deaths, the accession of rulers, victories, defeats, droughts, famines, floods, eclipses, are duly noted, but while the fortunes of Kings and states are recorded, this is without explicit interpretative comment. The *Annals* are a celebration of past deeds, rescuing them from oblivion: but they also contain lessons for the present, even if we are left largely to make our own connections and to infer the reasons for prosperity or decline.

In the *Zuozhuan*, by contrast, events are woven into a continuous, vivid narrative, with graphic portrayals of the characters of the chief persons involved – loyal or untrustworthy, upright or corrupt, cautious or foolhardy – interspersed with pithy judgements, some ascribed to Confucius by name, others just to an unnamed 'gentleman' (*junzi*). The story is punctuated by the praise or blame of the main agents.

Yet when the *Zuozhuan* sets down what purport to be the conversations of those agents going back more than 240 years, strict historicity has pretty clearly been subordinated to the dramatic needs of the narrative. It is true that the role of scribes or historians (*dashi*), as represented in the text,[14] includes the duty to record events as they happened, however unpopular that might make them in the eyes of those in power. Thus in the account of the assassination of Duke Zhuang of Qi by his chief minister, Cui Shu, we are told that first one historian and then two of his brothers recorded that 'Cui Shu killed his ruler', only for all three to be put to death one after another.[15] Another brother eventually got the entry into the record (and indeed the remark about the killing corresponds to one we find in the *Spring and Autumn Annals*) and we are even told that there was someone else ready to come and make sure the entry was made. Clearly we are meant to be impressed by this example of the dedication of historians to the truth, even when this offended ministers. At the same time the falsification of records, precisely to suit those in positions of power, no doubt happened often enough.[16]

Moreover we cannot rule out the possibility that this very story owes its origin to the authors of the *Zuozhuan* inventing a suitably edifying

---

[14] On the original role of the *shi*[1] as chief ritualist in the period prior to the Warring States, see Cook 1995.

[15] Duke Xiang 25th Year, 1099: cf. Vandermeersch 1994, p. 105, Lewis 1999, p. 130.

[16] Huang Yi-long 2001, gives a detailed analysis both of cases where astronomical events are not recorded (because not politically or at least not symbolically acceptable) and – conversely – of others where phenomena are invented for the sake of the omens they convey.

framework for that entry in the *Spring and Autumn Annals*. However, once the veracity of a record becomes a question, we can see that an important step has been taken – *away* from an account of the past (whether oral or written) that merely serves the purposes of celebration or legitimation (let alone of entertainment), *towards* one that may indeed continue to serve those purposes but recognises some obligation to *accuracy* and indeed derives its power from its ability to offer some justification for the claim to deliver that.

Sima Qian's project undoubtedly represents a far more sustained and self-critical attempt at an accurate universal history, although the points should not be exaggerated. On the one hand, a critical attitude towards his sources, and to what others believed, is evident in many passages. He corrects other accounts on matters of fact, such as chronology or geography (e.g. on the Kunlun mountains and the source of the Yellow River, e.g. *Shiji* 123: 3179.5ff). He explicitly disclaims knowledge of very early periods – of the times of Shennong (the supposed founder of agriculture) and before[17] – and he acknowledges that he has to leave gaps in his chronological tables. On the positive side, he claims to have access to archives from the imperial palace, he frequently refers to his own extensive travels, and he cites inscriptions, edicts and memorials apparently verbatim,[18] even though he also remarks that, with the Qin especially, much had been destroyed – and not just in the notorious episode of the burning of the books, ordered by Li Si, in 213 BCE.[19]

On the other hand, he starts his account with at least a token reference to the Yellow Emperor (supposed to have lived long before dynastic times) and like the *Zuozhuan*, the *Shiji* includes many quite imaginary conversations from early times. Sima Qian repeats such legends as that of Jian Di, the mother of Xie, the founder of the Yin, who became pregnant on swallowing an egg laid by a black bird. Again the Zhou dynasty is traced back to Jiang Yuan, who became pregnant after she had walked in the footsteps of a giant.[20]

Yet in that case, in the sequel, some undercutting occurs. The child Jiang Yuan bore was Hou Ji, Lord of the Millet, who in other early

---

[17] *Shiji* 129: 3253.5. He also expresses some doubts about stories about ghosts and spirits, though his denial of these is not unequivocal.

[18] For example, *Shiji* 130: 3296.1f. *Shiji* 121: 3115.5 claims that Confucius already used earlier records to create the *Spring and Autumn Annals*.

[19] There are two main, but by no means identical, accounts of this in *Shiji* 6: 255.6ff and 87: 2546.11ff, cf. also 15:686. This became a favourite theme with those who set out to blacken the reputation of the Qin and we may suspect some exaggeration in the accounts of how far Li Si's proposals were implemented.

[20] *Shiji* 3: 91.1ff, 4: 111.1ff.

Chinese texts is treated as a divine figure in charge of grain with a number of not merely human exploits to his name.[21] In Sima Qian's version, he was appointed by Emperor Shun to take charge of agriculture to save people from starvation, but his successes there are put down to his hard work and skill, rather than to any miraculous powers he might have. This gives a more naturalistic twist to the story, though Sima Qian does not go as far as some Greek writers might have done, in such circumstances, by explicitly dismissing traditional tales as absurd.[22] In particular, he does not bring to that task a concept that corresponds to *muthos* in the pejorative sense of fiction (not its only sense, as we shall see in a moment). Indeed he does not have a category that approximates to that at all, not even the term that was introduced into Chinese, but only much later, to cover some senses of 'myth', namely *shenhua*, literally spirit talk.

But the *Shiji* is not *just* history, nor its author just a historian, and both points are important. The work is organised in five main sections. First there are the 'Basic Annals', the accounts of the main dynasties from their foundation to their fall. These are followed, secondly, by chronological tables. Then comes a third section, a group of treatises, dealing with the calendar and astronomy, waterways, agriculture, music and ritual. The fourth section contains the memoirs of the 'hereditary families', but includes the biographies of Confucius and some other prominent figures. Finally a group of seventy chapters ('traditions', *zhuan*) contains biographies of statesmen, scholars and others, often paired or grouped together to illustrate particular types, and including chapters devoted to 'assassin retainers', 'money makers' and 'jesters'. This last section draws out certain general lessons from the fluctuating fortunes of historical figures otherwise anchored in the narrative account. But it is the third section, the treatises, above all, that incorporates material that goes far beyond what *we* normally expect in historical writing.

Yet the inclusion of that material is entirely appropriate, given first Sima Qian's own official position and secondly the overall aim of the work, where it will be helpful to compare it with other types of writing that are in no way historiographical but that share the *Shiji*'s ambition to convey information on matters of importance for government. First, as to the office that first Sima Tan and then Sima Qian himself occupied: Sima Qian refers to his father as *taishi gong*, and he quotes his father as claiming

---

[21] For example *Shijing* Mao 245, *Sheng min.*

[22] See, for example, below on Hecataeus. This is not to deny that Chinese historians repeatedly criticise one another. Already Ban Gu's evaluation of Sima Qian contains negative as well as positive points, *Hanshu* 62: 2737.1ff, 8, 2738.2ff, and hostile judgements recur in later commentators.

that members of their family had been *taishi* for generations.[23] On his father's death, he became *taishi ling*, or *taishi gong*, in turn, though that did not last. He fell out with the Emperor Wu Di because he defended the conduct of Li Ling, the officer who had commanded a disastrous expedition against the Xiong Nu, the barbarians often identified with the Hun. Sima Qian was arrested and would have been executed, but for the fact that he chose the humiliation of castration instead, precisely in order to be able to complete his father' work. Yet the story does not end there. Remarkably, according to the evidence in Ban Gu's history of the Han, the *Hanshu* (written about 80 CE), Sima Qian once again held office even after his disgrace, though not as *taishi*, but as *zhong shu ling* ('Secretariat Director', in Hucker's translation), in which role, indeed, according to Ban Gu again, he even won considerable honour.[24]

But what were the duties of the *taishi*? (For present purposes, I shall not go into the question of the differences between this and the other two titles, *taishi gong* and *taishi ling*, also used of Sima Qian[25].) English translations vary confusingly between Grand Scribe, Grand Historian or Grand Historiographer, Grand Astrologer, even Astronomer Royal.[26] When we encounter individuals with that title or, what seems the equivalent, *dashi*, whether in the *Shiji* or the *Zuozhuan*, we find them undertaking a variety of roles. These certainly included acting as the recorder of events (as we have seen in the story about Cui Shu's assassination that I mentioned from the *Zuozhuan*). But they were also consulted on ritual matters and they carried out divinations or interpreted those conducted by others and omens and prodigies generally.

It so happens that the predominant modes of divination associated with such figures in the *Zuozhuan* are those based on turtle shells and milfoil, rather than on the interpretation of astronomical signs or portents. However, there is no discontinuity between the divinatory and the astronomical interests of the *taishi*, as is apparent also from what we are told of Sima Tan's own training.[27] That included studies in astronomy as well as

[23] *Shiji* 130: 3295.2ff. Upholding the family's reputation was evidently an important motivation for Sima Qian's work. See Nylan 1998–9, who mounts a powerful case for the role of piety and of considerations of religious propriety in Sima Qian's thought.

[24] *Hanshu* 62: 2725.1. In contrast to Hucker 1985, p. 193, Bielenstein 1980, p. 212, glosses the *zhong shu ling* as 'Prefect of the Palace Writers'.

[25] All three expressions are used not just of Sima Tan but also of Sima Qian, even though the *gong* added in *taishi gong* is honorific, not the title of an office.

[26] See, for example, Needham 1959 xlv, cf. Watson 1961 (Grand Historian), Hulsewé 1993, Queen 1996, Hardy 1999 (Grand Astrologer), Dawson 1994 (Grand Historiographer), Nienhauser 1994a (Grand Scribe).

[27] *Shiji* 130: 3288.1ff.

in the classic divinatory text, the *Yijing* or *Book of Changes*. As a recorder of events, a *taishi* would certainly be concerned with the calendar (though not necessarily, to be sure, with calendar reform) and as a diviner he might well be called upon to interpret signs from heaven. When one of the later dynastic histories, the *Hou Hanshu* (25: 3572.1ff), comes to define the duties of the *taishi ling*, it specifies (1) being in charge of the calendar and ephemerides, (2) choosing auspicious dates and times for state business, sacrifices, funerals, weddings and so on, and (3) recording propitious and baneful omens as they occur.

Since a *taishi* would be expected to be learned in astronomy and ritual, the inclusion of treatises on those subjects in the *Shiji* makes good sense. But what about the essays on agriculture, or on aspects of music, such as acoustics, that go beyond ceremonial? Here we have to look further afield for precursors or models, to works such as the *Lüshi chunqiu*, and *Huainanzi*, compendia that offer comprehensive advice to rulers.

The first of these, the *Lüshi chunqiu*, was compiled under the direction of Lü Buwei (before 237 BCE), who was minister to the man who eventually became the first Qin Emperor, Qin Shi Huang Di, although Lü fell from grace before the unification of China was complete. The text he was responsible for compiling contains advice not just on how rulers, ministers and others should conduct themselves, but on music, medicine, agriculture and on the nature of the basic principles at work in the universe, in other words cosmology. Similarly from the second century BCE, the *Huainanzi* (put together under the auspices of Liu An, King of Huainan) set itself an ambitious programme encompassing pretty much the whole of useful knowledge.[28]

The *Shiji* itself does not, to be sure, have the pretensions to comprehensiveness that we find in such works. Yet the addition of the treatises was no

---

[28] A third such comprehensive treatise, the *Chunqiu fanlu*, should also be mentioned. This was attributed to Dong Zhongshu, a famous memorialist and statesman who lived from 179 to 104 BCE. It too, however, was a compilation, and how much of the text we have was composed by Dong Zhongshu himself is controversial, see Arbuckle 1989, 1991, Queen 1996. On the one hand Sima Qian evidently knew and admired Dong Zhongshu, including a short biography of him in which he praised his honesty and learning (*Shiji* 121: 3128.5 and 8). More importantly, in the final chapter of the *Shiji* 130: 3297.1ff, when Sima Qian defends his own practice as a historian, under hostile questioning from Hu Sui, he cites with approval Dong Zhongshu's interpretation of Confucius' role as that of 'giving instruction in the business of a ruler', where the best way of doing so, as Confucius himself is cited as saying, is by 'illustrating this through the depth and clarity of events'. (This is important testimony that Sima Qian represented himself as following Confucius' model in his own book, even though he enters a disclaimer, saying that he did not *make* a work as Confucius did, but merely *transmitted* a record of past affairs: 3299.1–3300.1.) On the other hand, neither of these chapters in the *Shiji* cites the *Chunqiu fanlu* as such, which is never mentioned explicitly in the *Shiji*, even though the commentators take as an allusion to it a remark at 14: 510.5, that Dong Zhongshu 'extended' the *Springs and Autumns*.

mere learned decoration. Rather, it was accepted that even quite detailed information on such subjects as music, astronomy, ritual, formed part of the technical knowledge that the Emperor, or his officials, would need to have and indeed put to use. Their mastery of such knowledge was, as we shall see, an important element in their claims to legitimacy. This needs some explanation. It was the Emperor's responsibility to ensure the welfare of 'all under heaven', in which context he was conceived as a mediator on whom good relations between heaven and earth depended. To carry out that task, he needed both correct ritual and accurate knowledge – of what was going on in the heavens, among other things, the kind of knowledge the astronomical treatises provided – and of course not just for him but also for his ministers. More on these issues later.

We come then to the key question of the modes of usefulness of the *Shiji* taken as a whole. What, to judge from this example, was Chinese 'historiography', if we can call it that, for? The answer depends on the balance between three points. First, although the *Shiji* was not directly commissioned by the Emperor (as the Emperor Ming was later to order Ban Gu to write the history of the later Han[29]), its authors held, as *taishi*, an official position, and depended on imperial approval for access to palace archives, for instance.

Secondly, the *Shiji* was certainly not *just* state propaganda. There is a clear contrast between it and the inscriptions that, from Qin Shi Huang Di onwards, Chinese Emperors (like some Persian Kings) put up in prominent positions, on their progress through their lands, to glorify their achievements.[30] Moreover Sima Qian continued his work, even after his disgrace. Whether indeed he then set out to incorporate more critical comments as tacit reproof of Wu Di himself is controversial.[31] On the one hand, encoded reprimands of rulers are a well-developed Chinese skill.[32] On the other, that was always a risky business, not least for someone who had fallen out with Wu Di once before.

The third point may, then, be the fundamental one. The usefulness of the work – to anyone from Wu Di down – and its claim to fame, were not just that it provided a record to memorialise the achievements of great men. Much depended also on its conveying valid information and

---

[29] See Hulsewé 1961, p. 38.

[30] There are several examples in 'Basic Annals' 6 with regard to the first Emperor, Qin Shi Huang Di, *Shiji* 6: 243, 245–7, 249–50, 261–2. Cf. Herrenschmidt 1996 for a discussion of Persian inscriptions celebrating the deeds of Kings, though in some cases these were placed in inaccessible spots where mere mortal observers could hardly inspect them.

[31] See Durrant 1995, Lewis 1999, pp. 308ff, and contrast Peterson 1994.

[32] See, for example, Schaberg 1997.

advice on the conduct of human affairs. The narrative is punctuated by remarks made by the *taishi gong* (whether this is Sima Tan or Sima Qian) that reflect on the lessons to be drawn from what happened, the morals of the stories, the misfortune that may overtake the corrupt, but also the unwary and the innocent. There is no trumpeted claim that the work is a 'possession for always'. But 'Basic Annals' 6 (278.9ff) cites Jia Yi quoting a folk-saying that 'the past remembered is a guide for the future': one should examine the ways of ruling in ancient times, test them in one's own generation and look for what fits. Again in 18 (878.4ff) while it is stated that the present is not necessarily like the past, the text adds: 'if one examines the ways in which men win position and favour and the reason why they lose these and incur disgrace, one will have the key to success and failure in one's own age'. Even though the text continues by implying that it is not necessary to consult the traditions of antiquity, they obviously provide a similar resource.

Moreover in the letter that, according to Ban Gu, *Hanshu* 62: 2735, he wrote to Ren An, Sima Qian talks about why he composed the *Shiji*. There he first compares himself with others, including Confucius and Lü Buwei, who chose 'writing about the past while thinking about the future' as a way out of the frustrations they felt in being thwarted in their attempts to influence affairs directly. So too, he says (2735.6ff), he gathered together old traditions and 'investigated the principles of success and failure and of rise and decline'. If later generations, he goes on, appreciate his work, then it will have been worthwhile.

Early Chinese historiography has often been compared with Chinese divination (which I shall be discussing in my next chapter), and the similarities and differences bear remarking, not least because such a text as the *Yijing*, the *Book of Changes*, offers not just a technique for prognostications, but a whole framework for the understanding of human experience. The *Shiji* itself does not aim to prophesy the outcome of events. It does not lay down rules for prognostication, even though in the astronomical treatises it associates particular heavenly phenomena with particular types of events, such as epidemics, wars, victories or defeats. Thus it says that a conjunction of the planet of Fire (Mars) with that of the Earth (Saturn) is a deadly omen for high officials, signifying famines and military defeats: whereas if *Fu Er* (a star in Taurus) twinkles, it means that there are those who spread malicious gossip and create confusion at the Emperor's side.[33]

---

[33] *Shiji* 27: 1320.10 and 1306.1, respectively.

But if we take a broader perspective, the *Shiji* certainly conveys lessons from which the wise ruler or statesman will be able to learn, inferring the likely consequences of types of behaviour or policies, and thereby putting himself in a better position to manage the present and anticipate the future.

From the point of view of officialdom, evidently, there was a double – bind – as the later dynastic histories were eventually abundantly to show. On the one hand, merely hagiographic historiography would give the ruler a warm glow, and was often promoted for propaganda purposes: yet the downside was that it offered little or nothing of value as advice. It just told the ruler what he wanted to hear, and though there are plenty of rulers who have wanted *just* that, some saw it as vacuous: and indeed the idea that advisers should stand up to their lords and where necessary admonish them, however unpopular it made them, is a well-developed theme in the stories surrounding Chinese philosophers from Mencius, if not Confucius himself, onwards.

Yet on the other hand, if the historian was allowed his head, then the more careful his research and the more independent his opinions, the greater the potential for subversion, the possible damage from the revelation of mistakes in policy or flaws in judgement. Conversely, from the side of the historian, the goal was to record, to evaluate and explain, to diagnose the reasons for success or failure. But the dire consequences of possible official disapproval always loomed.[34] The ongoing modern debates on Sima Qian's own position and attitudes towards Wu Di show how well he covered his tracks, leaving us his readers with exceptional hermeneutic space within which to evaluate *his* evaluations.

Greek *historie*, as is well known, covers far more than the writing of history, just as we found to be the case, though in a different way, with Chinese 'historiography' – so here too historiography had complex origins and certainly inherited no automatic god-given intellectual niche. First *historie* can be used either of a form of knowledge or of investigative research, and secondly, when it has the latter sense, it can be used of *any* inquiry – or of the knowledge or information it results in – with or without a specification with a *peri* clause, 'concerning', animals or plants, for instance, or nature as a whole. But those who practised one branch of inquiry did not necessarily engage in others – a point that we shall

---

[34] As Ban Gu's own fate testifies. He was denounced and imprisoned for 'refashioning' the history of the state, though he was later released and ordered by the Emperor Ming to turn to the history of the founding of the later Han. He was executed in 92 CE, effectively for siding with the wrong faction in the early years of the young Emperor He Di.

see is relevant to the ambitions of those who deal with subjects that are closer to historiography in our sense.

Two fundamental institutional points and one ideological one must be made at the outset. It is not as if any of the practices of *historie* in the classical period brought with it an official post, the equivalent to that of a *taishi*. Doctors, to be sure, were sometimes retained, for limited periods, as public physicians, but that was to serve as doctors, not to do research or practise *historie* in the sense of inquiry (though they might also do that).[35]

The second, related, institutional point concerns the audience Greek practitioners of *historie* were out to impress. Even though they sometimes worked at the courts of tyrants, Greek investigators made their reputations more by impressing their own peer group, or even the citizenbody as a whole, than by courting rulers (pale shadows, in any event, of Emperors responsible for the welfare of 'all under heaven').

It is true that certain changes occur in the Hellenistic period that affect the situation with regard to both those points. Alexander had historians (in our sense) in his entourage, and the execution of one of these, Callisthenes, serves to remind us that Greek historians could be just as much at risk as their Chinese counterparts – a point valid also for Rome. Again, as I shall be considering in the final chapter, the institutions set up by the Ptolemies at Alexandria, and imitated elsewhere, offered limited support for *historie* of various kinds.

Then the third, ideological, point concerns Greek attitudes towards the distant past. The Greeks of the classical period did not think of their own civilisation as having been instituted by Sage Kings many centuries ago. They had their heroes – Heracles, Theseus – and the period of the Trojan Wars was emblematic. But there was no equivalent to the notion of a mandate from heaven, passing down from one dynasty to another, over vast spans of time. When the Greeks encountered Egypt, some reacted to the evidence of past continuous culture there by registering their own, Greek, 'youth'.[36]

True, they had their stories of the founding of cities, the subject of local chronicles. But the earliest Greek historiography has no longstanding tradition of Annals to serve as models to imitate or to surpass. Local histories, the work of Ion of Chios, Charon of Lampsacus and the

---

35 *Historie* becomes an important methodological principle in the Empiricist school of Hellenistic medicine where it covers especially investigations into the textual records of earlier writers, that is, as we say, into the medical literature: see, for example, Frede 1987, ch. 13, Staden 2001, Sigurdarson 2002.

36 Plato, *Timaeus* 22b.

Atthidographers starting with Hellanicus, develop *along with*, and more or less at the same time as, the work of Hecataeus and Herodotus. If Herodotus had a model, some think that was epic, though the way the *Iliad* and *Odyssey* deal with wars, and foreign peoples, was very different from his.

Further back, when the Greeks picture a Golden Age, that is marked by discontinuities with the present. In Hesiod's myth of the metals, in the *Works and Days*, the ages are separate *gene*, the heroes, for example, the result of a distinct act of creation by Zeus, before he brought today's race of iron into being.[37] In the Age of Cronos, time is qualitatively different, flowing in reverse, so that old age precedes youth, the stuff, of course, of myth.

How far, indeed, we must now ask, was the key question, for early Greek historiography, indeed for *historie* as a whole, that of distancing itself from, precisely, myth? The scope for confusion, given the stretch not just of our own term myth, but that of the far from equivalent Greek *muthos*, is considerable. As Calame has recently insisted (1996, 1999), the early Greek historians, Hecataeus, Herodotus, Thucydides, were – none of them – intent on systematically rejecting myth in anything like the modern anthropologists' sense of sacred tales (whether one thinks of the 'Geste d'Asdiwal'[38] or of Hesiod's myth of the metals). Conversely, when Thucydides rejects other accounts of the 'archaeology' – of early Greek history – he criticises not just the poets, but also the *logographoi*, writers of *logoi*, where that term is not the antonym of *muthos* in the sense of fiction, but rather the synonym of *muthos* in the sense of story. Elsewhere too Thucydides has *logopoiein* in the sense of rumour-monger, while Herodotus uses *logopoios* to describe the kind of writer Hecataeus is.[39]

Yet however the point is expressed, the recurrent motif round which the self-image of early Greek historical writers was often articulated, relates to securing the truth. Hecataeus ridiculed the 'many tales' (*logoi*, indeed) of the Greeks as 'absurd': his own accounts, by contrast, so he claimed, are true (*alethes*, Fr 1). Herodotus, who is constantly evaluating the conflicting accounts of events he gathers from different informants, also uses the category of the absurd in dismissing the ideas of those who had given speculative accounts of world geography (IV 36, cf. 42) – where he may well have Hecataeus among others in mind.

The sequence continues in the next generation, with Thucydides. True, he does not name Herodotus: but he distances himself from those

---

[37] Hesiod, *Works and Days* 109–201, see Vernant 1983, ch. 1.
[38] Lévi-Strauss 1967.   [39] See Herodotus II 143, V 36, 125, Thucydides VI 38.

whose accounts are 'more suited to entertain the listener than to the truth' (1 21). Their stories are beyond verification or scrutiny (*anexelegktos*), having 'won their way to the mythical' (*muthodes*), where, in a collocation associated with unverifiability, that term clearly acquires pejorative undertones.

Such a motif is the counterpart, in historiography, of the common moves made in early Greek philosophy and medicine to downgrade other people's views as mere opinion, as speculation, even as rank superstition (*deisidaimonie*), and it corresponds to similar competitive pressures. Yet that way of putting it – using our categories, of historiography and philosophy at least – hardly does justice to the fluidity of the boundaries across which and within which polemic was conducted.

Herodotus, for instance, shares aetiological interests – on such topics as the causes of the Nile's flooding – with those we think of as Presocratic philosophers.[40] The Hippocratic treatise *On Airs Waters Places*, in its account of the Scythians, for example, shares some of Herodotus' ethnographic interests. The causes of the impotence of the Anarieis are discussed by both writers. Where the Hippocratic writer dismisses the idea that this has anything to do with the gods, Herodotus reports one story to that effect without rejecting it.[41] But another Hippocratic writer attacks a large part of the aetiological tradition itself. *On Ancient Medicine* criticises those who speculated about 'things in heaven and things under the earth', where his point, like Thucydides', is that such talk is beyond verification. A correct understanding of the physical constitution of humans is a *historie* that should be based, he claims, on medicine, a matter not of speculation, but of experience.[42] But as we see both from the disagreements between Herodotus and the author of *On Airs Waters Places*, and the criticisms of other ways of proceeding on the question of the human body in *On Ancient Medicine*, quite what counted as a genuine *historie* was far from agreed even by those who did agree that some such should be practised.

It is not the case, indeed, that all early Greek writers approved of *historie*, however they defined it. Heraclitus, who dismissed most of what most people believe as deluded, speaks with contempt of those who turned themselves into polymaths, naming Pythagoras as one who had done so

---

[40] See especially R. Thomas 2000. Similarly there are extensive geographical and ethnographic interests in such later historians as Diodorus, while in Strabo, conversely, historical material (in our sense) is incorporated into an otherwise largely geographical account.
[41] Herodotus I 105, cf. *On Airs Waters Places* ch. 22, *CMG* I 1 2, 72.10ff.
[42] *On Ancient Medicine* ch. 20, *CMG* I 1 2, 51.6ff, 51.17, cf. also ch. 1, 36.9ff, ch. 2, 37.1ff.

through *historie*. 'Pythagoras son of Mnesarchus practised inquiry (*historie*) most of all men': but 'much learning does not teach sense: otherwise it would have taught Hesiod and Pythagoras and again Xenophanes and Hecataeus'.[43] Claiming to practise 'inquiry' cut no ice with Heraclitus. Notoriously, Aristotle, who engages in *historia* on his own account, with regard to animals, the soul, nature in general, also uses that term in relation to the narrative account of events, in the *Poetics* (1451 b2–4), where he compares the 'historian' unfavourably with the poet on the grounds that the former deals with particulars and with what actually happened, the latter with the general and with what is likely to occur. In that passage, he says that even if Herodotus' text were versified, it would still be (a kind of) 'history'. But elsewhere, in *GA* 756b6ff, when discussing what Herodotus has to say about the fertilisation of fish in his Egyptian account, he downgrades him as a mere 'mythologist'.[44]

It was, to be sure, perfectly possible, as that text in the *Poetics* shows, to distinguish historiography from other types of *historia*, zoology, psychology, geography or whatever, viz. by their subject-matter. What they have in common is a search, indeed a research, for truth. That was the *claim*. But the challenging of boundaries, of methodologies, of results, all indicate the competitive pressures that existed. No early Greek historian had any prospect of employment. To make their way, they needed considerable skills of self-advertisement. Herodotus, we are told, read out parts of his work at Athens, if not also elsewhere.[45] But Thucydides says his work does not pander to the audience. His tactic to defeat the competition is to claim that his own work is no mere piece produced *for* a competition (*agonisma*, I 22).

There is, of course, more to the ambitions of early Greek historians than self-publicity. Herodotus' stated aims are both to commemorate the great achievements of the Greeks and the barbarians and to show how conflict arose between them. Thucydides disclaims knowledge of the distant past, but claims that his subject is the greatest war there has ever been. As for the usefulness of his work, the programmatic I 21–2 famously proclaims it as a 'possession for always'. It sets before the reader not just what happened, but what may be expected to happen again in

[43] Heraclitus Fr 40, cf. Frr 35 and 129.
[44] Aristotle denies that female fish could ever be fertilised by swallowing the milt of the male – citing his knowledge of the internal layout of the organs of reproduction. He did not need dissection to establish this point, for he could have learnt the essential facts from a fishmonger. Yet elsewhere dissection, explicitly defended in *On the Parts of Animals* I ch. 5, 645a26ff, for instance, was one of his most effective research methods in his inquiry into animals.
[45] See Marcellinus' *Life of Thucydides* in Jones and Powell 1900 I 54.

all probability – thereby neatly contradicting Aristotle *avant la lettre*. Just
as the plague at Athens is described so that it may be recognised should
it reappear (II 48), so similarly, in the moral and political domain, the
calamities that befell the Greeks as a result of *stasis*, strife, are those that
will always recur 'as long as human nature is the same' (III 82). Political
maladies, we may understand, follow as regular courses as physical ones –
turning the historian into the diagnostician, if not the therapist, of political ills. Of course Thucydides' lessons are general, not specific: nor
does he exactly propound causal theories for political change. But the
reader is meant to learn, at least in general terms, about the sources of
calamities, the strains of war, and the moral degradation that may follow
from internal strife.

The possible roles of historiography stretch from celebrating, commemorating, legitimating, to explaining, instructing, moralising, criticising,
admonishing. But the first three are appreciably easier than the last five,
in that the latter inevitably set up a tension between the historian and
his audience. On what basis, with what justification, does a historian
criticise? How can he expect his audience (whoever that is) to react when
he admonishes them? That is where not just skill in presentation, but
also the quality of research come in, to support the claim to speak the
truth: the writing of history that explicitly claims to be true raises, precisely, the question of justification and evidence. I have seen, I have
heard, I have investigated, I can quote the *ipsissima verba*.[46] I can tell how
it really was – an extraordinary claim, in all conscience, when we reflect
how absurd it would be to try to tell it *all*. *Histoire totale* is as chimerical
as *histoire événementielle* is inconsequential.

   Herodotus and Thucydides share with Sima Qian not just a com-
memorative, but also didactic and advisory ambitions. The beginnings
of historiography in both cultures are political. But the ways they negoti-
ate those functions vary, reflecting differences both in their own positions
and in the political realities they faced. Both ancient Greece and ancient
China (among other societies) came to use the active study of the past
as a resource for understanding the present and anticipating the future,
providing a powerful if certainly not unambiguous weapon in the evaluation of the current *status quo* or the recent conduct of affairs, potentially
justificatory, but potentially also critical, even subversive. However, the
routes Greece and China took to develop those potentials were different,

---

[46] Hartog 1988 provides a classic discussion of these themes in Herodotus.

and so too were their end-results. Call the one the official, the other the unofficial, route. Let me summarise the main points to have emerged from this first inquiry into the development of inquiries, in terms of their self-definition, manner of research, modes of criticism and audience.

First self-definition, and in both cases the relation of historical to other writings is complex. In the Chinese case this is because the earliest dynastic histories include, for example, astronomy, not as a mere appendage, but as contributing to their advisory role. Knowledge on such matters formed a significant component not just in the ruler's self-presentation, but in his claims to legitimacy. In the Greek case, *historie* was anything but the monopoly of what we call history, so it needed to carve out its domain by reference to its subject-matter – which it did with mixed success.

Historiography, in China, was an affair of state, and this even before there was an official Bureau of History to oversee the writing of official dynastic histories. Sima Qian, like Sima Tan, held office as *taishi ling*, with duties that comprised far more than just those of a scribe recording events. The support he could count on included access to state archives of a far more impressive kind than were cited by Herodotus or Thucydides – indeed than any that existed in any classical Greek city-state. So while research in all three cases involved personal inquiry, on the ground, the potential archival back-up was far greater on the Chinese side.

Then as to criticism and audience, one might suppose that the price the Chinese historians had to pay, given their official role, was exorbitantly high. Of course the Emperor and his ministers were not the sole targets of the *Shiji*. When Sima Qian was disgraced, he did not just give up, but continued his father's work, first out of piety to him, of course, but then also in the conviction of its usefulness. Yet he could not afford to offend Wu Di again. The critical comments the text ascribes to the *taishi gong* show an independence of judgement that belies the potential perils of their authors' situation. While that is testimony to Sima Qian's toughmindedness and courage, I argued that from the perspective of officialdom, the historian's independence corresponded, at least up to a point, with their interests too. There was not much to be learnt merely from flatterers, though woe betide those who took too critical a line. Besides, the celebration of glorious past deeds was not much of a celebration if it was compiled by hacks who did not even *appear* to be independent.

The early Greek historians had neither the advantages nor the drawbacks of an Emperor in the wings, none of the support an official position could offer, but none of the constraints either. (Later historians of the Greco-Roman world are, to be sure, another matter: but I am concentrating here on the *early* development of inquiry.) Not in anyone's employ, they could, in principle, criticise anyone they liked and as openly as they liked. Yet they too faced the problem of impressing and persuading an audience. Their chief constraint was the need to succeed in the fiercely competitive environment of those claiming special knowledge, whatever branch of *historia* they cultivated. The rejection of others' efforts – including via the use of the category of *myth* in a pejorative acceptance – was a common, if not quite obligatory, preliminary to your own bid for attention. But evidently your own performance was no more immune to attack, from rivals or from colleagues, in your own generation or the next, than those you yourself undermined.

The early Greek historians too wrote, in a sense, for the benefit of those in whose hands lay political power, not, in their case (mostly), Kings, let alone Emperors, so much as the citizens of the classical Greek city-states. True, Thucydides, exiled from Athens for his poor performance as commander in the Thracian campaign (v 26), was thereafter unable himself to participate directly in Athenian politics at all. But he reaches out, with his 'possession for always', beyond his contemporaries, to future generations of those whom *he* no doubt envisaged as participants in the political processes with which he was familiar. There is an irony here, in that he wants his work to be useful, including to his fellow-citizens: yet within the narrative he repeatedly and very vividly illustrates just how difficult it was to persuade the Athenians of where their true interests lay – let alone to get them to learn the lessons of the past.

I shall have more to say, in later chapters, on these and other aspects of the situation in which Chinese and Greek investigators worked – on the different problems they faced in getting their ideas accepted and implemented. We have already seen how historiography was perceived to be relevant to the future, as a source of ideas about what is likely to happen. The topic of chapter 2 will be the wider issues raised by the different manifestations of the ambition to predict.

CHAPTER TWO

The modalities of prediction

When introducing a discussion of the mainly historiographical aspects of *historia*, in the last chapter, I remarked on the dangers of using modern categories in a study of inquiry in ancient cultures. 'Science', in particular, is open to criticism both on the grounds of anachronism and on those of teleology. The ancients were not to know what that was to become, nor could they be expected to have anything like a scientific programme as one of their goals. We should focus, rather, on how *they* saw their aims and interests, while recognising how heterogeneous they could be.

One common interest exhibited in different ways in different types of inquiry is in prediction – but there we encounter another difficulty. In the form of divination, prediction figures among what used to be called the pseudo-sciences. In the early days of the history of science, in the middle of the nineteenth century, they were always an occasion of embarrassment. When the project of the history of science was one of charting first its emergence, then its onward and upward march, it was essential to be able to distinguish between those inquiries that did, and those that did not, contribute to that progress. Astrology, alchemy, physiognomy, later phrenology, all had to be dismissed as essentially deluded. The historian of science was not to be distracted by their presence in the same periods, even in the very same authors, as those he or she was interested in, except insofar as he or she had a duty to point out how mistaken the pseudo-sciences were. Ptolemy's *Syntaxis* was fine: but his *Tetrabiblos* had to be rubbished, when not just simply ignored.

A second phase in the study of divination began when its rationality came to be recognised. In the debates on the irrational that were common in psychology, philosophy and anthropology, from the 1950s on, it was remarked that techniques of divination have their own internal coherence and obey certain rules, and on that score and by that criterion

do not fail to be rational.[1] That helped to shift the debate away from
the 'delusions' of the pseudo-sciences, even though the sciences were still
generally the norm against which they were judged – as if they were
nothing but poor attempts at modern scientific understanding.

One of the durable features of those debates was the recognition of
the sociological dimension of the problems. The issues were not just to
do with knowledge claims in the abstract, but with who made them, with
what institutional support, or in the face of what institutional opposition.
Since the knowledge claimed for divination concerned the future, it held
out the promise of influencing it – a prospect that state authorities could
hardly ignore. The legitimacy or otherwise of the practices were not
just matters of the rationality of aims and methods, for issues of state
control, or its subversion, could be at stake. The unauthorised casting of
the horoscope of a Roman Emperor was high treason (cf. Barton 1994) –
just as in late imperial China private studies of astronomy and astrology
could be criminal offences.

At one end of the spectrum, a private individual may attempt some
prediction purely for his or her own private purposes – with or without the approval or consent of state authorities. At the other, there are
ritualised, institutionalised occasions when those in charge may be high
functionaries of state, or even the ruler in person. In such circumstances,
a challenge to the prediction could hardly fail to be construed as a challenge to the state authorities themselves. The more complex or recherché
the mode of prognostication, the more likely this is to necessitate specialists of some type, and the question then arises as to how they get to be
recruited. Access to membership of specialist groups might be a matter
of birth, or of training and apprenticeship, or of adjudged ability.

Obviously predictions may be attempted in just about every field of
human experience. Is today a good day for me to go fishing? If we make
war, shall we be victorious or suffer defeat? Comparative anthropological
studies (such as those of G. K. Park and O. K. Moore[2]) have shown that
sometimes, when a particularly tricky decision has to be taken, and it
might be invidious for an individual to be solely responsible for it, an
impersonal mode of divination may be used as the basis for a consensual
verdict as to what to do. In which direction should the hunting party set
out? Divination can resolve the issue without implicating any individual
with blame for failure: and such a procedure may also have the effect of

[1] Dodds 1951, K. Thomas 1971, Vernant 1974, Hollis and Lukes 1982.
[2] Moore 1957, Park 1963, cf. also Bascom 1969.

introducing a random element in the courses of action to be pursued. The hunting party does not always follow a set pattern in deciding where to try its luck.

Again when Big Men or rulers have to be advised, the context of discussion of what the signs foretell may provide a framework for that to happen without any of the parties to the advice being in danger of losing face. On the surface the talk is of how to interpret the omens and what they hold out for the future: but what is at issue is deciding what to do. Discussion of what the signs mean enables different views to be expressed about what should be done.

Evans-Pritchard famously problematised the question 'why me?', that is, why did what happened 'have' to happen to the individual concerned, the lightning strike, or the tree fall, just where it did, and just that question provides further rich areas for the exploration of hidden aspects of the present or the past (still divination, though retrodiction rather than prediction). Techniques of various kinds may be brought to bear, to uncover the personal or impersonal reasons why my crops failed, or the crops failed generally, why I was struck by disease or the whole city was. Have the ancestors been offended? What is offending them? Again, how would past generations, wiser than ourselves, have responded to the crisis? The spectrum extends from divination to the type of study of the past I discussed in chapter 1.

The vastness of the field is apparent, and I shall concentrate here simply on those aspects that are directly relevant to my central theme, of the development of different types of systematic inquiry. What did they owe to the ambition to predict? The proposal I shall explore is that the hope of being able to foretell the future, or otherwise to have access to hidden truths, may provide a powerful incentive to intellectual experimentation, analysis, research. So far from predicting, or even divining, being merely negative influences inhibiting the growth of inquiry, my argument will be the reverse, that they were, sometimes at least, positive ones encouraging it. So far from being mere superstitions, of interest only to the gullible, their practice led to the discovery of certain regularities and to a realisation of certain differences between different modes of prediction, notably between the conjectural and the rigorous. True, prediction figures also in many other guises, notably as a means of communicating with the ancestors, as advice, as admonishment, and as a way of removing indecision. But a study of its modalities can, I believe, illuminate its importance for the growth of inquiry more generally.

Pride of place, in any account of ancient modes of prediction, must go, not to China, nor to Greece, but to the evidence from Mesopotamia, both for its antiquity and its extent, and because it is suggestive already of two important themes. First the topic was evidently considered sufficiently important for many aspects of it to come under the direct control of the King, to whom a variety of officials, experts in different modes of prediction, usually reported. Among these we hear of ṭupšarru ('astrologer scribes'), barû ('haruspex diviner'), āšipu ('exorcist magician'), asû ('physician') and šā'ilu ('dream interpreter') – those are Parpola's translations.[3] One area of particular concern was the study of the heavens, where from some time around the seventh century BCE there was increasing confidence in the predictions offered over a certain range of phenomena. The second theme that our Mesopotamian data illustrate is, then, the growing sense of the control of a subject-matter.

First, however, we may note that predictions were certainly tried out in other fields as well. Babylonian medical prognostications share with some astronomical ones that they take the form of conditionals. If so and so (the sign), then so and so (the result or 'verdict'). The protasis sets out a significant indication (a sign generally, not a cause), the apodosis the expected outcome. Some protases specify a patient's 'symptoms' ('if his head is hot . . . the feet up to the lower part of the legs cold, and the tip of his nose black'), but others circumstances surrounding a case ('if a falcon flies to the right of the house of the sick man' or 'if there is a scorpion on the wall'). The apodoses state whether the patient will recover or die, and often identify the god or demon responsible ('the hand of Ištar', for instance, or 'the hand of Šamaš').[4]

Thus in Babylonian medicine the possibility of divine or demonic intervention is assumed. But there is a desire to anticipate the course a sickness will take, and this leads to an effort at synthesis, coordinating or systematising experience. The extent to which that synthesis was the product of empirical experience, or how far it was generated by its own internal, symbolic or associative, logic, is not an issue on which a confident judgement can be passed. Nor is it clear how far these prognostications represent an orthodoxy for the practitioners concerned. But the systematisation of possible sequences of signs and outcomes provides

---

3 Parpola 1993 p. xiii. Cf. Rochberg 2000 on the evolution in the sense of ṭupšarru and in the roles of those concerned.

4 I take these examples from Labat 1951, pp. 7, 11, 25, 79, 173. See also Oppenheim 1962, Bottéro 1974 and Stol 1993. As Heessel 2000 points out, references to the hand of a god or demon may be descriptive and diagnostic rather than, or as well as, causal.

a framework within which the healer could interpret his experience and give his patients an account of what was afflicting them and advice on what to do to remedy the situation. The patients feeling reassured would depend crucially on their prior acceptance of the symbolic associations that form the basis of the interpretation. 'Falcons on the right', they would say to themselves: ah yes: and begin to feel a bit better. Not so, if they were on the left.

With the study of the heavens, our data is of an altogether different quality and quantity. To be sure, the fullest documentation relates to the Seleucid period, from the third century BCE on, the Astronomical Cuneiform Texts, Goal Year Texts, Almanacs and so on that form the focus of Neugebauer's classic studies.[5] These incorporate sophisticated arithmetical models for a variety of astronomical phenomena. But they represent the culmination of a long process of development that goes back to early in the second millennium, and it is this that is of particular interest to my investigation here.

Two main stages in the earlier developments may be distinguished. First there is the vast omen literature, often taking the form of conditionals similar to those in the medical evidence. Already in the Old Babylonian period this is well attested in, for instance, the series of texts known as *Enūma Anu Enlil*, that was put together some time between 1500 and 1200, although it incorporates even earlier material. It, in turn, served as a canon of interpretation for later work. One famous text is the Venus tablet, referring to the reign of Ammiṣaduqa around 1600, which contains empirical data about the appearances and disappearances of Venus recorded in conjunction with certain predictions. The apodoses here (which have received much less attention than the data) include, for example, that the harvest will prosper, that there will be hostilities, or reconciliation, between Kings, and so on. In other tablets we find such presages as: 'if Jupiter approaches the Crook, the harvest at Akkad will prosper', or 'if a star flares up from the West and enters the Yoke, there will be a revolution'.[6]

But then from some time around the seventh century there was a shift both in what was being predicted and in the confidence and accuracy of at least some of the predictions.[7] Our main evidence comes from the Letters and Reports, the bulk of which were composed between 680

---

[5] Neugebauer 1975, cf. also Neugebauer and Sachs 1945, Swerdlow 1998.
[6] I take the examples in this paragraph from Reiner and Pingree 1975, pp. 13f, Reiner and Pingree 1981, p. 41, and Hunger and Pingree 1989, p. 115.
[7] See Brown 2000. The Letters and Reports are edited by Parpola 1970, 1983, 1993 and cf. Hunger 1992.

and 650 by court and temple officials reporting to the Assyrian Kings at Nineveh. Many of the phenomena that had figured in the protases of the omen texts came to be more rigorously classified and themselves predictable, not just in ideal terms but even in terms of deviations from those ideals. These include (1) the length of the month as determined by successive first visibilities of the new moon, (2) the phases of the planets, that is first and last visibilities, conjunctions and opposition with the sun, stationary points, and (3) both lunar and solar eclipses. Let us be clear about what is new in all of this. Changes in the height of the sun and in the length of daylight had (one may guess) always been recognised as conforming to certain general patterns, and so too the phases of the moon and the configurations of the constellations at different seasons of the year. But what happens in Babylonia – for the first time, so far as our extant evidence goes – was an appreciation of far more complex cycles.

The possibilities of determining, in advance, when a planet would become visible after a period of invisibility, or of saying when an eclipse of the moon or sun would occur, or at least was possible, offered an altogether new scope for prognostication. Admittedly much remained beyond that scope.[8] The ṭupšarru squabble not just about their predictions, but about what had been claimed as observed. One writes: 'He who wrote to the King, my lord, "the planet Venus is visible" . . . is a vile man, an ignoramus, a cheat . . . Venus is not yet visible.' (It may be, though we cannot confirm this, that this was a case where no actual observation was possible. The weather, according to these Letters and Reports, was often atrocious for observational purposes. The dispute would then have been not on whether that scribe just invented the sighting or mistook another star for Venus, but on the correctness of the model according to which Venus' visibility could be deduced.) But against that, their confidence grows concerning a range of phenomena, including on the conditions of possibility of eclipses. 'Does the King not know', one scribe writes, 'that the watch for the eclipse is hardly necessary?'. And another says: 'I guarantee it seven times, the eclipse will not take place' (but that did not stop him watching for it, even so). A clear difference opens up between

---

[8] Surprisingly enough – a problem that Rochberg has addressed – even after it was clear to the ṭupšarru that lunar and solar eclipses could occur only at conjunctions, at the full or new moon, there continue to be references to the possibility of eclipses on other days. Some have suggested that these are not proper, actual, eclipses, but just darkenings of the moon or sun as the case may be. But that seems less likely than the other possibility that the ṭupšarru continued to include such material out of deference to tradition, that is, because they appeared in *Enūma Anu Enlil*. If so, that has interesting implications for the way the scribes saw their own work – that is, not as departing from the models of *Enūma Anu Enlil*, let alone criticising them, but rather as working within and elaborating them.

a style of prediction that focusses on the good or bad fortune that will result *if* a celestial phenomenon occurs, on the one hand, and, on the other, one that predicts such celestial phenomena themselves.[9]

The development of that possibility did not mean that the phenomena in question were no longer considered ominous. On the contrary, eclipses, in particular, were still considered inauspicious – not that they were thought to be causes of evil to come, only signs of it. If you think it strange that a phenomenon perceived as regular can still be thought of as inauspicious, remember that some of our own contemporaries believe that when the 13th of the month falls on a Friday, that brings 'bad luck'. At the stage when the scribes were able to predict one or its possibility, they could and did warn the ruler, who set about diverting disaster from himself by the ritual of the substitute King (namburbû).[10] Some poor unfortunate who was thought dispensable was put on the throne, so that whatever misfortune happened would occur to him, not to the real King, who was addressed meanwhile as 'the farmer'. But when scribes could tell Kings what to do, that suggests how seriously their work was taken.

The study of the heavens was not undertaken for its own sake: rather it was driven by a desire to acquire, somehow, advance knowledge of what was in store for the King or state. Nor was it just celestial phenomena that were scrutinised for clues, for what we should call meteorological ones (storms, lightning, hail) also continued to be studied – where the phenomena themselves were far harder to foretell. But the study of the heavens brought to light certain regularities, which in turn provided a powerful incentive to investigate them further. Thus the desire to see into the future came to be fulfilled in a manner that had scarcely been anticipated, and with a degree of certainty that quite outstripped that which went with the pronouncement of good or bad fortune in general. The ambition to predict had here an unexpected outcome – and one that was of great significance for the potential it suggested.

I cannot here go into the further stages whereby astronomical knowledge was accumulated in Babylonia – the topics of considerable ongoing

---

[9] I take the examples in this paragraph from Parpola 1993, p. 54, Parpola 1970, p. 29, Hunger 1992, p. 251.

[10] On namburbû, see especially Bottéro 1992, ch. 9, cf. Koch-Westenholz 1995, pp. 111 ff. Some faint, but inaccurate, knowledge of this ritual may be reflected in Herodotus' story, VII 15 ff, where Xerxes asks his brother Artabanus to dress in his clothes, sit on his throne and sleep in his bed, to see whether the dream that had come to Xerxes would also come to him. In this story Artabanus is made to make some deflationary comments to the effect that the vision would not be so foolish as to mistake him for Xerxes even though he put on his clothes – though that does not dissuade Xerxes from going ahead with his trial.

debate. But three points are beyond dispute. First, that accumulation was stimulated by the desire to foresee the future. That applies to both sides of the distinction that we draw (but the Babylonians themselves certainly did not) between astronomy and astrology.

Secondly, the new knowledge acquired was sufficiently impressive, to the Babylonians themselves, that it provided the basis of continued study stretching over several hundred years.

Thirdly, the whole enterprise was carried out by officials, specialists who were directly controlled by the Kings to whom they reported, or who (in Achaemenid times) were based in temples by which they were financed.

In relation to those last two points, it is striking how that study continued more or less uninterrupted through the political upheavals in the Mesopotamian area, including major shifts in who was in control. The work begun in the Old Babylonian period continued when Babylonia fell under Assyrian rule in the late eighth century – when both Assyrian and Babylonian scribes composed the reports I have referred to. Indeed the effort continued both after Babylonia had destroyed the Assyrian empire in its turn, at the end of the seventh, and when the Persians, under Cyrus, overran Babylonia in 539. Evidently the work of the astronomers was too important for whoever was in power to ignore or discontinue.

The extant materials for the study of the different types of prediction practised in ancient China are even richer than those for Babylonia. I shall focus first on some general techniques, and then on the two specific domains of medicine and astronomy.

The earliest divinations are found on the inscribed bones and turtle shells from Anyang that are our chief evidence for early Chinese writing: Keightley has studied a series of such divinations relating mainly to the twelfth century BCE (see figure 1).[11] They concern military expeditions, the construction of towns, illnesses, journeys, births – of significance to the King or (what comes to the same) the state, and they served a dual purpose, for they were attempts not just to see what the future holds, but also to test what policies had the approval of the ancestors – though these two functions often run together. We are dealing with expensive, official, ritualised procedures, not used outside court circles, but the

---

[11] See especially Keightley 1988, cf. 1979–80, 1984, 1999, Djamouri 1999. The secondary literature on Chinese divination in general is immense. The following may be found particularly useful: Kaltenmark and Ngo 1968, Ngo 1976, Vandermeersch 1977–80, DeWoskin 1983, Henderson 1984, Kalinowski 1991, Allan 1991, R. J. Smith 1991, Jullien 1993, Loewe 1994, Farquhar 1996.

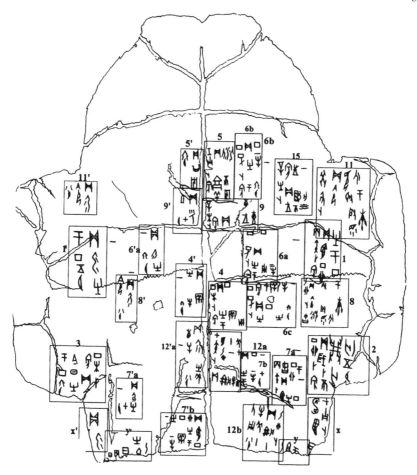

Fig. 1   Divination from the turtle shell. Holes are drilled in a turtle shell according to a symmetrical pattern and these are fired to give the answers to pre-formulated questions. These often take the form of pairs of possible outcomes: 'there will be success in hunting: there may not be', where the unfavourable result is qualified with the modal qi^1, 'may'. The illustration gives the transcription of marks on a turtle shell that has been used for no fewer than thirty divinations. Quite how the cracks formed by firing the holes were read to give the outcomes in question is still debated.

evidence confirms their cardinal importance, for state concerns, from earliest times.

Other less costly techniques also came to be developed. The text that came to form the basis of one of the most commonly used modes of foretelling the future – and indeed of understanding the human condition in general – was the great classic, the *Yijing* or *Book of Changes*.[12] Versions of this go back to the ninth century, though the compilation in its present form, with the major accompanying commentaries (the so-called Ten Wings), belongs rather to the end of the Warring States. Divination there was based on the interpretation of combinations of six lines (each either broken or *yin*, or unbroken, *yang*) forming a total of sixty-four hexagrams. For this purpose sticks of milfoil or yarrow were used – obviously a cheaper procedure than firing turtle shells. Some knowledge of milfoil divination may be presumed to be widespread. But to get the most out of the often highly elliptical and allusive text of the *Yijing* itself called for the highest linguistic, literary and philosophical skills. That was when the *Yijing* was treated not just as a handbook for prediction, but as a book of wisdom.

Although the *Yijing* hexagrams remained the most popular form of this style of divination, a variant, using eighty-one tetragrams rather than sixty-four hexagrams, was developed at the end of the first century BCE by Yang Xiong in the *Tai Xuan Jing*.[13] That aimed too to give a systematic account of the world and to make explicit what could only be derived from the *Yijing* by what Sivin has called heroic feats of hermeneutics. Among other types of divination practised, Ban Gu has an elaborate system of correspondences using five-phase theory in the *Hanshu*,[14] around 80 CE, and a few centuries later, in the *Nan Qishu*, there is a would-be complete astronomical system based on the calculated positions of the *taiyi*[1], or Grand One, a deity conceived as circulating among the circumpolar Celestial Palaces (see figure 2). This and other cosmic board techniques have been studied by Ho Peng Yoke.[15]

---

[12] On the *Yijing* see especially Shaughnessy 1996 and Shaughnessy in Loewe and Shaughnessy 1999, pp. 338ff.

[13] See Nylan and Sivin (originally 1987) in Sivin 1995b, ch. III.

[14] *Hanshu* 27A: 1317ff. We shall be returning to five-phase correspondences below.

[15] See Ho forthcoming, cf. Harper 1978–9 and 1980–1, Cullen 1980–1. In the *Nan Qishu*, the basic board consists of three fixed concentric circles (round the empty central circle), They identify the number of the 'palace', and incorporate correlations with states or regions of China. In the outermost circle are put the calculated positions of *taiyi*[1] and other celestial elements, the Great Generals, the Deputy Ministers on the 'Guest' and on the 'Host' side and so on. This involves moving clockwise or counterclockwise round the circle according to conventional rules from a specific date – the 'Superior Epoch'. The whole configuration then enables the terrestrial situation to be determined, especially whether it favoured attack or defence, the Host or the Guest side. Thus in figure 2 we have a configuration that gives a retrojection for 403 CE, where *taiyi*[1] in palace 7 is said to be blocked by the Host Great General in palace 1 (the Greeks would have said quartile) while the Opposing Guest Great General is in an even worse position in palace 3 (in opposition). That correlated with the Emperor Andi being forced out of his earthly

太 乙 陽 遁 十 六 局

太乙在七宮璉天
計神在大義
壬目交昌將天過
主算單一
主大將一宮
客目始擊大錢
客算三十二
客恭將九宮

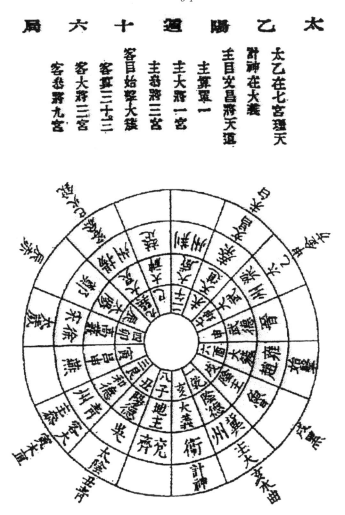

Fig. 2   Cosmic board from the *Nan Qishu*.

palace by Huan Xuan. The writer responsible for the first extended account of the system was Xiao Zixian (489–537), considered a genius at the time, though the system was so complicated that many later commentators abandoned attempts at an interpretation. However, his being in a position to offer advice certainly owed something to his belonging to the same clan as the Emperor. It should be emphasised that the system depended entirely (1) on the selection of the date for the Superior Epoch, and (2) on counting to arrive at positions for each element according to accepted, but arbitrary, rules. No observation of the heavens was involved. I am indebted to Ho Peng Yoke for discussions of this issue.

To see where prediction may serve as a vehicle of advice, we may turn back to the *Zuozhuan*, which we considered in chapter 1 as one of the precursors of Sima Qian's *Shiji*. Its admittedly often fictional accounts of events are punctuated with divinations, by the turtle shell (*bu*), by milfoil (*shi*[II]) and by the interpretation of portents, ranging from the strange behaviour of animals, to droughts, dreams and eclipses. Sometimes several techniques are combined and one played off against another. However the people who pick and choose among them, just to get the result they want, are understood to be unprincipled types and often come to a sticky end. There is a certain ambivalence with regard to *wu* (better translated 'mediums' than the customary but misleading 'shamans') who are reputed to be able not just to foresee the future but also to bring or stop rain: some pay for their predictions with their lives (cf. *Zuozhuan* Duke Xi, 21st year, 390). But elsewhere more official figures of different types[16] are called upon to interpret signs. They are far from always in agreement, even about the right technique to use, but they all assume there is a message, generally a moral one, to be had, and they make the most of the opportunity – for comment and advice – that this presents. The key point is the one I noted before, that talk of what the signs suggest is the occasion for discussion of delicate issues and for counsel. Moreover the response the diviners receive – their being listened to or ignored – turns rather more on *their* perceived uprightness of character than on any technical ability they may be thought to possess.

Omens are a way in which heaven communicates with rulers, encouraging them or remonstrating with them, warning them, for instance, that the mandate from heaven was under threat. That idea, indeed, remains largely intact when, in other late Warring States or Han authors, particular beliefs or practices are challenged. Expenditure on divination may be a waste of resources (says Xunzi in the third century BCE).[17] What is so special about turtles or milfoil that they can yield predictions, asks Wang Chong (first century CE), though he still thinks that fortunate people happen, as a matter of fact, to encounter auspicious omens, unlucky people inauspicious ones.[18]

A moral dimension is often present also in classical Chinese discussions of disease, where quite a few patients seem to get ill because of their own self-indulgent behaviour.[19] But in that context techniques of prediction

---

[16] These included the *dashi*, whom we discussed in ch. 1.
[17] *Xunzi* 21: 74ff, Knoblock 1988–94, III 109.   [18] *Lunheng* 71, *juan* 24, 994ff.
[19] Reference to divine or demonic forces at work is less common in classical Chinese medical texts than in Babylonian ones. That patients fell ill because of their self-indulgence is a point made

were cultivated that were very different from those we have considered so far from China. In addition to the great medical classic, the *Huangdi neijing*, and to the medical texts from the Mawangdui tombs,[20] we have a particularly valuable source in the biography of the doctor Chunyu Yi, contained in Sima Qian's *Shiji*.[21] (We are dealing in all three cases with material from the second or first centuries BCE.) The Chunyu Yi biography sets out the details of twenty-five of his patients' case-histories. Some of these die (though never as a result of his treatment): but in every case his prognoses are vindicated, at least as to whether the patient would recover or die, and sometimes even concerning *when* they would do so.

He uses a variety of techniques, including for example the colour (*se*) of the patient's face – the term also covers his/her expression. But his key method, mentioned in almost every case, is prognosis from the pulse (*mai*). He implies that he was taught this by his teachers who handed on certain books to him: when he refers to the 'Method of the Pulse', it is sometimes unclear whether this is a text, or teaching, lore. But pulse prognosis, as practised here, evidently depended crucially on the manual skills of the practitioner. Chunyu Yi develops quite a vocabulary to describe the pulses, said to be 'big', 'calm', 'long', 'strung' and so on, from which he infers the movements of the qi^{II} in the body. Thus in case 1, he got the liver qi^{II}, said to be 'turbid but calm', but those terms, turbid (*zhuo*: muddy) and calm (*jing*[I]) are both also used of the pulse itself.[22] The descriptions are set out in highly theory-laden terms, or rather description and interpretation run together. This is no matter on which lay persons could trust their own judgement – you had to learn to recognise what you felt – and the scope for mystification is evident. At the same time there was great potential here for development, for building up experience correlating the signs observed with the courses and outcomes of diseases.

The Chinese study of the heavens – the second specialist field of prediction I chose – shows certain interesting analogies to and some differences

commonly enough also in Greek medical case-histories. See, for example, *Epidemics* III cases 4 and 5 in the first series (L III 44.11–46.8, 46.10–48.21) and cases 10 and 16 in the second (L III 130.4–132.11, 146.8–148.5).

[20] On the various recensions and structure of the *Huangdi neijing*, see Yamada Keiji 1979 and Keegan 1988; on the Mawangdui medical texts, see Harper 1998.

[21] Chunyu Yi himself lived in the second century BCE. These case-histories are the subject of a forthcoming study by Hsu.

[22] See Kuriyama 1999, Hsu 2001 and forthcoming. Both terms are also used of the qualities of musical sounds. Such correlations between pulse qualities and harmonic theory are not surprising, given that the phenomena in both cases depend on the quality and movements of qi^{II}.

from its Babylonian counterpart. First it was, in China too, a matter of state importance. The rulers, later the Emperor, were personally responsible for the welfare of 'all under heaven'. So they could certainly not afford to be caught out in the orderly performance of their seasonal duties. To that end, already in Han times, an Astronomical Bureau was set up, with a considerable staff, charged with overseeing the two main branches of the study of the heavens, *lifa* and *tianwen*. The former included first and foremost calendar studies, but also other computational work, for example in connection with eclipses. The latter is the study of the 'patterns in the heavens', comprising cosmography and the observation, recording and interpretation of celestial phenomena deemed to be ominous. Evidently the contrast between these two is rather one between mainly quantitative and mainly qualitative studies, not between what we would call astronomy and astrology.

The history of the imperial Astronomical Bureau is amazing. It lasted more than 2,000 years, until the last dynasty, the Qing. This had a good deal to do with the convergence of interests between, on the one hand, the Emperor and his ministers, and on the other, those who staffed the Bureau. The former, as explained, had a direct interest in having the most accurate information available on matters that *lifa* and *tianwen* covered. But it was also in the interests of the astronomers that this imperial concern should be maintained – for their jobs, after all, depended on it. Their actual performance was mixed. On the one hand, there were notable successes, in calendar regulation, in determining cycles of eclipses and of planetary phenomena, and in general in discriminating between what is predictable and what is not. There their work had the effect of pushing back the frontier of the truly portentous, not that that category was ever abolished completely[23] On the other hand, in the case of some of their mistakes – when an eclipse that had been predicted did not occur – that was sometimes (in the Tang) excused with the argument that the non-occurrence was a sign of the special virtue of the Emperor. Such was his virtue – so it was claimed – that an eclipse that would otherwise have happened, did not. The incorrectness of the prediction was not chalked up *against* the astronomer, but *for* the Emperor. Yet that type of excuse did not, in general, obviate the need to make the most accurate observations possible.

Some of our post-Han sources indicate that a job in the Bureau was sometimes treated as a sinecure. The officers did not bother to carry out

---

[23] See Sivin 1995a, ch. II. On political interferences in the matter of what did or did not get recorded, see Huang Yi-long 2001.

the regular observations: rather they made up the records on the basis of what had been predicted – which the observations were supposed to check, of course. Yet when the calendar got out of step, there was the possibility, in the long run the inevitability, of this being found out. Sometimes this happened as the result of the work of individuals outside the Bureau – who, if they made successful proposals for reform, might well find themselves drafted into it.[24] But it would be wrong to suggest that improvements came only from outside what was, admittedly, an essentially conservative institution. Moreover, conservative as it was, it far outstripped not just the Babylonian palaces and temples, but rivals from any ancient or modern society, for sustained observation, over the centuries, both of cyclical phenomena and of irregular ones. Their records have proved, indeed, a valuable mine of information on such topics as novae and supernovae for modern investigators researching into their occurrence.[25]

Turning now to the mass of material relevant to our problems from Greece, I shall concentrate on four interlocking points especially. First, there is the diversity in the domains where prediction was practised and in the techniques employed. Second, there is the high prestige that generally attached to prediction from early times. Third, new types of prediction came to be developed in the classical and Hellenistic periods (where we may focus once again on medicine and astronomy). Fourth, there is the competitiveness that existed between different modes. In comparison with both Babylonia and China, prediction may be said to be less heavily bureaucratised in ancient Greece, even though some aspects were seen to be important for the state, and we need then to examine what difference that made.

Many types of prediction were attempted, in Greece, from early times.[26] Animal sacrifices were made and the victims' entrails (liver, gall-bladder especially) inspected for any sign that might be thought ominous.

[24] This was the experience of Shen Gua in the eleventh century, and even of the Jesuit Schall in the seventeenth; see Sivin 1995a, ch. III and Huang Yi-long 1991. The phenomenon may go back to the Han. Cullen 2000 has examined the debate in the Bureau about taking the ecliptic, rather than the equator, as the circle along which the regular movement of the sun should be tracked. Two of the key figures in introducing this reform were Jia Kui who had only a peripheral office in the palace, who submitted an important memorial in 92 CE, and Zhang Heng, in the decade 120–130, during which he twice held office as *taishi guan*, or Grand Clerk.
[25] See Xi Zezong and Po Shujen 1966, Xi Zezong 1981, cf. Clark and Stephenson 1977, Stephenson and Clark 1978, Huang Yi-long and Moriarty-Schieven 1987, Li 1988, Huang Yi-long 1990 (who emphasises that the difficulties of interpreting ancient descriptions should not be underestimated), Stephenson 1997.
[26] The most comprehensive survey of Greek divination remains that of Bouché-Leclercq 1879–82, cf. Vernant 1974, Barton 1994.

The flights of birds were similarly scrutinised. Dreams, or at least some of them, were thought to be significant for the dreamer or for others, and elaborate theories for their interpretation came to be developed (as by Artemidorus in the second century CE). Oracles were consulted, where special interpreters might be needed to elucidate what had been said. Each of these modes can be illustrated already in Homer, where reactions to their use vary from the awestruck to the sceptical. Thus when in *Iliad* 12 the seer Polydamas interprets a fight between an eagle and a snake it has captured as an omen that the Trojans will be thwarted of victory, Hector rejects this with 'one omen is best: to defend one's country'. But that apparently fine expression of unconcern for the seer's prediction must be put into perspective. Hector, for his part, gains his confidence from the promises he says he has had from Zeus: besides, in the event, Polydamas turns out to be correct.[27]

Many of the seers, diviners, prophets, represented in early Greek literature are greeted, like Polydamas, with disbelief, suspicion, derision, contempt (we may compare the reaction to some Chinese *wu* – and even to some *dashi* indeed). Cassandra's fate is to foresee the future but never to be believed. Teiresias, in Sophocles' *Oedipus Tyrannus*, is accused of malice, envy, corruption.[28] The possibility of political manipulation of predictions was recognised. The priestess at Delphi, or the interpreters of her pronouncements, could be suborned.[29] Many assumed that when the outcome of a state sacrifice was reported as unfavourable, that was just an excuse for doing nothing – as often when the Spartans refused to leave their own territory on the grounds that the omens were inauspicious.

Yet the fact that individual seers were frequently accused of cheating, obfuscation, charlatanry, should not be equated with any general Greek disbelief in the practice of divination as such. Many texts imply, to the contrary, that it was highly regarded. Solon cites seer-craft alongside medicine and poetry as arts under divine aegis.[30] In Aeschylus Prometheus includes divination, *mantike*, with medicine, navigation and metal-work, among the arts and resources that he bestowed as benefits on humans.[31] Nor is it just in poetry that we find this theme. In the Hippocratic treatise *On Regimen*, when *technai* are used to throw light, by analogy, on the human body, the first mentioned is divination.[32]

---

[27] *Iliad* 12 200–50.
[28] *Oedipus Tyrannus* 387ff. Similarly Aristophanes repeatedly satirises both named soothsayers and prophets in general, as at *Peace* 1045–1126, *Birds* 958–91, *Knights* 115ff, 1002ff.
[29] See for example Herodotus VI 66, 75.   [30] Solon 1 53ff.
[31] *Prometheus Vinctus* 484ff.   [32] *On Regimen* I chs. 12–24, *CMG* I 2 4, 136.5ff.

But another Hippocratic work shows another side to the picture. The author of *On Regimen in Acute Diseases* emphasises the difference between medicine and divination.[33] He criticises his medical colleagues for their disagreements with one another. This gives medicine a bad name. Lay people are in danger of concluding that it is no better than divination, *mantike*. This is just one of many Hippocratic works that seek to dissociate their styles of medical practice from various popular or traditional beliefs. *On the Sacred Disease*, especially, attacks those who held that gods or demons could cause or cure diseases, criticising the 'purifiers' as charlatans, quacks, *magoi*.[34] The author's own techniques of diagnosis may look to us quite speculative, and his therapies ineffective, but they stay within the orbit of *phusis*, nature, the key concept (as I have argued elsewhere[35]) used to mark out the territory of the new-style self-proclaimed rationalists in both medicine and philosophy. Since every kind of disease has its natural cause, that leaves no room for supernatural intervention either in the causing of diseases or in their cures or (some of the philosophers would add) anywhere else, come to that.

Doing justice to both the differences and the similarities between that new-style naturalistic, and older, traditional, types of medicine is more complex than might appear. First as to the differences. Such works as *Prognosis* and the *Epidemics* specify the signs the doctor should use in arriving at his diagnosis.[36] They include the famous Hippocratic facies (*Prognosis*, ch. 2) and particular attention is paid to the excreta, stools, urine, sputa, vomit. I note in passing that the pulse is not among the diagnostic indicators in Hippocratic works: it came to be used in Greece only after Praxagoras (around 300 BCE) though it then underwent massive theoretical elaboration, including some attempts to apply a mathematical analysis based on music theory.[37] However, without that, the Hippocratics already had a battery of natural signs to refer to, and one of the aims of the detailed case-histories in the *Epidemics* may well have been to enable correlations to be made between signs and outcomes. As with Chunyu Yi, there was great potential here for further investigations.

Yet some of the techniques and concepts of the Hippocratics are closer to those of other styles of medicine than some of the polemic leads us

---

[33] *On Regimen in Acute Diseases* ch. 3, L II 242.3ff.

[34] The first chapter of *On the Sacred Disease*, especially, engages in a sustained polemic, analysed in detail in my 1979, ch. 1, pp. 15ff.

[35] Lloyd 1991, ch. 18.

[36] The whole of the treatise called *Prognosis* is devoted to this topic: cf. also *Epidemics* I ch. 10, L II 668.14ff especially.

[37] See Galen on Herophilus, K IX 464.1–4, cf. Staden 1989, pp. 276–82, 354–6.

to expect. Dreams were the key technique used in temple medicine, in the shrines of Asclepius for instance. The faithful 'incubated' (spent the night in the shrine) and their dreams were then interpreted as indicating a therapy – or better still, they woke cured. But dreams are also included among the signs the doctor should attend to in *Epidemics* I (ch. 10, L II 670.8), and *On Regimen* IV gives detailed guidelines for their interpretation: except that now dreams are just indicators of the physical state of the body, not signs from god. Dreaming of springs and wells indicates trouble in the bladder, for instance: a rough sea is a sign of disease of the bowels, and so on.[38] The theme continues right down to Freud, of course.

Again, when the Hippocratic doctors practise prognosis, they do so sometimes in terms that echo those used by the seers. Both *Prognosis* and *Epidemics* I speak of the doctor 'telling in advance' 'the present, the past and the future', for all the world like Calchas in Homer or the Muses in Hesiod's *Theogony*.[39] Medical prognosis has both a defensive and a promotional role. If the doctor has foretold the death of the patient, he will not be blamed – defensive. If he can tell his patients not just the outcome of the disease, but also its past course and their present condition, then they will more readily entrust themselves to his care – the promotional role. The ambivalence of Greek naturalistic medicine, claiming to deal purely with factors that had a rational explanation, yet still sometimes using the discourse of seer-craft, can be seen again in Galen in the second century CE. He tells us that he was so successful in prognosis that his rivals claimed he must be a magician.[40] He repudiates this, putting it all down to his skill in the interpretation of the pulse and the like. Yet he clearly exploited every opportunity to impress his clients, relishing, even, the reputation he got as a wonder-worker.

New styles of prediction, and competitiveness, are also features of Greek astronomy, where two important differences from Babylonia and China stand out. First the Greeks had no Astronomical Bureau, nor generally any official positions. The difference between the reception of Greek work on the calendar and the Chinese experience is particularly striking. Although Meton, Callippus and others in the fifth and fourth centuries undertook studies in that area, the application of their results

---

[38] A series of such correlations is suggested in *On Regimen* IV ch. 89, e.g. *CMG* I 2 4, 220.18ff, 224.3ff. See Lloyd 1987, pp. 34–7.

[39] *Prognosis* 1, L II 110.2f, *Epidemics* I ch. 5, L II 634.6ff, cf. *Iliad* 1 70, Hesiod, *Theogony* 38. However, other texts warn the doctor *not* to engage in extravagant predictions, e.g. *Prorrhetic* II chs. 1f, L IX 6.1ff, 8.2.

[40] See Galen, *Prognosis*, ch. 7 at *CMG* v 81, 106.21ff especially, cf. ch. 3, 84.5ff, ch. 5, 94.18f. Cf. Kollesch 1965, Vegetti 1981.

was haphazard even in Athens itself – while other Greek city-states generally persisted in the use of their own distinct lunisolar calendars.[41]

But then the second difference relates to the type of theory attempted. From Eudoxus in the fourth century BCE onwards, the Greek goal was to provide a geometrical model from which the apparently irregular movements of the sun, moon and planets could be derived and so explained. The detailed interpretation of the models of Eudoxus and Callippus is, it is true, controversial, as also is the extent of their knowledge of Babylonian data.[42] Yet two fundamental points are clear. First the geometrical character of the models is not in any doubt. The irregularities of planetary movements were interpreted as the resultant of the combinations of the simple circular movements of a number of concentric spheres. (That was not, in my view, simply a matter of a fascination with the perfection of the circle, for circles are also easier to handle geometrically.)

Then the second point that is not in serious doubt is that it did not give determinate solutions to the movements of each of the planets. In other words it was not a quantitative, but merely a qualitative account. It explained how stations and retrogradations can in general occur, but did not provide all the detailed parameters needed for each planet.[43] Yet once a qualitative model was in place, that raised the possibility of proceeding to such determinate solutions.

So the contrast with Babylonia is twofold. Babylonian arithmetical methods allowed for the reduction of apparent irregularities to regularities by way of periodic tables incorporating steplike or linear zigzag functions. Exactly what that corresponded to, in physical terms, was unclear and evidently of no interest to the Babylonians. The Greek ambition was to derive the movements from the geometrical properties of the models and in that sense to explain them, and to do that, whether or not a physical account of the constitution of the spheres (what they were made of) was also attempted. Yet in the matter of prediction, Eudoxus' model was obviously far less able to give good determinate results than the corresponding Babylonian tables. He was way behind them there.

---

[41] On the Athenian calendar, see Pritchett and Neugebauer 1947, Waerden 1960, Meritt 1961, and on Meton's work more generally, Bowen and Goldstein 1989.

[42] See most recently Mendell 1998a and Yavetz 1998, cf. Goldstein and Bowen 1983.

[43] Simplicius (*In Cael.* 495.26ff) reports the values Eudoxus adopted for the two main periodicities of the planets (the sidereal or zodiacal, and the tropical), and they tally with, and may well have been derived from, Babylonian data. Modern reconstructions of the parameters of the two inner spheres that yield the hippopede that explains retrogradation are conjectural, and even on the most optimistic interpretations of those that Eudoxus may have adopted, the model fails as a quantitative account for Mars, Venus and Mercury.

Among the many developments in later Greek astronomy, there are just two that must be mentioned here. First there is the eventual realisation – within certain limits – of the possibility that Eudoxus' theory had opened up, that of a fully quantitative account giving both geometrical explanations and precise predictions of the movements of the planets. That was the achievement of Ptolemy's *Syntaxis*, based not on concentric spheres but on epicycles and eccentrics, and drawing extensively on Babylonian as well as Greek observational data.

Then the second important development for which Ptolemy is again one of our chief sources relates to the contrast between what we would call astronomy and astrology. True, Ptolemy does not mark this in just those terms. But the opening chapter of the *Tetrabiblos* (I 13.32ff) distinguishes clearly between predicting events in heaven, and predicting, on their basis, what may happen on earth. The former, he held, can claim to be demonstrative. The latter is uncertain and conjectural, yet potentially of great utility. It too used mathematics, in the casting of horoscopes: yet views about the characters of the planets – which were beneficent, which maleficent, for example – were derived from tradition and could not claim certainty. But it was because these characters were assumed to be part of their essences, their natures, that they could be thought of as influences. The vocabulary not just of power (*dunamis*) but of nature (*phusis*) is widely used in the opening chapters of the *Tetrabiblos*. The very concept that the Hippocratics and early philosophers had employed to *undermine* traditional beliefs was now brought into play to *justify* them.

The range of positions taken on this issue in Greco-Roman antiquity is remarkable. Ptolemy thought that both studies have their place. But some considered astrology to be subversive, while others held it to be deluded (Cicero's *De Divinatione* is a mine of arguments *pro* and *contra*[44]), while yet others (the Epicureans, some Sceptics) doubted the validity of astronomical theorising itself. This is all symptomatic of Greek polemic, and it is that polemic that may be thought to be a major contributing factor in the forging of a contrast between astrology and astronomy in the first place. We noted the absence of anything like an Astronomical Bureau in ancient Greece, setting an official agenda. In Greece, as we saw with regard to historiography last time and as will be illustrated further in later chapters, the free-for-all between competing intellectuals often led not just to rival solutions to agreed problems, but to radically

[44] See Long 1982, Denyer 1985, Beard 1986, Schofield 1986.

different views on what the problems were and on the viable means of investigating them.

We may now take stock, in conclusion, of what our very rapid surveys suggest. We have seen that the ambition to predict is enormously widespread and diverse. Successful prediction is a feature that we all recognise in science, where it is sometimes held to be one of its defining characteristics. But modern science has no monopoly of that *ambition*. Under its stimulus, all sorts of different techniques were tried out, in ancient times, on everything from the study of the stars, to the weather, to the outcome of diseases, from matters of state policy to the fortunes of individuals.

Evaluating these procedures is more complex than might appear. Many seem to us to be dead ends – some seemed to the ancients themselves to be so, as we noted for Xunzi on divination in China, and for the rejection of astrology by some Greeks. But *which* were, and *why*, are tricky issues, and we should beware of concluding prematurely to any radical differences in the gullibility of the ancients and ourselves. The first complication relates to the aims of the talk about what may or will occur – for that affects the basis on which the performance is judged. The chief role of a prediction may, we suggested, be admonitory, or it may simply serve to resolve indecision – where what matters is the status or character of the person offering the advice, the seer who can claim foresight into human affairs.

Where the basis is evidential, the connections observed or assumed vary – from causal relations to merely symbolic ones.[45] When the cause of a particular effect is known, the latter can be taken as an indication of the former (the smoke of the fire that produces it) though not all effects have unique causes. Conversely, effects can be anticipated (within limits) where causes have been established and identified in the particular case (one of the standard ancient Greek examples is dropsy from the mad dog's bite). But more often predictions related to non-causal connections, some just symbolic, but others representing regular conjunctions: the arrival of swallows heralds spring (at least if you are in Greece). Finally some signs are significant not because they betoken, but because they breach, regularities, as is the case with miracles, or as the Chinese claimed for the

---

[45] The distinctions between signs of different types are explicitly debated by the Stoics and Epicureans, among Greek philosophers, see for example Sedley 1982, Burnyeat 1982. But in Indian logic too there are analyses of inferences based on signs in the Nyaya school, see Matilal 1971, 1985, Zimmermann 1992.

non-occurrence of certain eclipses – though to understand something as such an exception to a rule means having some idea of the rule.

Often there is no conclusive test of a prediction: the outcome is indeterminate. No one could tell for sure what would have happened if the advice had not been taken. But sometimes, for sure, there were obvious mismatches between what had been foretold and what actually happened. In such cases, there are well-known difficulties in diagnosing what has gone wrong. In ancient times, but not just in ancient times, the practitioner was often blamed rather than the practice, and not just when the practice served state interests or was otherwise well entrenched, though when that was the case, the scope for mystification was considerable. Yet in modern science too, as Lakatos especially pointed out,[46] when precisely counter-examples should spell the demise of a theory as a whole is a tricky matter of judgement. If a theory has proved its worth over a range of problems, then the refusal to abandon it in the face of objections is sensible – until those objections have to be recognised as overwhelming.

While mismatches, whether excusable or not, were the lot of many ancient predicters, we also found signs of the increasing efficacy of prediction as patterns of regularities were discovered. In some cases, phenomena that came within the scope of reliable prediction *lost* their ominous character. But that did not always happen – as we saw in Mesopotamian astronomy. There the search for connections of one sort led to the discovery of others. The ṭupšarru were hoping to learn from the heavens what was of significance for the state: in the process they identified certain regularities in the heavenly phenomena themselves, though that did not diminish their significance as signs.

We might be tempted to conclude, from that last example, that inquiry, when geared to prediction, developed in a rather random fashion: the ṭupšarru just stumbled on those regularities. But that would be to discount the elements of judgement involved, first in recognising the regularities for what they were, and then in pursuing the programme of further research they suggested. The development of medical prognosis serves to make a similar point. The pulses were read very differently by Chinese doctors and by Greek ones: but both saw the possibility of establishing correlations between them, the internal condition of the patient's body and the outcome of a complaint, and they pursued their investigation with some energy. The problem was always that of evaluating the results,

---

[46] Lakatos 1978, chs. 1 and 2 especially.

and plenty of thought was given to that, in all three civilisations, even while, in each, there was also a good deal of inflation on the subject, especially by interested parties.

In certain respects, however, the fortunes of prediction varied in different ancient civilisations. Attempting, in public, to undermine what others believed was a peculiarly Greek phenomenon. Yet to put that into perspective, criticism of other scribes is expressed in Babylonia and so too are doubts about certain modes of prediction in China. What appears as another striking difference in degree is that much Babylonian and Chinese work was carried out in powerful state institutions, courts, temples, bureaux, while many (though not all) Greek investigators operated outside such structures. It is already clear that not all the advantages lie on one side, that of state support, or of going it alone, but the further discussion of the comparative strengths and weaknesses of different institutional frameworks will form the central topic of chapter 6. But before that, we have further aspects of the development of inquiry to consider, notably the ambition to understand things by discovering their numbers or by exploring their mathematical relations. That will be the subject of my next chapter.

CHAPTER THREE

The numbers of things

From the belief that mathematics reveals invariant truths it is all too tempting to conclude that mathematics itself is invariant. That view is then often combined with a thesis about the development of science, namely that it depends on a shift from the qualitative explanation of phenomena to their quantitative understanding. That is generally represented as the key factor in the changes that took place in what used to be called the scientific revolution of the sixteenth and seventeenth centuries, and in support Galileo is regularly cited for the notion that the book of the universe is written in mathematical language.

The flaws in such a package of beliefs are obvious. First, there are the objections I have raised before against a teleological history of science – writing that history from the perspective of what was to come, as if the individuals concerned could have known what that was. But then even a modest acquaintance with the extant mathematics from Egypt, Babylonia, India, Meso-America, Greece, China, reveals an immense diversity, first in the problems investigated, secondly in the styles of reasoning cultivated, thirdly in the relationships between 'mathematics' (however interpreted) and other types of inquiry, and fourthly in the roles and value of 'mathematics' in society. Finding the numbers in things has often been held to be the key to understanding, but that has been with very varying views both as to how to find them, and as regards the nature of the understanding to be obtained.

I shall certainly not be able to do justice to all the cross-cultural ramifications of this topic here: that would take a monograph by itself. I shall concentrate just on the rich materials from China and from Greece, first to reveal something of that variety. What different modes of the search for the numbers of things, or their other mathematical relations, were cultivated, and with what ambitions? That will lead me to questions of values and to the ideological associations of some aspects of these studies. The strategic issue I shall broach in conclusion is why mathematics developed so differently in these two ancient civilisations.

Following my usual methodological principle of adopting actors' rather than observers' categories, we should first review how some of the key Greek and Chinese terms were used. This is not just a matter of remarking, for instance, that Greek *arithmos* does not correspond to our 'number', but has a more restricted reference, namely to positive integers greater than one. As Ho Pengyoke showed, the range of *shu*[1] in China, the word generally translated 'number', is much wider than that suggests.[1] It covers, for instance, 'several', 'counting', 'scolding', 'fate and destiny', 'art' as in 'the art of', and 'deliberations'. *Shuxue* or *shushu*, that is the study or arts of *shu*[1], will, accordingly, comprise far more than just any investigation of, or using, numbers or quantities – and the same applies also to *suan*, another word for counting that figures, for example, in the titles of the two major classical Chinese mathematical treatises that date from 100 years either side of the Common Era. These are the *Zhoubi suanjing* (conventionally translated as the *Arithmetic Classic of the Zhou Gnomon*: though more than just 'arithmetic' is involved, as we shall see) and the *Jiuzhang suanshu*, that is the *Nine Chapters of the Arithmetical*, or better, again, *Mathematical, Art*. Again Greek *mathematike* does not tally with our 'mathematics' either. The noun *mathema* comes from the verb *manthanein* which has the entirely general meaning of 'to learn' and the commonest Hellenistic use of *mathematikos* (and of the Latin *mathematicus*) is for the astrologer.

Such differences might be thought to undermine the viability of comparison as a whole. But provided we bear in mind the differences in the intellectual mapping of the disciplines concerned, we can study how numerical relations were investigated and used. That is where the common ground lies.

While there are many modes by which an understanding of things may be sought, two of the most basic are counting and measuring. Both were prized as indicative of culture itself in both Greece and China. Prometheus revealed number to humans as the most excellent of devices (*exochon sophismaton*) in the *Prometheus Vinctus* (459), and that is long before Plato has god doing geometry. In China, balance beams and plumblines, along with the carpenter's square and compasses, the marking cord and level, were the so-called six standards, associated with culture heroes such as Fu Xi and Nü Gua at the origins of civilised life. Both Greeks and Chinese recognised that without number there would be no commercial

---

[1] Ho Pengyoke 1991.

transactions, no monetary ones certainly, no keeping of accounts, no land surveying, no census, no taxation – in a word, no civilised life: I mean no social order or control. Yet the modalities of those practical applications already differ as between the two societies, as did – what I am chiefly concerned with here – how number figures in the understanding of things, and how that can be extended by research – which numbers are significant, which things are especially worth counting and how indeed they are counted.

A first straightforward point relates to a difference in arithmetical notations. The Chinese used a place-value system with a decimal base that does not strike us as too unfamiliar, for all that their calculations with counting-rods may.[2] But the Greeks used letters as the symbols for numbers, alpha for 1, beta for 2, iota for 10, rho for 100 and so on. That has generally been criticised as pretty cumbersome, and indeed it takes some getting used to in practice. But that is not my point here, but rather the fact that this notation provides an immediate association between numbers and things by way of the letters that stand for their names. The name of any person or thing could be said to correspond to a determinate number. Alexandros, for instance $(1 + 30 + 5 + 60 + 1 + 50 + 4 + 100 + 70 + 200)$ comes out at 521, and Elenê gives 98 and so on. It is certainly not the case that all Greeks believed that there was a profound significance in these associations. Some did, while others, as we shall see, were highly critical of such ideas. Nevertheless the notation lent itself to such play, which is inconceivable without it. The Chinese did not go down that particular speculative route.

Yet the *general* idea that, somehow, numbers provide the key to understanding things can be found in different forms in both Greece and China. In Greece there is the Pythagorean belief that the underlying properties or relationships between things are expressible numerically. Aristotle also ascribes to the (or rather some) Pythagoreans the doctrine that all things *are* numbers, though whether he is reporting their view, or rather interpreting it, is disputed. It is now generally accepted that his own philosophy of mathematics, whereby mathematics studies not independent mathematical entities, but rather the mathematical properties of physical objects, makes him an unreliable witness on this point. Thus he may well be spelling out what he believes to be the consequences of the Pythagoreans' positions, rather than what they actually said.[3]

---

[2] For brief accounts of the use of the counting rods, see Needham 1959, pp. 70ff, Li and Du 1987, pp. 6ff, Volkov 1994, Martzloff 1997, pp. 209–11.
[3] Aristotle, *Metaphysics* 985b26ff, 986a15ff, 987a13ff, Huffman 1993, and see Lear 1982 on Aristotle's philosophy of mathematics more generally.

It is true that much later, neo-Pythagorean writers made some ambitious, not to say extravagant, claims. In the third century CE Iamblichus, especially, expresses the unqualified view, in his *On the Common Mathematical Science*, that 'mathematics' enables one to understand the whole of nature and its parts. That sounds promising. But we have to bear in mind that under mathematics he included, among other things, prognostic astrology and the symbolic associations of numbers, as well as a variety of attempts at giving a quantitative account of the four elements. However, already in the fifth century BCE, as we can tell from the evidence for Philolaus, both harmonics and astronomy were fields in which the mathematically expressible relations underlying physical phenomena were beginning to be explored[4] (I shall have more to say about them later).

Two other ideas also certainly go back before Aristotle, firstly the belief that certain numbers carry a particular symbolic charge, and secondly the building up of systems of correlation in part through mathematical relations. Aristotle pours his scorn on, but he has not just invented, the idea of the special significance of the number ten. He even claims that it influenced the Pythagoreans to postulate a counter-earth in their astronomy – to bring the moving heavenly bodies up to ten – but there is more to that than he lets on: he elsewhere suggests that that extra body may have been used to help explain eclipses.[5] Our sources, friendly or otherwise, advance a number of speculations, for example that 10 is the sum of the first four integers themselves associated with point (1), line (2), triangle (3) and pyramid (4). But whatever may have been the reasoning, the decad came to be represented as having, for the Pythagoreans, a religious significance, as when they were said to swear by him who handed down the *tetraktys* (the triangular figure representing 10 shown in figure 3).[6] From one point of view, the one that is generally picked up, this might suggest the traditional, even folkloric, elements in Pythagorean thought. But from another, it illustrates, rather, how distant their religious beliefs were from conventional Greek ones.

Similar problems of interpretation arise with regard to the use of the *sustoichia* or table of opposites, for which once again our earliest evidence is in Aristotle.[7] Ten pairs of opposites are there represented as, in some sense, the principles of other things. Items in each column are, by that very arrangement, associated with one another. Some such correlations

---

[4] Huffman 1993, part III ch. 4, pp. 231 ff, part IV ch. 3, pp. 364ff.

[5] Aristotle, *Metaphysics* 986a6–12, *On the Heavens* 293a23–b30.

[6] Porphyry, *Life of Pythagoras* 20, Iamblichus, *Life of Pythagoras* 150.

[7] Aristotle, *Metaphysics* 986a22ff: limit/unlimited, odd/even, one/plurality, right/left, male/female, at rest/moving, straight/curved, light/darkness, good/evil, square/oblong.

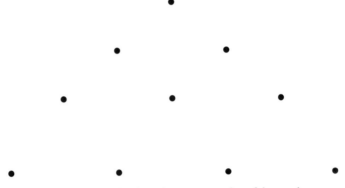

Fig. 3 *Tetraktys*: symbolic triangular representation of the number ten.

are, to be sure, traditional or conventional enough (as the association of
right with male, left with female). But that applies less to the more mathematical principles, square and oblong, straight and curved, one and
plurality, odd and even. The first pair, limit and unlimited themselves,
appear as the ultimate principles on which cosmic harmony depends in
Philolaus, where again we have a tantalising glimpse of a metaphysical
system based, in part, on mathematical ideas.[8] But however it was generated, the *sustoichia* provided a framework that enabled associations between highly disparate phenomena to be suggested, partly, though it is
true not entirely, through mathematical relations.

The evidence for early Chinese thought seems at first sight to suggest
rather similar patterns of speculation, though as we shall see there are
also important differences at a deeper level. *Yin* and *yang* themselves
are not, in origin, mathematical, but relate primarily to dark and light,
to the shady and the sunny sides of a hill or a river bank, for instance.
But the system of divination set out in the *Yijing* (which we mentioned in
chapter 2) depends on combinations of broken (*yin*) and unbroken (*yang*)
lines, and there the latter are associated with the odd numbers nine and
seven, the former with the even numbers six and eight. In the chief
traditional version, the hexagrams are built up by sorting sticks of milfoil
or yarrow into piles, where the remainders from certain operations will
yield those four numbers, nine and seven being termed the greater and
the lesser *yang*, six and eight the greater and the lesser *yin*. In popular
modern versions, the sixes, sevens, eights and nines are got by throwing

[8] Huffman 1993, part II ch. I.

coins in threes and counting the heads and tails as threes and twos respectively.

The point of similarity between *yin/yang* and the Pythagorean Table of Opposites is that both offer a grid to which just about every kind of object or event can be related. The *Yijing* (we said) had not just a divinatory function, but a cosmological one, offering insight, to the skilled interpreter, not just into the present situation and likely future developments, but into the whole human condition. But the fundamental difference between *yin/yang* and much Greek thinking with polarities is that *yin* and *yang* themselves are not stable, fixed entities, but dynamic, interrelational, aspectual. What is *yin* in one respect may be *yang* in another: an old man may be *yang* in relation to a young one in terms of political power, but *yin* in respect of stamina. Moreover in the hexagrams themselves, there are rules that govern the changes in the lines themselves, when a *yin* line transforms into a *yang* one, or vice versa. That is after all fundamental to the system set out in what is *called* the *Book of Changes*.

The *Yijing* operates with binary oppositions. But other systems of correlations that do not (just) depend on *yin* and *yang* also figure extensively in Chinese thought. The concept of the five phases, *wuxing*, only becomes prominent in accounts of physical change in extant texts from the third century,[9] though thereafter it comes to form the basis of much Han cosmological thought. This is not an element theory, in the sense that we understand in Greece, where the elements are the basic constituents of things and in themselves unchanging. The five phases, wood, fire, earth, metal, water, are the stages or transformations that occur, processes rather than substances, related to one another in cycles of production and of conquest (figure 4). But from our present point of view, the key feature that concerns us is that the five came to be correlated with a whole range of other factors, cardinal points, tastes, smells, colours, musical notes, star-palaces, heavenly bodies, planets, weather, rulers, ministries, measuring instruments, kinds of living creatures, kinds of domestic animals, 'grains', sacrifices, sense-organs and affective states.[10] Obviously some of these groupings have a more transparent rationale than others. The fifth 'cardinal point' is the centre, and that is unproblematic enough. But to get to five seasons, late summer had to be added to the usual four,

[9] The point is the subject of current controversy where the issue hinges chiefly on the interpretation of the evidence for Zou Yan in the early third century BCE. This has been subject to a recent analysis by Sivin 1995b ch. IV. On the more general questions of the origins and development of the five phases, see Kalinowski 1991, Harper 1999a, pp. 86ff, Lloyd and Sivin 2002, ch. 5 and appendix.
[10] See Needham 1956, pp. 262ff, contrast Graham 1989, pp. 340ff.

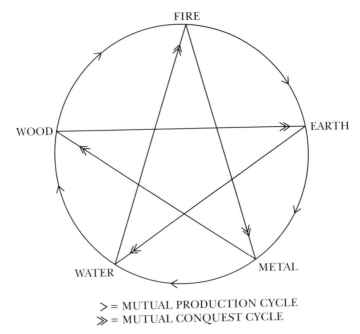

> = MUTUAL PRODUCTION CYCLE
>> = MUTUAL CONQUEST CYCLE

Fig. 4   Transformations of the five phases. The mutual generation cycle follows the sequence picked out by single arrows on the circumference of the circle, that is, wood, fire, earth, metal, water. The mutual conquest cycle follows the chords indicated by the double arrows, where wood overcomes earth, metal overcomes wood, fire metal, water fire and earth water.

despite the disruption this entailed to a definition in terms of solstices and equinoxes.

But once a fivefold grouping was found, or could be suggested, then its members could be brought into relationship with other sets of fives.[11] The planet Mars ('Sparkling Deluder'), for example, was associated with fire, summer, the south, the colour red, the ministry of war, the tongue as sense-organ, and joy as affective state. While there is far from total uniformity, as between different texts, on the precise correlations proposed, what they all have in common is that the members of each group of five are coordinated with the members of others.

The temptation, at this point, is to use the label 'numerology' to dismiss all of this as rubbish. But that is to miss the point. What such systems offer are ways of suggesting orderly relations between very diverse phenomena. What was thereby revealed was not causal relations.

[11] Yet other systems of correspondences based on the numbers four and six were also proposed, see Graham 1989, pp. 325ff.

The nature of the understanding achieved was not explanatory, but associative. Each item was brought into a network of relations with other items and so given its place in a single comprehensive framework. Different items or groups of them could then be seen as exemplifying similar structures and as illustrating, even if they could not be deduced from, the same general laws or principles.

But in other contexts, in China and in Greece, the extraction of the numbers of things was not just a matter of observing or suggesting certain correlations. The study of the heavens yields some impressive examples, where the regulation of the calendar immediately raises the problem of reconciling lunations with yearly solar returns, neither of them reckonable exactly in terms of whole numbers of days. That the tropical year is not exactly 365 days was known early on in both civilisations.

Here too, to be sure, there is much reflection on the significance of particular days or months. In Greece, we have Hesiod making all sorts of suggestions, in the *Days*, about does and don'ts on particular days. 'Few know', he remarks,[12] 'that the twenty-seventh of the month is best for opening a wine-jar . . . Few call it by its right name . . . And again few know that the fourth day after the twentieth is best while it is morning: towards evening it is worse.' 'One praises one day, another another, but few know.' We need Hesiod himself, evidently, as our guide.

Analogously, in China, the monthly ordinances, *yueling*, texts,[13] lay down what should or should not be done in each month, what the Emperor should eat and drink, down to the colours of the dresses to be worn by the court ladies. The recommendations here envisage the Emperor and his officials, a grander audience than Hesiod's, and they are less personal or idiosyncratic, drawing on a greater depth of tradition, though with similar pretensions to special knowledge.

But such calendrical lore is a far cry from the work of those who sought to determine periodicities, to calculate the mean motions of the sun and moon, to plot the trajectory of the planets and to draw up reliable eclipse tables. A text from the *Zhoubi suanjing* sets out what can be achieved in this domain if the correct method is used.[14] The pupil, Rong Fang, approaches his master, Chenzi, and says: 'Master, I have recently heard something about your Way. Is it really true that your Way is able to comprehend the height and size of the sun, the [area] illuminated

---

[12] Hesiod, *Works and Days* 765–828, especially 814ff, 818, 820–1, 824.

[13] Different versions of such ordinances are presented in the *Lüshi chunqiu* (around 240 BCE), in *Huainanzi* (around 140 BCE) and the *Liji* (collected after 79 CE). See, for example, Major 1993, pp. 217ff.

[14] *Zhoubi suanjing* 23–4, see Cullen 1996, pp. 176ff.

by its radiance, the amount of its daily motion, the figures (*shu*[I]) for its greatest and least distances, the extent of human vision, the limits of the four poles, the lodges into which the stars are ordered, and the length and breadth of heaven and earth?' To which Chenzi replies: 'It is true'. Although Rong Fang is initially defeated by the problems, Chenzi puts it to him: 'Your ability in mathematics is sufficient to understand such matters if you sincerely give reiterated thought to them'. Indeed he claims that 'all these things are attained to by mathematics' – *suanshu*, the art or method of numbers.

The questions about which Rong Fang asks are a mixed bag. The boundaries of the twenty-eight Chinese star or lunar lodges (*xiu*), for instance, were conventional. They play a similar role to the constellations of the zodiac, though their widths varied. But one key method, for determining the height of the sun, for example, was the use of gnomon-shadow differences.[15] On the assumption that the earth is flat, a comparison between the noon shadow lengths, at the summer solstice, of three eight-foot-high gnomons located at distances exactly 1,000 *li*[I], 'leagues', apart (a *li*[I] was about a third of a mile or half a kilometre) on a due north–south line, is made to yield a value for the height of the sun (see figure 5). As for the dimension of the sun, that is to be got by sighting it down a bamboo tube such that the angular diameter of the sun exactly fits the bore of the tube (see figure 6). Then given the distance of the sun (100,000 *li*[I] along the hypotenuse) and the measurements of the bore and the tube, the size of the sun can be obtained by similar triangles.

The serious underestimate of the shadow-length difference is the first main problem: it is assumed that the difference is one Chinese inch (a tenth of a Chinese foot) for an 8-foot high gnomon for every 1,000 *li*[I] – when the real figure for the latitude of central China would be more like one inch for every 150 *li*[I]. We are dealing, evidently, with an at least partly hypothetical set-up, even though direct observation seems to be claimed of the sighting down the bamboo tube.

Both methods, as has been pointed out, have their analogues in ancient Greece. Archimedes sighted the sun down the bore of a tube not to get the size of the sun, but to fix the upper and lower limits of its angular diameter.[16] Eratosthenes used gnomon-shadow differences, taken again at noon at the summer solstice at Alexandria and at Syene, to arrive at his estimate of the circumference of the earth (see figure 7).[17] He had

---

[15] There is another example of this in *Huainanzi* 3, see Cullen 1993, pp. 269ff, cf. Volkov 1996–7, pp. 145–58.

[16] Archimedes, *Sandreckoner*, ch. 11, HS II 222.11ff.

[17] Eratosthenes' estimation is reported by Cleomedes, *On the Circular Movement of the Heavenly Bodies* I 10, 90.20ff, and is the subject of extensive scholarly discussion, see Lloyd 1987, pp. 231ff.

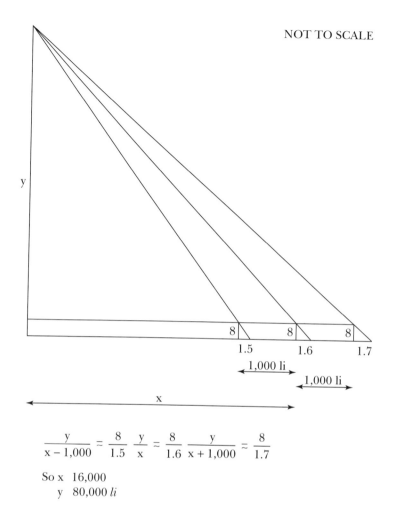

NOT TO SCALE

$$\frac{y}{x-1,000} \approx \frac{8}{1.5} \quad \frac{y}{x} \approx \frac{8}{1.6} \quad \frac{y}{x+1,000} \approx \frac{8}{1.7}$$

So x 16,000
   y 80,000 *li*

Fig. 5   Gnomon shadow differences used to determine the height of the sun, as in *Zhoubi suanjing*. The lengths of the shadows cast by three 8-foot high gnomons, distant from each other 1,000 *li*[l], on a north–south axis, are measured at noon on the summer solstice. It is assumed that the earth is flat. The height of the sun can then be derived from similar right triangles. The actual figures for the shadow lengths quoted in the text (that is 1.7, 1.6 and 1.5 feet) tally exactly with the conventional assumption that a distance of 1,000 *li*[l] gives a difference of one Chinese inch (one-tenth of a Chinese foot), but this is a gross exaggeration (the actual figure being an inch for approximately every 150 *li*[l]). The accuracy of this assumption was already the subject of comment in Li Chunfeng's seventh-century commentary.

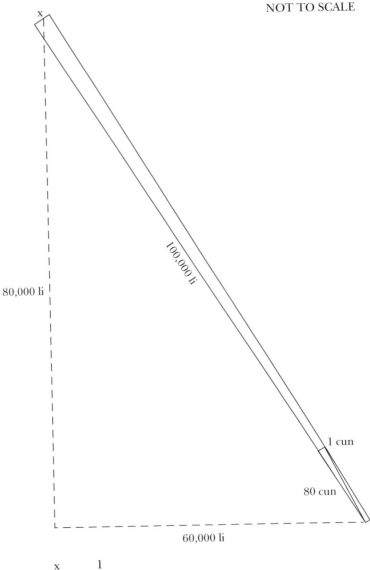

x

80,000 li

100,000 li

1 cun

80 cun

60,000 li

$$\frac{x}{100,000} \approx \frac{1}{80}$$

So x is 1,250 *li*

Fig. 6 Determination of the circumference of the sun by sighting down a bamboo tube as in *Zhoubi suanjing*. The sun is sighted down a bamboo tube of length 8 feet and diameter 1 inch and it is said to fit the aperture of the tube exactly. Given the further assumption that the sun is distant 100,000 *li*[1] along the hypotenuse (corresponding to a height of 80,000 *li*[1] from the sub-solar point) the dimension of the sun can be got from those of the tube by similar triangles.

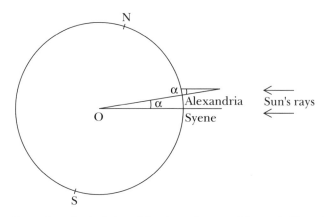

Fig. 7 Eratosthenes' calculation of the circumference of the earth. Eratosthenes assumed (a) that the earth is spherical (already proved by Aristotle), (b) that the sun is at such a distance from the earth that its rays may be taken to fall on the earth in parallel lines, (c) that Alexandria and Syene are on the same meridian (in fact Syene is 3 degrees East of Alexandria) and most crucially (d) that the distance between them is 5,000 stades. (How he arrived at that figure is not at all clear.) It was reported that at Syene at noon on the summer solstice the gnomon cast no shadow (our sources note that the same applied not just at Syene but to an area around it), and at Alexandria the shadow made an angle of 7 and a half degrees. The circumference of the earth can then be calculated at 250,000 stades (though it is not certain which of several 'stades' Eratosthenes was using). Other sources report that he gave the circumference as 252,000 stades, which may have purely been an adjustment to give a more convenient figure for subdivisions of the circumference, namely 700 stades for each degree.

practical problems, too, first with the assumption that Syene is due south of Alexandria (when it is actually 3° east of it) and secondly with estimating the distance between the two (taken as the suspiciously round figure of 5,000 stades). Nor do we know which value of the stade to apply to his procedure – which affects our judgement of the accuracy of his result, a figure of 250,000 stades (before adjustment) for the circumference of the earth – though even on the worst case interpretation that is less than 20 per cent out, and it may have been much closer than that: on the best, it is only 0.1 per cent out.

But while the Chinese and Greek methods were essentially the same, mathematically, the key difference between them lies in the starting assumptions made. Eratosthenes assumed, what Aristotle had already proved, namely that the earth is spherical. Moreover he took it that the sun is at such a distance from the earth that its rays may be treated, for practical purposes, as if they were parallel. The *Zhoubi*, by contrast, operates with the common-sense assumption that the earth is flat. With that assumption, the sun's distance can, in principle, be got from the difference in the shadow lengths.

Here, then, were methods that, whether in their Greek or Chinese versions, offered – as the ancients themselves thought – the *prospect* of extraordinary results. Just as some Pythagoreans held up mathematics as the key to new insight into things, so too the exchange between Rong Fang and Chenzi registers a sense of the power of the art of numbers. Moreover, as in Greece, the point is echoed in other, not specifically 'mathematical' writings. In the *Suwen* recension of the medical classic, the *Huangdi neijing*, Qi Bo remarks that the men of high antiquity, who knew the Way, harmonised themselves with disciplines based on what is regular, or, as he puts it, on the working or the art of numbers, *shushu*.[18] Just as the prestige of *mathematike* in Greece spread into other domains, so too this happened in China to the art of numbers. In both cultures, doctors, for instance, sought to determine the critical days of diseases on the model of other periodicities. Yet there was this difference, in that case, that in China they were often directly correlated with the sixty-day calendrical cycle, while in Greece the days were counted from the onset of the disease, and it did not matter which month you were in.[19] That was just as well since Greek calendars varied as between one city-state and another, both the names of the months, and their starting-dates, and the systems of intercalation used.

Two related issues thus emerge, first the question of which problems would yield to an attack based on mathematics and on what assumptions, and secondly that of the adjustments or corrections that might need to be made to the results obtained or indeed to obtain them. The recurrent problem there was how much of the complexities of the empirical data had to be sacrificed for the sake of small numbers, simple relations, equalities. Harmonics was one area that illustrates both the prospects and the problems.

Take first Chinese explorations of the relationship between the five notes of their standard pentatonic scale, and the twelve pitch pipes (*lü*), which give the twelve notes of what we would call the 12-tone scale. This is discussed at some length in *Huainanzi* and in the *Shiji*, among other works.[20]

---

[18] *Suwen* 1 1 7. It is striking that, in the one case from Han times when the dissection of a human body is referred to (see below, chapter 5 note 9), among the points recorded are the measurements of some of the viscera, cf. Kuriyama 1999, pp. 223–4.

[19] In some contexts, in China, not just particular days, but particular hours within a day, were deemed significant for medical practice. Harper 1999b has an interesting discussion on the similarities between the discourse, and roles, of doctors and diviners in China.

[20] See *Huainanzi* 3.21b, on which see Major 1993, pp. 112ff, and *Shiji* 25: 1249.2ff, see Chavannes 1898, III pp. 313ff, Picken 1957.

Huainanzi suggests correlations between the pitch pipes and the seasons of the year, for example between each pitch pipe and one of twelve positions of the handle of the Big Dipper, as that constellation moves round the celestial pole through the seasons.[21] The idea here is that each pitch pipe resonates spontaneously with the q^{II} of the season.[22]

But then *Huainanzi* also sets out a schema correlating five of the pitch pipes with the five notes of the pentatonic scale and explaining how the other pitch-pipe notes can be generated in sequence from them.[23] The first five notes are plain sailing: if we take them as corresponding to C

[21] *Huainanzi* 3.19b, Major 1993, pp. 106ff. The order of the pitch pipes in this sequence is (in Major's translations) Great Budding, Pinched Bell, Maiden Purity, Median Regulator, Luxuriant, Forest Bell, Tranquil Pattern, Southern Regulator, Tireless, Responsive Bell, Yellow Bell, Great Regulator. In another schema, *Huainanzi* 3.12b, Major 1993, pp. 88ff, each of the pitch pipes is used twice and correlated with fifteen-day periods in the sun's annual movement.
[22] The way in which this idea came eventually to be undermined and refuted is discussed by Huang and Chang 1996.
[23] *Huainanzi* 3.21b–22a, Major 1993, pp. 112–14.

Table 1. *Chinese harmonics: the generation of the chromatic scale*

Pitch pipes in generation order	Pentatonic notes	Modern interpretation	Interval	Number assigned In Huainanzi 3
Yellow Bell	*gong*	C	Fifth	81
Forest Bell	*zhi*	G	Fourth	54 (×2/3)
Great Budding	*shang*	D	Fifth	72 (×4/3)
Southern Regulator	*yu*	A	Fourth	48 (×2/3)
Maiden Purity	*jue*	E	Fifth	64 (×4/3)
Responsive Bell		B	Fourth	42 (×2/3)
Luxuriant		F sharp	Fourth	57 (×4/3)
Great Regulator		C sharp	Fifth	76 (×4/3)
Tranquil Pattern		G sharp	Fourth	51 (×2/3)
Pinched Bell		D sharp	Fifth	68 (×4/3)
Tireless		A sharp	Fourth	45 (×2/3)
Median Regulator		F		60 (×4/3)

It should be noted that the production of what *we* call a higher note is called the inferior (*xia*) generation, that of a lower note the superior (*shang*) one: see Needham and Robinson 1962, pp. 173ff.

G D A and E in modern notation, they are got by alternate ascents of
a fifth and descents of a fourth. *Huainanzi* supplies numbers. The first
pentatonic note, called *gong* ('palace' or 'ruler') is correlated with the
pitch pipe Yellow Bell, and is assigned to the number 81. The other
four are then equated with 54, 72, 48 and 64 respectively (produced
by multiplying by 2/3 and 4/3 alternately). So far so good. But as the
other notes of the remaining pitch pipes are generated, first the strict
alternation of ascents and descents is interrupted (you get two descents
one after another, from B to F sharp and then to C sharp: this is to stay
within a single octave) and then the numbers equated with the notes are
rounded – and not always to the nearest whole number. Thus Responsive
Bell, the first after the five pentatonic notes, is assigned to 42, though by
strict arithmetic 64 multiplied by 2/3 is 42 2/3.

Interestingly enough, a different solution to the problem figures, if our
text is correct, in the *Shiji*.[24] There the sequence of alternate ascents and
descents is adhered to – but at the cost of going outside a single octave –
and no rounding adjustments are made. But that in turn means that we
have to cope with ratios such as 32,768 to 59,049. Indeed *Huainanzi* too
recognised (at 3.21a) that if whole numbers are used, then, starting from
unity, numbers up to three to the power of 11, that is 177,147, will be
needed.

On the one hand, these texts show a clear interest in much more than
just the symbolic correlations between numbers, notes and seasons, in
the numerical analysis of sequences of fifths and fourths. On the other,
they illustrate how, once mathematisation of harmonic phenomena is
attempted, problems arise. Rounding adjustments need to be made, or
very large numbers tolerated, the proportions being as complex as some
of those they appreciated had to be used in such other contexts as the
determination of eclipse cycles or calendrical concordances.[25]

How did the Greeks get on? Here too there were disagreements
among theorists, indeed more fundamental epistemological ones than in
Chinese harmonics.[26] Here too there were some success stories and, in
the application to astronomy, much wild speculation. Even with regard
to the successes, fantastic accounts circulated about how Pythagoras (in
person) discovered that the intervals of the octave, fifth and fourth are

[24] On the textual difficulties of *Shiji* 25: 1249.2ff, see Chavannes 1898, III pp. 313ff.
[25] Thus the Triple Concordance system, adopted in 104 BCE, gives a lunation of 29 43/81 days and
a year of 365 385/1539 days, and a concordance cycle where 1,539 years equals 19,035 lunations
and further equals 562,120 days. See Sivin 1995a ch. II, who notes (p. 12) in this context that the
apparent precision is specious.
[26] In what follows I draw extensively on Barker 1989 and 2000.

expressible as 2:1, 3:2 and 4:3. In one he passes a smithy, hears concordant notes (so we would be led to believe) and gets the ratios from the weights of the hammers – except that that is impossible, for the notes will vary, rather, with the anvil.[27]

Those ratios, at least, were common ground to otherwise quite divergent Greek theoretical analyses. One approach, exemplified by Aristoxenus, insisted that the unit of measurement should be something identifiable by perception. Here a tone is defined as the difference between the fifth and the fourth, and in principle the whole of music theory is built up from these perceptible intervals – by ascending or descending fifths and fourths in a way that is reminiscent of Chinese harmonics. This approach accepted that musical intervals can be construed on the model of line segments and investigated quasi-geometrically.

But another mode of analysis, according to which the tone is understood as the difference between sounds whose 'speeds' stand in a ratio of 9:8, was more exclusively arithmetical. In this, the so-called Pythagorean tradition, represented in the Euclidean *Sectio Canonis*, musical relations are construed as essentially ratios between numbers and the task of the harmonic theorist is to deduce various propositions in the mathematics of ratios, for example that there is no ratio of integers that corresponds to a half or a quarter tone.[28]

These radically different modes of analysis were associated with quite different answers to such questions as whether the octave, fifth and fourth are exactly six tones, three and a half and two and a half tones respectively. If the tone is identified as the ratio 9:8, then you do not get an octave (2:1) by taking six such intervals (9:8 to the power of 6). Again the excess of a fifth over three tones, or a fourth over two, has to be expressed by the ratio 256:243 (not by the square root of 9/8).

First there was a dispute over whether a purely arithmetical analysis of harmonic phenomena can, or should, be given. But that was linked with an even more fundamental disagreement. Was perception to be the criterion, or reason, or some combination of the two?[29] Both extreme positions are attested. Some thought numbers rule, and if what we hear appeared to conflict with them, too bad for our hearing. For example, they spotted that the ratio 8:3, which corresponds to an octave plus

[27] This story is found, in one or other version, in no fewer than five different texts, for example Nicomachus, *Harmonics* ch. 6, 245.19ff. See further Lloyd 1979, p. 144 and n. 95.
[28] [Euclid] *Sectio Canonis* propositions 3 and 16, cf. Barker 1978 p. 4, 1981, p. 3, 2000, p. 253 n. 9.
[29] This is a recurrent theme in Ptolemy's *Harmonics* I ch. 1, and indeed throughout that work, see Barker 1989, pp. 270ff, 276ff and 2000, ch. 2, pp. 14–32.

a fourth (2:1 times 4:3) does not conform to the patterns of the main
concords, 2 to 1, 3 to 2 and 4 to 3 (these all have the form of either a
multiplicate ratio, that is n:1, or a superparticular one, n+1:1, where n is
a positive integer greater than 1). So that interval cannot *be* a concord,
whatever it may sound like.

At the opposite end of the spectrum, Aristoxenus, we said, claimed that
everything had to be got by perception. But even between the extremist
positions, those who were for reconciling the findings of perception with
those of mathematics, were faced with the question of how precisely that
accommodation was to be achieved. Ptolemy for his part undertook in
his *Harmonics* an ambitious twofold task (cf. Barker 2000). First there was
that of deriving what is perceived as tuneful from rational mathematical
principles: why indeed should there be any connection between sounds
and ratios? What hypotheses should be adopted to give the mathematical
underpinning to the analysis? But just to select some such principles was
not enough, for these then – in the second task – had to be brought to
an empirical test, to confirm that the results arrived at on the basis of
theory did indeed tally with what was perceived by the ear in practice to
be concordant or discordant as the case might be.

Attempts to find correlations between musical intervals and celestial
phenomena take us into more speculative territory. The Greeks were not
content with equating certain notes with the yearly movements of the sun
and stars, as we found in *Huainanzi*, with the notes corresponding to the
season of the year. Rather, the Greek claim was that each of the planets,
sun and moon produced one of a series of notes that were in concordant relationships with one another. In the earliest version – reported by
Aristotle[30] – the speeds of the heavenly bodies vary with their distances,
yielding concordant notes that produce 'the harmony of the spheres'.
The fact that we do not hear these sounds was explained on the grounds
that we have been used to them from birth, and so no longer notice
them – a plea that Aristotle himself dismissed with contempt.[31]

That doctrine antedates any precise, detailed knowledge of planetary
periodicities in Greece, and one might have thought that once that was
available, any such idea would have been abandoned. Whatever geometrical model was used for the motions of the planets, sun and moon,
their periods simply cannot be got to tally with the simple ratios of 2:1,
3:2 and 4:3. Yet it was not just the more speculative philosophers who
maintained it, in one or other of a variety of versions, in the wake of
an influential endorsement of the idea in Plato's *Republic*.[32] Ptolemy is

[30] Aristotle, *On the Heavens* II ch. 9, 290b12ff: see Lloyd 1996a, ch. 8, pp. 174ff.
[31] Aristotle, *On the Heavens* 290b30ff.   [32] Plato, *Republic* 617b.

prepared to countenance it in a modified form.[33] Nor was it just the Greeks who were fascinated by the idea, for it continues, in one version or another, down to Kepler at least. The attractions of this idea of cosmic harmony evidently outran doubts and disagreements about just how it was supposed to work.

Two other areas should now be considered very briefly, before I take stock of this first section of my discussion. These are optics and statics, neither at all well represented in our Chinese sources, although the mutilated remains of Mohist works provide glimpses of their interest in optics.[34] So far as statics goes, I have mentioned the cultural importance attached to weighing and measuring in China, though there the interest was chiefly in practical applications, and in standardisation, not in theoretical analysis.

Greek theoretical optics was part physical (what is the nature of light? Is it an actuality or does it move?),[35] part geometrical, part experimental. Geometrisation, in Euclid and others, generally meant axiomatisation (on which more in due course). Certain assumptions are first set out, for example that visual or light rays can be treated as straight lines, and then certain theorems demonstrated on their basis. As with most axiomatisations, there are problematic features. It is puzzling, for instance, that in Euclid's *Optics* visual rays are assumed *not* to form a continuum: there are *gaps* between them.[36] But even more surprising are the adjustments made in the course of the experimental verification of the laws of refraction set out in Ptolemy.[37] The ambition here was not just to prove that refraction occurs when light passes from one medium to another, but to determine its amount, for different angles of incidence, for three pairs of media, air to water, air to glass, and water to glass. Ptolemy reports his results, but he has evidently doctored them, since they all turn out to tally with a general law (which he nevertheless does not state explicitly) that takes the form $r = ai-bi^2$, where r is the angle of refraction, i the angle of incidence, and a and b constants for the media concerned. In this case we have not just simplifications, or the roundings of figures, but their 'correction' to fit the theory they were presumed to exhibit.

We do not get numbers or experimental verification in Archimedes' statics, a particularly pure example of axiomatic-deductive reasoning

---

[33] Ptolemy, *Harmonics* III chs. 9, 14, 15, cf. Barker 1989, pp. 381ff, 524ff.
[34] See Graham and Sivin 1973.   [35] Damianus records the dispute at *Optics* 24.7ff, 16ff.
[36] Euclid, *Optics* Definition 3, 2.7ff, Propositions 1, 3 and 9, 2.22ff, 4.26ff, 16.7ff. The interpretation of this material is, however, much disputed: see Brownson 1981, p. 174, A. M. Smith 1981, A. Jones 1994.
[37] See Ptolemy, *Optics* v chs. 11, 18 and 21, 229.1ff, 233.10ff, 236.4ff, Lejeune, see Lloyd 1987, pp. 245–7, A. M. Smith 1996.

that abstracts from all the complexities of real-life weighing. In charac-
teristically Euclidean fashion he first sets out his assumptions (the first
postulate states, among other things, that 'equal weights at equal distances are in equilibrium')[38] and then proceeds to the deductive proof,
for example of the law of the lever, first for commensurable, then for
incommensurable, magnitudes.

The striking feature of the idealisations here is that on the one hand
they permit the purely geometrical analysis of the problems, but on the
other they correspond, in the main, to assumptions commonly made in
everyday practice. Everyone who bought and sold goods using a balance,
whether of the equal-armed, or unequal-armed (steelyard) variety, implicitly assumed that when the arm was level, the weights on either side
are in reciprocal proportion to the distances. Archimedes discounts such
factors as the imperfections in any wood or metal bar, the effects of friction in the movement of such a bar about a fulcrum and the flexion and
weight of the bar itself. But then those simplifications too correspond to
ordinary practice. In our Greek sources we find references, for instance,
to cheating in the market place by those who used a wooden beam with
a knot at one end.[39]

From one point of view all that Archimedes has done is to tell people
what they knew already. But from another, that is anything but true.
First, he has made explicit the proportionalities that hold. Secondly,
he demonstrates his results through the geometrical analysis of the
distribution of weights. Third, his extension of that analysis to the
incommensurable case is pure mathematical virtuosity, since it is of no
practical consequence.

There are greater similarities between the Greek and the Chinese experience, in the mathematisation of certain inquiries, than is generally
allowed for by the stereotypes representing the Chinese, for instance, as
incapable of geometry (belied by the *Zhoubi* examples I took) or merely
interested in practicalities – not true of their harmonic theories, nor of
many other aspects of their mathematics. My favourite example is their
work on the value of the circumference–diameter ratio (or π) which they
attacked by calculating the areas of inscribed regular polygons (much in
the way that Archimedes does in *On the Dimensions of the Circle* – though
he circumscribes them as well). In the *Nine Chapters* and the associated
commentaries, we find them starting with a regular hexagon, where the
perimeter is three times the diameter (showing that π must be greater

38 Archimedes, *On the Equilibrium of Planes* Proposition 1, HS II 126.6ff.
39 See the pseudo-Aristotelian *Mechanica* 849b34ff.

than three). But they then work out the areas of successively larger polygons, doubling the sides each time, to the point where the area of a
regular polygon of 192 sides is being determined and that of polygons
with up to 3,072 sides is being contemplated (by the time we get to
Zhao Youqin in the thirteenth century, that figure rises to 16,384-sided
ones).[40] So much for Chinese mathematics being always fixated on the
practical.

Much mathematisation, on both sides again, was fanciful or mysti-
ficatory, and some seemed so to some ancient critics themselves. Some
applications only worked by dint of some adjustment to the results. Large
numbers got in the way of the claim to have shown how simple the universe was: yet they could also be put to advantage, to show the prowess of
those who knew how to manipulate them. Phoney precision spreads out
into other domains, as is shown by the example mentioned in chapter 2
of the Greek attempt to apply music theory to the analysis of the pulse.
There was order to be discovered. That stimulated the search in both
China and Greece. But in both societies, announcements of its discovery
were sometimes premature.

This takes me to the last two topics I promised to discuss, the question
of values and ideologies, and the problems posed by the differences in
the way mathematics developed in China and Greece.

Both Chinese and Greeks shared the notion that the world as a whole –
'heaven and earth' in Chinese terms, the cosmos in Greek ones – is
orderly, but the forms their notions of orderliness took differ, providing
interesting insights also into their divergent notions of intelligibility. In
China, the regular relations between heaven and earth are, in a sense, the
responsibility of the Emperor who acts as a mediator between them. On
him depend not just the welfare of 'all under heaven', but also the orderly
relations between heaven and earth themselves. They are a matter of due
processes of change: yet these could be disrupted. When irregularities
occurred, that could be taken as a warning, a sign of danger or even
that the Emperor's mandate was coming to an end – though the non-
occurrence of an eclipse (as I remarked in chapter 2) could be taken as a
sign of his virtue. Order in the heavens, in that sense, could not be taken
for granted.

In Greece, by contrast, *cosmic* regularities are unchanging. This is not
just in the Platonic view, where the Demiurge or Craftsman imposed
order on precosmic chaos, and his work is subsequently immutable other

---

[40] *On the Nine Chapters of the Mathematical Art* 1. 104–6. On the later attack on the problem by Zhao
Youqin see Volkov 1997.

than by himself – and he would certainly not want to change it. Aristotle too, without a transcendent Craftsman, held that the order in the heavens is unchanging. Even anti-teleologists, such as the Epicureans, held that there were regularities governing the physical interactions of things, even if uncaused swerves had to be postulated to account, for example, for the earliest stage in the formation of a cosmos.

That in turn means that while we humans may experience difficulty in discerning the order of things, we should expect it to be there – not necessarily a mathematical order, to be sure, but especially impressive if that were the case. Which numbers are significant may be, and indeed was, disputed. Aristotle, for one, was contemptuous of those who exaggerated the importance of what he treats as mere coincidences. What was the connection between the number of the stars in the Pleiades and the age at which children lose their teeth? Both happen to be seven (so some would say), but so what?[41] Yet Aristotle admits the significance of the ratios governing the principal musical concords, and even offers, on his own account, a similar, more speculative, explanation as to why certain colours should be beautiful: these are the proportional blends of the primary ones – when bright and dark are blended in the ratios of 2:1, 3:2 or 4:3, for instance.[42]

While many Greeks represented cosmic order on the analogy of order in the political domain (and thus far might look close enough to Chinese ideas), the trouble was that what order should be in that latter domain – the political ideal – was in Greece the subject of radical dispute. Both oligarchs and democrats prized equality: but they meant very different things by it.[43] The democrats insisted that equality meant equality for everyone, all citizens, that is: it was not as if women and slaves were to be included. Even so, we should not underestimate the radical nature of the idea that every citizen's voice should be heard and everyone's opinion counted equally in the procedure whereby a decision was taken by majority vote. But the oligarchs countered that equality consisted in the shares allotted to different groups being adjusted to their deserts. Those who were more deserving (because of birth or wealth, for instance) should have a greater allocation. Some people, in other words, were definitely more equal than others. But that political dispute quite undermined any consensus on the equation or interdependence of the

[41] Aristotle, *Metaphysics* 1093a13ff.
[42] Aristotle, *On the Senses* 439b25ff, 31ff. At 442a12–17 he contemplates a similar theory in relation to flavours.
[43] See especially Vlastos 1953, 1973, ch. 8, on the range of the term *isonomia*.

cosmic and the political orders, any straightforward agreement that they were part of one and the same order indeed, let alone any notion that order depended, in some sense, on the conduct of the Emperor.

I remarked at the outset that what counts as 'mathematics' in a given society, what modes of reasoning are cultivated, and with what aims, are questions to which we should expect to give different answers. What can we say on that issue, now that we have looked at some of the actual applications of *mathematike* in Greece and *shushu* in China?

In both cases we have encountered very considerable variety. In both cases we have at one end of the spectrum the symbolic associations of numbers and their use in divination, and at the other their use in the analysis of harmonics and in the study of the heavens. Generalisation within Greece, or within China, alone, might, in those circumstances, seem risky, let alone any attempt to arrive at comparative judgements between the two. Let me nevertheless hazard some conjectures, not about the entire spectrum of interests, but about two important and contrasting concerns.

On the one hand I have pointed to the common, though far from universal, Greek preoccupation with axiomatic-deductive demonstration. This is the distinctive feature of Greek mathematics in the Euclidean tradition, and it is what gave mathematics its particular cachet, as a model for knowledge in other fields as well. This was the way Euclid himself proceeded, both in his *Elements* and in the *Optics*, the way Archimedes did in his statics and elsewhere, even the way Galen hoped to prove some of his results in the entirely non-mathematical domains of anatomy and physiology.[44]

The great strength of the model was that, given self-evident axioms and valid inferences, it yielded incontrovertible results. That may seem reason enough for the Greeks to have developed it. But when we reflect that neither the Chinese nor any other ancient mathematical tradition did so, there would appear to be more to it than mere intellectual attractiveness. What more may be answered in part, I suggest (though I shall return to the issue in chapter 6), by the negative models provided by the styles of argument cultivated in those other peculiarly Greek institutions of the law-courts (*dikasteria*) and political assemblies. It was dissatisfaction with the merely persuasive arguments used there that led some philosophers and mathematicians to develop their alternative, to

[44] Galen's ambitions in this regard are analysed in Lloyd 1996c, cf. Barnes 1991, Hankinson 1991.

capture the high ground, in the intensely competitive circumstances of Greek intellectual life, by identifying the true, indeed the only way to secure incontrovertibility. The philosophers, Aristotle especially, provided the definition of strict demonstration, and the mathematicians in the Euclidean tradition showed what could be done with it in practice.[45]

But on that model, everything depends on the axioms. You get out what you put in. The axioms of logic, such as the principles of non-contradiction and excluded middle, were generally accepted, and so too were some mathematical ones, such as the equality axiom (take equals from equals and equals remain). But elsewhere that was far from being the case. Euclid's parallel postulate (that non-parallel straight lines meet at a point) was challenged already in antiquity, though attempts to prove it did not then lead, as they later did, to the discovery of non-Euclidean geometries: they only led to some flawed, because circular, proofs.[46] But it was especially in relation to physical assumptions that problems arose – with the axioms, that is. It was one thing to postulate that, in relation to the sphere of the fixed stars, the earth is of negligible size and can be treated as a point.[47] It was another to postulate that all natural movement was either to or from the centre of the universe or in a circle round it.[48] The quest for more than just hypotheses – for self-evident truths, no less – was more elusive than many Greek theorists let on, but the ambition to find them corresponded to an ambition to secure a demonstration that would silence the opposition once and for all.

The Chinese, by contrast, set themselves very different ideals, not certainty, nor incontrovertibility, but to find the guiding principles that unify the different strands of mathematics – the art of numbers. That is remarked on, for example, by Liu Hui in his Preface to his commentary on the *Nine Chapters* – one of the admittedly rare occasions when an early Chinese mathematician reflects self-consciously on his work.

---

45 Yet as I document in Lloyd 1996a pp. 56f, the fifth- and fourth-century orators employ precisely the same terms for their kind of proving – beyond reasonable doubt – that were to be used by Aristotle of his strict axiomatic-deductive demonstration. When Aristotle puts it in the *Nicomachean Ethics* 1094b25–7 that no one would accept a mathematician's merely plausible arguments any more than one would demand proofs, *apodeixeis*, from a rhetorician, he is deliberately ignoring the point that the orators did precisely claim to 'prove'. His own position depends, here, in other words, on taking his view of what strict proof entails, and yet in his *Rhetoric* he allows a different style of *apodeixis*, labelled, precisely, rhetorical demonstration. Cf. Lloyd 1996b ch. 1. The evidence is discussed in Lloyd 1990a ch. 3 and 1996a, especially ch. 10.

46 Both Ptolemy and Proclus attempted proofs: see Proclus, *In Euc.* I 191.21 ff, 365.7 ff.

47 Various astronomical theories that depended on the assumption that the earth is of negligible size in relation to the dimensions of the circle of the fixed stars are set out and discussed in Lloyd 1987, pp. 307 ff.

48 See Proclus, *In Ti.* III 146.21 ff.

Though the *Nine Chapters* are, we should say, just devoted to sets of mathematical problems, Liu Hui chooses, in his introductory remarks,[49] to relate it to the discovery of the eight trigrams, to the inauguration of the calendar and the tuning of the pitch pipes – many of the themes I have been discussing in this chapter. His own studies of the text led him, he tells us, first to remark on the division of *yin* and *yang*. That might sound just like window-dressing, the kind of rhetorical ploy to be expected of a member of the literate scholarly elite. But it would be quite wrong to dismiss it as such, since the principal theme of his introduction is, precisely, the *unity* of mathematics. He is not interested in deducing it all from a single set of axioms: there are no axioms at all in Chinese mathematics before the arrival of the Jesuits. His own interests lie elsewhere, in what links different mathematical procedures together.

The various categories (*lei*) of the mathematical art are all related to one another. They may be divided into different branches, but they all belong to the same trunk or root. The ideal, for the Chinese mathematician, is to find the essential points that unify the subject, the *gangji* as he calls them. Within each chapter, much attention is paid to how the quantities are 'equalised', 'made to communicate', 'homogenised', but – to follow up a point first made by Karine Chemla[50] – these are not just terms for first-order activities, within the discussion of particular problems. They operate at a second level as well, where the equalising and homogenising work on the first-order procedures themselves, bringing *them* into communication with one another.[51]

For one Greek tradition, at least, the numbers in things, and the mathematical analysis of physical phenomena more generally, provided the route to certainty. But for one Chinese one, the goal was unification. On the Greek side, one may remark the tension between, on the one hand, the fundamental disagreements, on political ideals, on epistemological questions, on the principles on which physical and cosmological theory should be based, and, on the other, the hankering after incontrovertibility. The Chinese, for their part, had no ambition to try to deduce the whole of mathematics from a single axiomatic base. But on that score, their goal, too, had its potential political resonances, in the value set on unification. Both societies use number to illustrate orderliness; both recognise number as essential to social arrangements; in both those who were expert in the manipulation of numbers gained prestige from that and made the most of the opportunities for display that that presented.

---

[49] See Qian Baocong 1963, p. 96.   [50] See Chemla 1992 and 1994 especially.
[51] Cf. the references to finding similarities and extending categories in *Zhoubi suanjing* 24.11 ff.

But the Greek mathematical universe was (in principle) independent of humans, objective, ungainsayable, the Chinese one a source not of incorrigibility, but of cohesion, of resonance, of unity. Such at least is the conjecture that I would propose.

A concern for abstract theory, and a sense of the importance of practical applications, are themes that have figured several times in this chapter. Our next study will take as its central topic the question of the extent to which systematic inquiry, in China and Greece, was geared to the development of devices held to be of practical utility.

CHAPTER FOUR

Applications and applicabilities

Thus far our inquiry into inquiry has focussed, for the most part, on what may be called theoretical interests: the research into the past, the ambition to predict the future, the attempt to understand phenomena by associating them with numbers or discovering their mathematical relations. But what, we may now ask, did the undertaking of systematic research owe to a perception of its possible practical applicability? In what areas was practical utility the chief stimulus to research? Conversely, how far did the actual technological advances made in early societies depend on input from the side of the 'theorists'? Once again I shall concentrate on ancient Greece and China, which both provide rich materials on the issues.

I must note straight away that what counts as 'practical' or what as 'useful' is problematic. As we shall see, certain ancient authors claim that their inquiries are directed at what is practical and that their devices are useful, even when they just seem designed for amusement or for show. They are toys. In some cases their 'usefulness' seems limited to that of securing, for their inventors, a reputation for ingenuity. We need to keep an eye both on the mode of utility sought and on the nature of the theoretical analyses offered.

Certain assumptions have often been made both about the ancient Greeks and about the ancient Chinese that – if we accepted them as valid – suggest an almost polar contrast between the two civilisations. The ancient Chinese are generally recognised to have been highly prac-tical people, to have been deeply interested in, and on the look-out for, possible technological advance, and to have succeeded in producing in-vention after invention, in one field after another, in many cases long before the West had any inkling of the idea or device in question. In-deed, it is a commonplace that the West derived its knowledge of the use of movable type in printing, of the compass in navigation, of gunpowder, and many other items either directly or indirectly from China.

The stereotype of the ancient Greeks is, in many respects, the opposite, namely that of a society that despised manual labour or anything that savoured of it, where the intellectuals prized theory for its own sake and were indifferent to the practical applications of the ideas they proposed.

As with many stereotypes, these have *some* basis. But first there are some methodological problems that have to be addressed, and then I should mention a couple of immediate objections, before we turn to some of the detailed evidence.

First, on methodological issues, we have to be careful to compare like with like, so far as periods are concerned. If we are to assess the relative interests or indifference, the successes and failures, of Greeks and Chinese, we should take equivalent time spans. It obviously will not do to compare the achievements and attitudes of Greco-Roman antiquity with those of China right down to the early modern period, to, say, the sixteenth century – though in some studies that is precisely what happens.

Secondly, we have to pay attention to several kinds of bias in our sources. The picture of Greek intellectuals being profoundly unconcerned with the practical applications of their ideas stems largely from texts that belong to a particular, Platonist, tradition. That is true of Plutarch, who in much-quoted passages in the *Marcellus* not only cites Plato's disapproval of practical work in mechanics, but attributes a similar view to Archimedes, claiming that he thought engineering was vulgar and wanted to be remembered just as a mathematician.[1] Those views correspond, to be sure, to Plutarch's own. He was not interested in technology: he was a priest at Delphi. But if we take into account the whole range of Archimedes' interests, it soon becomes clear that Plutarch's portrait of him is a nonsense. Those interests included not just his brilliant military inventions, but also the application of the screw to the water-lifting device named after him (figure 8). Again, the implication of the famous aphorism, 'give me a place to stand, and I can move the whole earth',[2] is that he was anything but indifferent to the applications of the various mechanical principles (of the lever, and of compound pulleys) with which he was associated. That illustrates both the idea of making a principle work, and its being taken to extremes: we shall find more examples of that later.

To only a slightly lesser extent the stereotype on the Chinese side also reflects a partial reaction to the evidence. The idea that the Chinese

[1] Plutarch, *Marcellus*, chs. 14 and 17: cf. also Carpus quoted by Pappus, *Collectio*, VIII 3 1026.9ff: cf. Cuomo 2001, ch. 6.
[2] Pappus, *Collectio*, VIII 19 1060.2f.

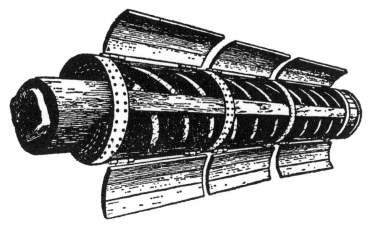

Fig. 8   Archimedean screw made of oak, for lifting water, from a mine at Sotiel in Spain.

were always on the alert for possible practical applications of their ideas has, to be sure, some foundation. But in what is broadly labelled the 'Confucian' tradition, the life of the gentleman, *junzi*, was one primarily devoted to self-cultivation and to virtue. There are plenty of texts from authors belonging to the literate elite that express the low esteem in which most craftsmen and labourers were held – by those authors at least. The chief Confucian virtues were *ren* (humanity), *yi*[I] (righteousness), *li*[II] (propriety), *zhi* (knowledge) and *xin* (trustworthiness) and they did not leave much room for the entrepreneurial, technologically oriented spirit that nevertheless is prominently represented in other strands in Chinese society. Mencius (I A I) indeed explicitly condemns the orientation towards profit (*li*[III]) in the advice he offers to King Hui of Liang.

One aspect of the bias in our sources is represented by the particular viewpoints adopted by particular authors with their own agenda. Another is the very different impressions we may derive from, on the one hand, the archaeological record, on the other our literary sources. Each type of evidence has its own strengths and weaknesses. The literary texts sometimes describe objects that were never in fact made: but they may reveal the attitudes of their authors directly. The archaeological remains, by contrast, confirm some at least of the devices actually employed, but do not, of themselves, tell us about the aims and ambitions of those who used them, let alone of those who invented them.

These methodological remarks already indicate some of the unsatisfactoriness of the stereotypes I mentioned at the beginning. A scorn for

manual labour is as common among members of the Chinese literate
elite as it is among certain Greek authors. But that does not give the
whole picture – either on the Chinese or on the Greek side. I am not just
thinking of Archimedes, but of a whole series of writers whom we know
from direct or indirect evidence to have been interested not just in the
theoretical principles of mechanical devices, but in those devices themselves. They include Democritus in the late fifth century BCE, Archytas
and Eudoxus in the fourth, Ctesibius in the third, Philo in the second,
Hero in the first century CE, Pappus in the early fourth, to whom we can
add a variety of Latin authors, notably Vitruvius in the first century BCE.

To make any progress in our understanding of the questions I raised
at the outset, our best tactic is to begin by reviewing the chief data in
some of the more important fields in turn. I shall consider each of three
main subject areas, first warfare, then agriculture, then civil engineering,
though it will be immediately apparent that there is some overlap between
that third area and the other two. These three, between them, certainly
do not cover everything that might be discussed under the heading of
the practical applications of theory: but they will give us some idea of
the scope of the problems.

WARFARE is a subject that no state, no ruler, can afford to ignore. But
ideas about the aims and methods of waging war, and about the win-
ning of battles, have varied enormously, as also has the attention paid to
improving the efficiency of armies whether by employing better tactics
or better weaponry. Both the Greeks and the Chinese were conscious of
certain differences between their own ideas, techniques and practices,
and those of the foreign peoples with whom they were familiar. Contacts
with other peoples were one source of influence on Greek and Chinese
battle tactics themselves. We are told by Vitruvius (x 13) that certain types
of siege engines that came into general use in the Greco-Roman world
originated among Tyrian and Carthaginian engineers. The Chinese derived their horses (used first in chariots, then in cavalry engagements)[3]
from the people of the steppes (see figure 9).

At the same time efficiency was not the sole criterion, at least in Greece.
For the Greeks, the use of the bow was thought inferior – morally –
to fighting hand to hand with spear, sword and shield. From Homer
onwards, the individual's performance in battle was a crucial factor in
the moral evaluation of the man. The *Iliad* is organised around the

---

[3] See Shaughnessy 1988, Yates 1988, on the later development of cavalry tactics, probably from the
third century BCE.

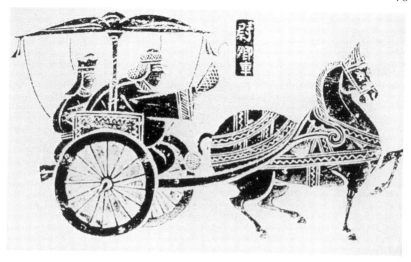

Fig. 9   Chinese chariot for ceremonial purposes.

consecutive *aristeia*, deeds of valour, of the Greek heroes who take centre stage in turn in the absence of Achilles. But even when victory in battle depended, as it later did, on the disciplined manoeuvring of the heavy-armed troops – the hoplites – in the massed formation of the phalanx, playing one's part was the prime test of courage, *andreia*, literally manhood.[4]

Evidence of the increasing complexity of warfare begins already in Herodotus and more especially Thucydides. Thucydides refers to the development of the trireme, the ship on which victory at sea for long depended.[5] In his accounts of the various sieges that took place during the Peloponnesian war, he refers at one point to a primitive kind of flame-thrower.[6] Not much later, in the fourth century BCE, we have our first extant specialist Greek military treatise, the *poliorketika* – siege-warfare – of Aeneas Tacticus, part (it seems) of a series of works he wrote on military matters, the rest of which have not survived. Siege-warfare in particular, and military stratagems and strategy in general, were the

[4] We may recall how Socrates won praise for his bravery in rallying his comrades in the Athenian retreat from Delium, see Plato, *Laches* 181 ab, *Symposium* 220e ff.

[5] Thucydides I 13. The development of Greek naval vessels was subject to what Garlan has called 'gigantisme' (1972, p. 143, with reference to Athenaeus, *Deipnosophistae* v 203e ff). The construction of larger and larger ships was a response to symbolic ambitions rather than to practical ones.

[6] Thucydides IV 100. This was the device the Boeotians and their allies used to take Delium. A cauldron full of lighted coals, sulphur and pitch, was hung from one end of a hollow beam. Air forced through the beam from the other end by means of bellows sent flames on to the walls setting them alight and causing the defenders to abandon their positions.

topics, subsequently, of works by several Greek and Latin authors, Philo, Asclepiodotus (first century BCE), Frontinus (first century CE), Polyaenus (second) and Vegetius (fourth) among them.

This allows a direct comparison to be made with China, since there too we have extensive extant written sources. These start with the two classics, the *Sunzi* and *Sun Bin*, where we can now supplement the Song editions with the versions of the treatises that have recently been excavated from Han tombs dating from between 140 and 118 BCE.[7] The variations between these show that these works existed in different recensions, but also confirm that some version had already been put together by the second century. How much further back they may go is more controversial. But these classics serve as model for later treatises on the art of warfare that run into their thousands. In addition, we know that one of the major philosophical groups of the Warring States period – before the unification in 221 – namely the Mohists, were particularly interested in the study of the defensive aspects of waging war.[8] While, like many others, they sought to become the advisers to rulers, they were distinctive in that the advice they offered related not just to matters of government, but also to the defensive tactics to be adopted in warfare, especially to the question of how to fortify cities to enable them to withstand sieges – very much the topic that provides the central theme also on Aeneas' work at the other end of the Asia-Europe land-mass.

A comparison between these Chinese and Greco-Roman works yields immediately several points of similarity and two important contrasts. Both Aeneas and *Sunzi* stress the importance of experience, of military intelligence (knowledge of the enemy's strength, whereabouts and intentions) and especially of morale. Both describe the use of spies; both devote attention to the problems of passwords and signalling; both describe various tricks or ploys to gain a psychological or tactical advantage over the enemy.

But for *Sunzi* the supreme skill of the commander consists in securing victory with a minimum of cost, indeed if possible without having to fight a battle. The idea is that you so manoeuvre your troops that the enemy comes to realise the hopelessness of his own position and surrenders without an engagement. For *Sunzi* the value of victory is seriously diminished if the enemy's land is destroyed or his population decimated: the prime prize is to take over and occupy the territory of the vanquished

---

[7] Ames 1993 incorporates the new evidence from the MSS finds at Yinqueshan, cf. also Lau and Ames 1996.
[8] *Mozi* chs. 52–71: see Yates 1980.

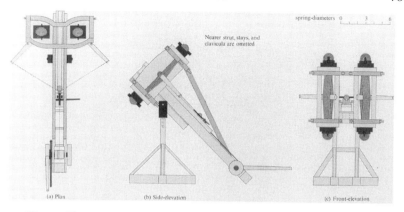

spring-diameters 0   3   6

Nearer strut, stays, and
clavicula are omitted

(a) Plan   (b) Side-elevation   (c) Front-elevation

Fig. 10   First-century BCE stone-throwing ballista described by Vitruvius as
reconstructed by Marsden.

more or less unharmed. Yet in the classical period neither Athens nor
Sparta aimed to take over the other's territory, even though Athens did,
of course, expropriate the island of Melos.

A second major difference lies in the preoccupation, throughout the
pages of Aeneas, with the possibility that the city being defended may be
betrayed by disaffected elements in the population who disagreed with
the policies of those in command. He gives advice on the dangers of having a lot of poor people, or debtors, in the defending army, and on how to
counter the plots of would-be revolutionaries.[9] Considerable sections of
the work are devoted to guarding against the possibility of the city-gates
being opened *from within*.[10] The problems posed by *political* disagreements, among the *citizen* body, on the conduct of the war, just do not figure
in our Chinese texts, for all that disagreements between *generals* often do.

The second type of text that has come down to us on the Greco-
Roman side deals with military weaponry. Archimedes' reputation as a
practical genius depended partly on the stories of the engines he devised
to repel the forces of Marcellus besieging Syracuse: but our evidence
there is second-hand and anecdotal. However, Philo, Vitruvius and Hero
all deal with the construction and improvement of the various types of
catapults – scorpions and ballistae – designed to hurl bolts or stones, in
both torsion and non-torsion varieties (see figure 10).[11] Starting with the
arrow-shooting *gastraphetes*, or cross-bow, these underwent considerable

---

[9] Aeneas Tacticus 3.3, 10.25, 12.1, cf. Whitehead 1990.
[10] E.g. Aeneas Tacticus 18.1 ff.
[11] Marsden 1971, p. 270, gives a chronological table setting out the main developments of non-
torsion and torsion catapults in Greece so far as our evidence allows these to be reconstructed.

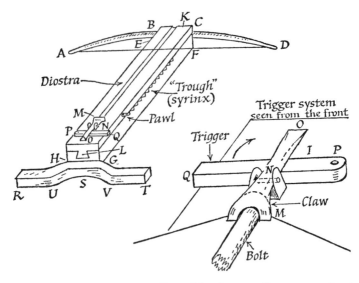

Fig. 11   Gastraphetes as dscribed by Hero, *Belopoeica* 75.10–81.2, as reconstructed by
Landels.

developments from the early fourth century BCE (see figure 11), as did
other types of weapons and siege-engines (battering-rams, for example,
and 'tortoises' designed to protect attacking forces and so on).

Thus Philo devotes several pages of the *Belopoeica* to a description of
a repeater catapult that he ascribes to one Dionysius of Alexandria (see
figure 12).[12] A single ratchet mechanism, controlled by a handspike, first
drew back the string, then armed it with a bolt, and then released the
trigger, enabling continuous fire to be maintained. However, Philo goes
on to note the weapon's chief weakness, namely that during fire it had
to be kept absolutely steady, which in turn meant that the aim could not
be adjusted.

A further text in Philo reports greater success and is particularly significant in attributing this to the sustained research of Alexandrian engineers
directly supported by the Ptolemies. The problem these engineers investigated and solved was that of isolating the factor on which the efficiency
of torsion catapults depends – namely the diameter of the holes for
the twisted skeins of sinews that provided the power – in other words
the mass of those sinews themselves. By carrying out systematic tests, we
are told, they were able to find the formula correlating the weight of the

---

[12] Philo, *Belopoeica* 73.21–76.20, cf. Marsden 1971, pp. 146ff, 177ff.

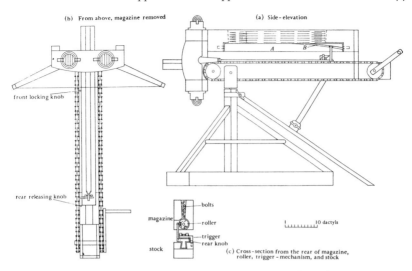

Fig. 12   Dionysius' repeater, as reconstructed by Marsden.

stone to be hurled with the diameter of the bore.[13] While there can be little doubt that most improvements in weaponry, both in China and in the West, were the hard-won outcome of experience on the field of battle, some on the Greek side would appear to have come from deliberate experimental research into the principles at work. Here is a prime example of the interaction of theory and practice, though it is important to add first that the circumstances of the Ptolemies' support were exceptional, and secondly that, in some of their theoretical explorations, some Greek authors went far beyond the limits of what was practicable: some of the devices in the technical literature were, in other words, *just theoretical* elaborations.

On the Chinese side, the emphasis is not so much on experimental research to prove a mathematical formula setting out the relevant proportionalities. On the other hand, there is a deep concern with what will work and with efficient performance. The main Chinese weapon was the cross-bow, introduced maybe as early as 400 BCE, an extremely powerful weapon, once equipped with an efficient trigger mechanism and once the problems of arming it were overcome (see figure 13).[14] Among later

---

[13] Philo, *Belopoeica* 50.14ff, cf. Marsden 1971, pp. 106ff. The formula involves, among other things, the extraction of the cube root of the weight (of the stone to be hurled) and Philo notes that if there is no rational cube root, it is necessary to take the closest approximation.

[14] On the development of the cross-bow in China, see especially Needham and Yates 1994, pp. 120–83.

Fig. 13   Chinese cross-bows being armed

improvements were magazine and repeater versions that are later than, though independent of, that described in Philo, but that did not suffer from the fundamental weakness he noted in the Greek weapon, namely a single aim for any given volley.

Changes in weaponry attract comment, outside the specifically military treatises, in such texts as *Huainanzi*, and, as noted, Mohist writings contain sections devoted to siege-craft, including siege-engines and the measures needed to fortify cities to withstand them. But the chief difference between the situations of those Chinese writers and their counterparts in Greco-Roman antiquity lies in the *dependability of the support* the Chinese military analysts could count on. The Ptolemies, we said, certainly gave such support to their engineers for the period of the research that Philo refers to. But that was very much the exception that illustrates the rule. We could certainly not claim that Greco-Roman engineers were less ingenious, less curious, less inventive, in their attempts to improve weapons of war, than their Chinese counterparts. Indeed the Greeks went further than the Chinese in their admittedly only partially successful efforts to reduce the problems to mathematical terms. Yet where the Chinese had a net advantage was in the organisations that existed for exploiting and implementing new ideas once they were proposed. Although the success of Chinese advisers in gaining the ear of rulers obviously varied, what rulers and advisers alike shared was an intense concern for every aspect of the art of war and a sense of the need to explore any possibility of an advantage and a determination to do so.

These comments will prove relevant also to the next domain we have to consider, namely AGRICULTURE. Every society, large or small, must be concerned with ensuring an adequate food-supply and most call on considerable collective knowledge of the relevant local ecological conditions to achieve that end. In hunting, fishing, herding, sowing and planting, once certain methods and techniques prove to be effective, there may be little incentive – indeed possibly great risk – in trying to change them. Experimenting with new crops has always been a dangerous business, has it not? In the domain of agriculture, in other words, the forces of conservatism have generally been particularly strong. Departure from tried and tested methods has, accordingly, to be motivated either by necessity – say the need to feed an increasing population – or by some perceived desirable end, the acquisition of wealth or prestige.

The actual conditions for the practice of agriculture in ancient China were very different from those of ancient Greece.[15] China possessed, what Greece generally lacked, considerable stretches of cultivable land, suitable for grain in the North and rice in the South. Conversely, animal husbandry played a less prominent role there than in the Mediterranean basin. However, what we are concerned with here is whether or to what extent deliberate measures were taken to improve agricultural

---

[15] In what follows I draw extensively on the pioneering study of Bray 1984.

productivity. In principle, agriculture offers certain opportunities for the application of theory to practice. Were those opportunities taken? Who was responsible, and what were their aims or motives?

We may begin with two fundamental differences in the perception of the importance of agriculture in our two ancient civilisations. First, for the ancient Chinese, agriculture came under the auspices of important divinities and culture heroes, Shennong, the tutelary deity or spirit of agriculture, Hou Ji, the Lord of Millet, and Yu the Great. Of course the Greeks had Demeter, the Romans Ceres. But they did not combine the role of corn goddesses with presiding over technological skills, which were the province, rather, of Athena and in a different way of Prometheus. Yu the Great was responsible for taming the flood, for land clearance, for inaugurating agriculture itself. Flood stories in Greece or the ancient Near East, by contrast, did not culminate in the celebration of the activities of a hero-figure whose efforts *countered* the flood and so enabled agriculture to begin.

The second important difference relates to the role of the Prince or Emperor himself, who in China was personally in charge of agriculture and presided over agricultural activities season by season. Thus he inaugurated the ploughing of the fields every year, just as the Queen started the picking of the mulberry leaves for the silkworms.[16] In *Huainanzi* the ruler does not just sacrifice to the appropriate deities at the appropriate moments of the year: he oversees each and every important agricultural activity. If he fails in his duty, the consequences this text predicts are dire, the failure of crops, drought, unseasonable rains, floods, fire, disease, and not just 'natural' calamities but others, such as the invasions of barbarians and the proliferation of bandits.[17] To be sure, the Romans had a ruler – Cincinnatus – who came from ploughing the fields to rule. But even though Columella, in reporting that story,[18] nostalgically approves of the connection between ruling and agriculture, that just points to their normal dissociation in Roman eyes.

Agriculture, one may say, had a far higher ideological profile in China than in the Greco-Roman world, and this is reflected in the amount of literature devoted to the subject. Agricultural topics are discussed in texts from the third to the first centuries BCE in the *Zhouli*, *Guanzi* and *Lüshi chunqiu*, for example sections defining the responsibilities of the many

---

[16] E.g. *Yantielun* (the *Discourse on Salt and Iron*) 17. This is a text that purports to record a discussion held at court by imperial edict in 81 BCE. The text itself is likely to have been composed in the next fifty years.

[17] *Huainanzi* 5, 1a ff.   [18] Columella, *On Agriculture* 1 Pref. 13.

different types of officials concerned, planning the most efficient use of the available land of different types, specifying what should be done in each season and stressing the importance of the care of agricultural implements.[19] Specialist treatises begin not much later, as well as monographs dealing with particular crops and the vast *bencao* literature dealing with medicinal plants, pharmacopoeia in other words.[20]

Ancient China suffered, we know, from time to time, from terrible famines, brought about by floods or drought or crop failures of one kind or another. Nevertheless the increase of yields by crop rotation, by large-scale irrigation works, by hybridising strains of corn and rice, by manuring, was impressive.[21] New devices for harrowing, ridging, seed-drilling, rolling, were introduced, and the design of the plough underwent considerable modification. These advances came, in the main, from the peasant-farmers themselves, rather than from the members of the literate elite who wrote the treatises.[22] The latter were not, on the whole, themselves innovators: yet they *recorded* the innovations that were made, and, given the prestige and imperial support their writings often enjoyed, this helped to ensure the diffusion of those innovations.

In the Greco-Roman world, too, we have extensive extant writings, ranging from didactic poems such as Hesiod's *Works and Days*, through general works discussing household and estate management, such as Xenophon's *Economica*, to specialist treatises dealing with plants and plant uses (as by Theophrastus) or with agriculture as a whole. Those last go back to the fifth century BCE, though our chief extant examples are from Latin writers of the second century BCE to the first century CE, the works of Cato, Varro and Columella. Some of the mechanical devices useful in agriculture, meanwhile, are described in other treatises as well, in Vitruvius, for example, or in Pliny's encyclopedic *Natural History*. These devices include most notably the mills and presses used in the manufacture of oil and wine (figure 14), the water-wheel (figure 15), water-lifting devices and even such complex machines as the Gallic corn-harvester (figure 16): the machine is very effective, but the terrain must be level; the

---

[19] See, for instance, *Zhouli* 2.17 p. 24, *Guanzi* 1 4, 16a–b, 1 5, 19a–b, v 13, 1 b–2b, VIII 20, 7a–8a, cf. Bray 1984, pp. 47 ff, 55, 70.

[20] Our first complete extant specialist treatise, the *Qimin yaoshu*, dates only from the sixth century CE. Eventually, in the Yuan dynasty (thirteenth century) the state set up a Bureau of Agriculture, *sinongsi*, to control this whole area of the economy. But already the *Shiji*, 30: 1428, mentions a minister for agriculture, *danongcheng*.

[21] See Bray 1984, pp. 7 ff, 138 ff, 289 ff.

[22] See Bray 1984, p. 90, and 2001. Thus the *Qimin yaoshu*, which was written originally in the main for landlords, came to be reproduced, printed indeed, in the early eleventh century by order of the Emperor for public use.

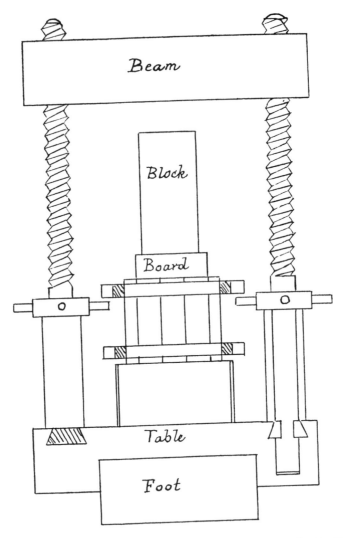

Fig. 14 Drachmann's reconstruction of the twin-screw press described by Hero,
Mechanics III 19.

design is close to that first adopted when the combine harvester came
to be reinvented in modern times – not that the Gallic antecedent was
known to the reinventors.[23]

[23] For an overview of the subject, see Drachmann 1963 and Landels 1978.

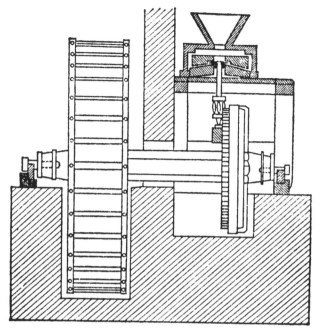

Fig. 15   Roman water-mill according to Vitruvius as reconstructed by Moritz.

Fig. 16   Gallic corn-harvester reconstructed from the reports in Pliny and Palladius.

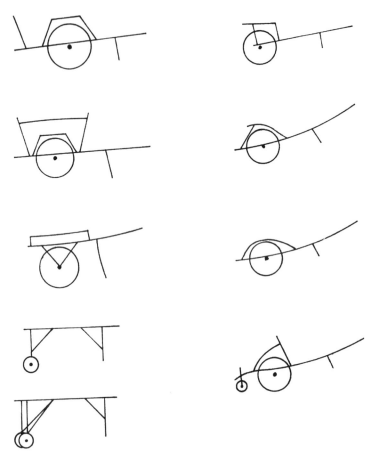

Fig. 17   Types of Chinese wheel-barrows.

Some of these Greek and Roman machines exhibit a considerable so-phistication, and those that employ the screw in its various forms (screw-presses or the Archimedean screw) depend on an understanding of the geometrical principles involved, as well as the all-important empirical know-how necessary to manufacture screws. Although the Greeks and Romans missed out on some simple devices, such as the wheel-barrow (figure 17), in other areas they exhibit both curiosity and inventiveness.

Yet one key difference marks the Greco-Roman literature out from the Chinese. This is that the specialist agricultural treatises are mainly addressed to private estate-owners – to give individual rich landlords the information they needed for the profitable running of their estates. They could be the audience of Chinese works too, but in China the prime target was often grander – to provide the Emperor with the wherewithal to ensure the prosperity of all under his control. True, Vitruvius does address his 'architectural' treatise to Augustus, and his hopes of thereby securing favour and employment are strictly comparable to those of many Chinese writers who presented memorials to the throne with similar ambitions. Yet Vitruvius writes first and foremost as an architect-engineer, not as an agronomist. He entertains no general expectation that the mechanical devices for use in agriculture that he describes will forthwith be taken up and exploited right across the Roman empire. Indeed in the case of the water-wheel, we can confirm from the archaeological record that its diffusion through the Greco-Roman world was both slow and limited in extent.

At this point the factor that many would invoke to explain the technological weaknesses in the Greco-Roman world is the widespread dependence on slave labour, often represented as the chief factor inhibiting the search for and exploitation of labour-saving devices.[24] Their relevance to the problem must certainly be granted, but should not be exaggerated, for three main reasons.

First, slaves, while expendable, still involved their owners in the expense of their upkeep and were far from necessarily always cheaper than machines. That depended crucially on the outlay needed for the machines.

Moreover, secondly, as between the Greco-Roman world and China, although chattel slaves were not common in China, the use of other types of unfree labour, such as conscripts, certainly was. I shall come back to this when considering civil engineering in the next section.

Thirdly, in the domain of agriculture itself, the existence of slaves will hardly be enough to explain the slow diffusion of mechanical devices,

---

[24] See Finley 1965, Pleket 1973, Scheidel 1994, Cartledge, Cohen and Foxhall 2001. Two further factors that have also been much discussed in the literature are (1) the lack of the idea of the desirability of material progress, and (2) the privileging of the natural over the artificial or mechanical, in Greco-Roman antiquity. A full discussion of these is beyond the scope of this chapter, but it is worth remarking, with regard to (1), that this is as much a part of what needs to be explained as a contribution to an explanation. With regard to (2), it is interesting that several of the writers on mechanics claim either that mechanical devices imitate nature, or that they should be seen as using nature (see Vitruvius, x 1 4 and 7 4, Pappus, *Collectio* VIII 2, 1024.26ff). Conversely, some natural phenomena are compared with mechanical devices, as planetary motions are likened to 'machines' in Vitruvius, x 1 4, even though Proclus used it as an *objection* to epicycle and eccentric models for the movements of the sun, moon and planets, that these *reduced* them to the movements of machines, *In Ti.* III 56.29–31.

for the simple reason that they were everywhere present throughout the Greco-Roman world. If we ask why the water-wheel was not immediately exploited, once the principle had been discovered, or why the Gallic combine harvester was never used in antiquity outside Gaul, then the existence of slaves *by itself* hardly provides the whole answer, since it offers no discriminating factor. Among the other considerations we have to add is the one we noted before, the lack of state structures taking overall responsibility for agricultural production. In the Greco-Roman world this meant that decisions concerning the running of estates, about the use of slaves or of machines, rested with individual landlords and their perception of where their private profits – or prestige – lay.

The third main subject area I identified is what I called CIVIL ENGINEERING, where there are obvious overlaps with military engineering (as in the siege-engines mentioned before) and with agriculture – insofar as irrigation projects, for example, in China especially, could involve considerable problems of planning and construction.

On the Greek side, the chief large-scale projects undertaken in the early classical period related to the building of cities and particularly to their embellishment, with public buildings, theatres, gymnasia and especially temples. Much remains unclear about how precisely the 'architects' in charge worked, the extent to which they made use of models or plans, how they made the often very subtle adjustments on site to produce the effects they did, as for example in connection with entasis (the curvature of columns and entablatures). But here is certainly an example where major works were undertaken on a corporate basis, not (as was usually the case in the running of estates) for private profit, but rather for public prestige.

Moreover considerable mechanical devices came to be deployed in connection with monumental building. Vitruvius (x 2 1 ff) describes how the problems of transporting large blocks of marble were overcome, reporting the devices used by Chersiphron and his son Metagenes in this connection in the construction of the classical temple of Artemis at Ephesus. One such consisted essentially in a pair of rollers between which the marble block was suspended, enabling it to be dragged along. That suggests that already in the sixth century BCE considerable ingenuity was being brought to bear to surmount the difficulties, as there was also in connection with lifting devices, where Vitruvius provides evidence of the development of elaborate cranes, especially those using compound pulleys (see figure 18).[25]

---

[25] Vitruvius, x 2 1 ff, see Drachmann 1963, pp. 141 ff.

Fig. 18   Part of a relief from a Roman sepulchral monument showing a treadmill being used to work a crane, incorporating compound pulleys.

Here is another instance where we can be sure that the theoretical principles involved attracted attention and study. We can infer that from the stories about Archimedes.[26] When he was challenged by King Hiero about his claim to be able to move the whole earth, he is said to have arranged a demonstration in which, with a system of compound pulleys, he dragged a fully laden merchant ship across land single-handed. The story is preposterous, but we can still see it as useful evidence for an *interest* in exploring the extrapolations of mechanical devices. Similarly the potential applications of the lever and related devices are the subject of elaborate discussions in Hero and Pappus.

The second main area where more than just a private individual's interests were at stake, was in the matter of the delivery of water-supplies to cities. This culminated in the vast networks of aqueducts that served Rome, feats of great engineering skill and again the topic of much ancient discussion. It is clear that those responsible never solved satisfactorily the problem of measuring the quantities of water delivered from sluice gates or openings of different apertures set at different angles to the flow of water: rather they used very rough-and-ready rules of thumb, not precise methods of calculation.[27] While the major aqueducts were Roman achievements, the supply of water to the *polis* of Samos had already been the subject of another, different feat of engineering in the sixth century BCE, when Eupalinus constructed a tunnel through the mountain behind the city to achieve this end.[28] As an inspection of the site reveals, he was confident enough of his technique to start tunnelling from both ends simultaneously (see figure 19). The theory of how to do this by using geometrical methods is set out in Hero's *Dioptra* (15, 238.3ff) (see figure 20). But it is now abundantly clear that Eupalinus did not proceed by triangulation, but used dead reckoning with sights set up in a straight line over the top of the mountain.

On the Chinese side, the construction of elaborate temples took second place to that of massive tombs. Many of them, we are told, were equipped with complex devices to deter anyone who might try to enter. These included stones that dropped into place automatically to block

[26] Plutarch, *Marcellus* ch. 14.7–9.
[27] See Landels 1978, pp. 53ff, on Frontinus' arithmetic on this question, and cf. Cuomo 2001, p. 169, on his discovery of the discrepancies between the inputs and outputs in the water-supply.
[28] See the archaeological reports in Kienast 1995. There is a further reference to tunnelling through a mountain to secure a town's water-supply at CIL 8 2728, referring to Saldae in the middle of the first century CE. On that occasion the two tunnels, started at either end, got badly out of line and failed to meet and a specialist engineer had to be called in. That inscription makes clear that the alignment was secured by posts over the top of the mountain. Cf. Cuomo 2001, p. 158.

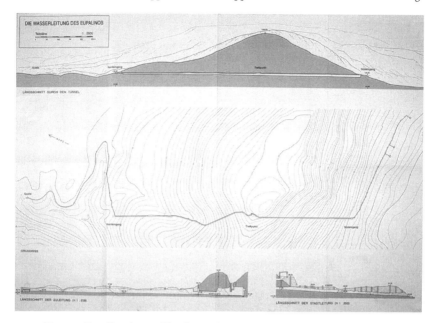

Fig. 19 Eupalinus' tunnel in plan and elevation according to Kienast 1995.

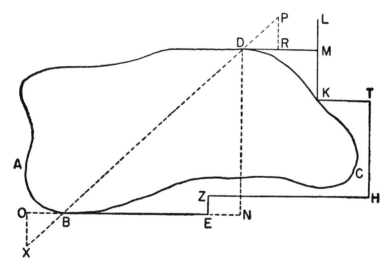

Fig. 20 Technique for tunnelling using triangulation as described by Hero, *Dioptra* 15: 238.3ff.

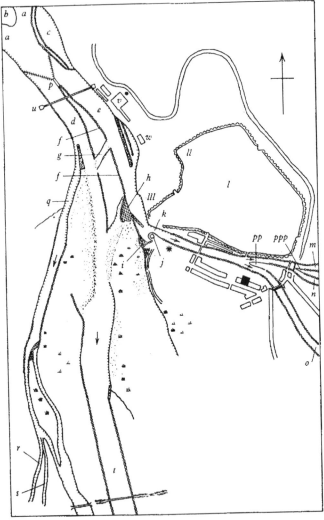

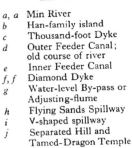

a, a	Min River	*k*	Cornucopia Channel;		
b	Han-family island		the rock cut		
c	Thousand-foot Dyke	*l*	Guanxian City	*r*	Derivatory canal
d	Outer Feeder Canal;	*ll*	Jade Rampart Mountain	*s*	Derivatory canal
	old course of river	*lll*	Phoenix Nest Cliff	*t*	Old course of river,
e	Inner Feeder Canal	*m*	Derivatory canal		flood course, etc.
f, f	Diamond Dyke	*n*	Derivatory canal	*u*	Suspension bridge
g	Water-level By-pass or	*o*	Derivatory canal	*v*	Temple of the
	Adjusting-flume	*p*	Fish Snout; primary division-		Second Prince
h	Flying Sands Spillway		head of piled stones	*w*	Temple of Yu
i	V-shaped spillway	*pp*	Left secondary division-head		the Great
j	Separated Hill and	*ppp*	Left tertiary division-head		
	Tamed-Dragon Temple	*q*	Right main derivatory canal		

Fig. 21(a)   Li Bing's waterworks at the River Min at Guanxian.

Fig. 21(b) (*cont.*) Looking upstream to the division of the River Min.

an entrance if a door was forced, and cross-bows that fired, again automatically, if anyone attempted to pass. The construction of the tombs themselves (sited always after extensive geomantic investigations) is one of the two most vivid illustrations of the Chinese ability to plan and carry out massive projects of civil engineering. In the case of the first Emperor's tomb, outside modern Xian, guarded by the famous terracotta warriors, we are told by Sima Qian (*Shiji* 6: 265.2ff) that 700,000 conscripts worked on it. All who had been involved in its construction and provision with treasure were subsequently executed – so they had no chance to divulge its secrets.

The second main illustration of those same Chinese capabilities is provided by vast irrigation projects, again involving the marshalling of immense labour forces and demonstrating extraordinary skills in overcoming practical difficulties. The most famous of these is the project started by Li Bing, around 270 BCE, and continued by his son Zhengguo.[29] They divided the river Min north of Chengdu and thereby solved at a stroke both the problem of the recurrent flooding to which the river was liable, and that of providing water to irrigate vast stretches of what is now the province of Sichuan. One uncontrollable river was thereby turned into two controllable ones (see figures 21a and b). To achieve this dual aim,

[29] See Needham 1971, pp. 284ff. Li Bing and Zhengguo both figure in Sima Qian's *Shiji* 29.

Li Bing had to overcome the problems of the seasonal variations in the quantities of water in the river, and those of silting, over and above the main one of dividing the main channel of the river into two. Although theory, in the sense of applied physical theory, was not much involved, here, even so, practical ingenuity of the highest order was displayed.

Grand generalisations about the development of technology in China or in the Greco-Roman world inevitably fall foul of the actual diversities we find between periods and across fields. To have any pretensions to comprehensiveness, my rapid survey of just these three main areas would need to be supplemented by a review of such other domains as transport, navigation, time-keeping devices, astronomical and geological instruments (such as Zhang Heng's famous second-century CE water-driven armillary and his seismoscope: see figure 22),[30] metallurgy, the applications of pneumatics, catoptrics and acoustics, not to mention such other fields as pharmaceutics which involve non-mechanical applications of theory. But while recognising that I have had to be selective, I shall now ask how far we can answer the principal questions I posed at the outset. What part did theorists play in the advances in technology that were made, in these three fields at least? How far did they manifest an interest in applying their theoretical ideas to practical problems? To what extent did the actual advances we can identify happen without any theoretical input at all? Should all these questions be answered differently for China and for the Greco-Roman world, and if so, what was responsible for the differences?

We may use the last question as a point of entry for suggesting answers to the others. There is, I argued, a far greater similarity between China and the Greco-Roman world than the contrasting stereotypes of practical Chinese and impractical, head-in-the-clouds Greeks would allow for. Many members of the Chinese literate elite were as reluctant to get their hands dirty as were many educated Greeks or Romans.

Against the stereotype of the theoretically oriented, impractical, Greeks, a considerable body of counter-evidence can be adduced. Some of the mechanical devices recorded in the literature are, to be sure, no more than toys, exhibiting a certain ingenuity but of no practical consequence. Such are the ball rotated by steam described by Hero, at *Pneumatics* II 11, 228.13ff (figure 23) (drastically misnamed his 'steam engine'), and many of his pneumatic and hydraulic devices, designed to amuse diners at a symposium, or to impress religious worshippers, as in

---

[30] Zhang Heng is referred to in the *Hou Hanshu*, 89. His seismoscope is discussed by Sleeswyk and Sivin 1983.

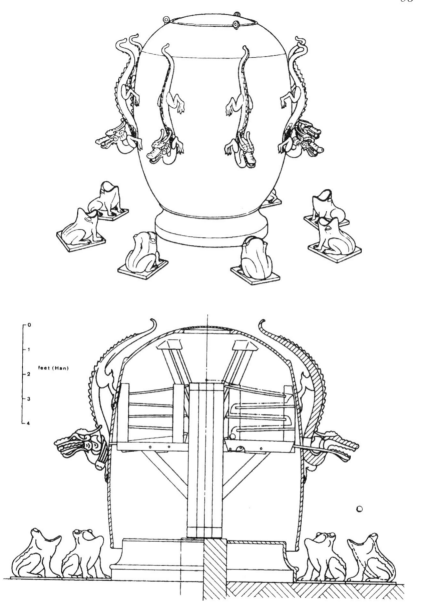

Fig. 22   Zhang Heng's seismoscope as reconstructed by Sleeswyk and Sivin.

Fig. 23   Hero's ball rotated by steam, as described in the *Pneumatics* II, 228.13ff.

his idea for temple doors that open automatically when a fire is lit on an altar (figure 24).[31] That was no practical proposition, but plenty of his other gadgets can be made to work. One such device is a water-pump incorporating one-way valves that was used as a fire-extinguisher. Even though Pappus amazingly included the gadgets of the 'wonder-workers' among what he calls the 'most necessary' parts of the mechanical arts, not all Greek mechanics was like that.[32] Improvements in weapons of war, in lifting devices using compound pulleys, in the development of

[31] Hero, *Pneumatics* I 38, 174.11 ff, cf. statues made to pour libations, I 12, 80.4ff. Elsewhere Hero describes trick drinking horns (from which two different liquids can be poured) or mixing vessels (that replenish themselves from a hidden reservoir), e.g. *Pneumatics* I 9, 64.14ff, I 22, 112.13ff, II 20, 260.5ff, II 28, 288.9ff, for which Chinese parallels can be found (Needham and Robinson 1962, pp. 34f, Needham 1965, pp. 156f). On the one hand there was clearly a market for such gadgets, and on the other they certainly offered the mechanical writers good publicity as illustrations of the range of their performance as well as of their ingenuity.

[32] Pappus, *Collectio* VIII 2, 1024.12ff. Pappus there purports to be recording the views of those associated with Hero. According to these, the 'most necessary' parts of mechanics include not just the use of pulleys, catapults and water-lifting devices, but also the construction of spheres to illustrate the movements of the heavens, and a variety of gadgets produced by so-called 'wonder-workers'. Among the last he mentions Hero's pneumatic devices, his production of automata – imitating the movements of living things by means of sinews and ropes, as in the extant treatise on the 'automatic theatre' – and hydraulic devices such as water-clocks, to which is added Archimedes' work *On Floating Bodies*, even though our extant treatise is purely geometrical in character. A similar very variegated list, ranging from war engines to wonderful devices based on air currents, weights and ropes, figures in Proclus' definition of mechanics, at *In Euc. El.* 41.3ff. By contrast, Vitruvius distinguishes the 'useful' from 'necessary' at X 1 4–5, and initially gives a restricted list of the latter, comprising the manufacture of clothing, agricultural devices, transport and the use of the balance 'to defeat fraud'. He has less to say about devices that serve merely for pleasure or amusement (*ad delectationem*), though he introduces that category when he defends the usefulness of the hodometer (X 9 7).

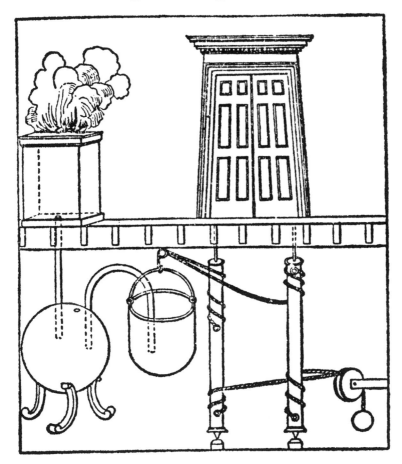

Fig. 24 Hero's scheme for opening temple doors by the condensation of steam from lighting a fire at an altar.

applications of the screw in oil and wine presses and in water-lifting devices, all owe something to the researches of Greek and Roman theorists.

It is certainly the case that many of the actual technological advances we can trace in both civilisations cannot now be assigned to named inventors – nor maybe could they ever have been. Many, probably most, were the work of anonymous individuals or groups directly engaged in the business of food-producing and processing, of fighting battles or whatever. Yet both civilisations produced a considerable technical literature devoted to the description and analysis of practical problems. If the driving force was often necessity, many gifted individuals saw the opportunity (and took it) to make a reputation for themselves and were duly celebrated for their achievements, as hydraulic engineers, builders, inventors, whether in the military or the civil domain. While some texts content themselves with recording the devices used, some individuals and groups (the Mohists, Li Bing, Zhang Heng, Archimedes, the Alexandrian engineers, Hero) evidently engaged in more or less sustained investigations into the problems on their own account.

Yet certain differences may be detected, first in the nature of the theoretical discussions to be found in that literature, and then, more fundamentally, in the matter of the structures that existed for the implementation of new ideas.

On the first score, two features appear particularly striking, first the Greek predilection for geometrical idealisations, and second the Chinese focus on exploring the propensities of things, *shi*[III]. I have remarked before that in such fields as statics, Greek geometrical analysis led both to a successful isolation of the key factors in play, and to the bonus that the results could be presented in the form of axiomatic-deductive demonstrations. Yet elsewhere idealisation could mean the neglect of problems relating to the efficiency of actual machines. The effects of friction are typically discounted, not just in Archimedes' extrapolations of the powers of compound pulleys, but also in the repeated calculations we find in Hero concerning the force needed to move a given weight, whether using pulleys or cog-wheels or levers.[33] Again in his discussion of the inclined plane, Hero starts from the idea that, in principle at least, any weight can be moved on a horizontal plane by a force less than any given force (diminishing to zero), even though in practice he recognises that this is not the case.[34] In this instance, there is a second equally unsuccessful attack on the problem by Pappus,[35] who adopts the assumption that Hero explicitly denied, namely that on a horizontal plane the force needed to move a weight varies directly with the weight in question. We have noted before the prestige that proof *more geometrico* enjoyed with many Greeks. Yet in cases where geometrisation was bought at the cost of eliding or ignoring the key factors on which the efficiency of machines depended, that move was a mixed blessing, or rather no blessing at all.

On the Chinese side, geometrisation was not the route that theoretical analysis of these questions took, though that cannot be put down to an alleged Chinese lack of interest in geometry as such – we saw good reason to doubt that blanket allegation in chapter 3. But over a range of

---

[33] See Hero, *Mechanics* II 25–6, 158.17ff (levers), II 3, 98.29ff, II 23f, 154.13ff (pulleys) and I 1, 2.4ff, II 21, 146.31ff and *Dioptra* 34, 292.16ff (cogwheels). See Drachmann 1963.
[34] Hero, *Mechanics* I 20ff, 54.10ff, especially I 23, 60.9ff.   [35] Pappus, *Collectio* VIII 17, 1054.4ff.

technological problems, the Chinese interest is less in attempting to *master* the materials they worked with, than in getting those materials to work *for* them. Li Bing's success would be better described not as overcoming the river Min, but as getting it to cooperate with his aims. Similarly, in warfare, the goal of the Chinese strategist was not to annihilate the enemy, but to have him do what you want – surrender. The means to this end was the exploitation of the potentialities of the situation, from the lie of the land to the disposition and morale of your own and the enemy forces. Both the early military classics, *Sunzi* and *Sun Bin*, have chapters devoted to *shi*[III], understanding and using the propensities of things,[36] and as François Jullien has shown, the concept plays a similar role, as the focus of interest and theoretical elaboration, across a variety of fields where the goal is effect.

Different emphases, such as these, may, then, be found in the *motifs* given prominence, when Chinese, or when Greek or Latin, authors discuss the keys to the solution of practical problems. But there are far more marked differences, between the two civilisations, in the matter of the exploitation of whatever new ideas the theorists and others proposed.

The exceptional nature of the Ptolemies' support for their military engineers just highlights the contrast with the *norm* in the Greco-Roman world. Where, in that world, civic or state interests *were* at stake – in temple building or in the construction of aqueducts – there we find great projects seen through to successful completion. But that was the *norm* in China, increasingly so after the unification of the empire under Qin Shi Huang Di, with the systematic engagement of the Emperor himself (and so of all his many officials under him) in agriculture, in warfare, in the welfare of all under heaven. It was not that the Emperor sought to ensure the prosperity of his people *solely* in a spirit of disinterested magnanimity. Rather, that prosperity had often been, and continued to be, taken as a sign of his virtue and of his mandate from heaven. So where the Roman agronomists (for example) targeted private land-owners whose desire for greater efficiency was driven largely by the profit motive, many of the Chinese – not unmoved by profit themselves of course, despite Mencius – were further influenced by the ideal of the welfare of the empire as a whole. But that was not just in a spirit of idealism, but also one of self-interest, for the apparently altruistic ideal of the welfare of the empire coincided with the egoistic one of a secure job in the imperial service.

---

[36] See *Sunzi* ch. 5, Ames 1993, pp. 71 ff, *Sun Bin* ch. 9, Lau and Ames 1996, p. 86. For the wider ramifications of the notion, see Jullien 1995.

CHAPTER FIVE

The language of learning

The results of inquiry have normally to be expressed in language, and an important way in which inquiry may become self-reflexive is on the question of the adequacy of language as a tool to express its findings. The two main problems I address in this chapter are first the question of the creation of a more or less specialised language to convey the results of research and indeed to conduct it in the first place, and secondly the type of reflection on language use that may advance or hinder those researches. I shall concentrate, once again, on the evidence on these issues from ancient Greece and China, though I am well aware that other ancient cultures, and especially India, have much to contribute to our understanding of the problems.

First, however, two preliminary but important points must be raised, namely the question of how far wisdom is expressible in words in the first place, and secondly the esoteric use of language, designed not to communicate openly, but rather just to an exclusive group.

The inexpressibility of the highest truths is an idea that can be illustrated from both China and Greece. The famous opening sentence of the *Daodejing* states – as it is usually rendered – that the way that can be told is not the constant way. That captures the main point, for sure, but does not convey the play, here, on the senses of the word *dao*, both 'way', and 'guide', show the way, and so in the middle of the three occurrences 'told'. What we have is: *dao ke dao fei chang dao*: the way that can be shown-as-a-way is not the constant way. In any event, criticism of glibness, and admiration for the sage who can communicate without speech, are themes that recur, in the *Lunyu* (*Analects*), in *Xunzi*, in the *Lüshi chunqiu* and other texts.[1] In the hierarchy of Chinese values, facility in speech generally ranks low.

[1] *Lunyu* 1 3, 5 5, 11 23, 15 11, 15 27, 16 4, *Xunzi* 22: 49ff, *Lüshi chunqiu, lan* 6: 18, where two texts, especially, 18, 2: 1155 and 18, 3: 1167, emphasise that there were ancient rulers who gave their words weight by speaking rarely, and that there were sages who communicated without speech.

In Greece, the inexpressibility of the highest truths becomes an important theme in late antiquity, in Plotinus and Proclus, for example, though sometimes the point is combined with a strong sense of the value of dialectical skills, at least in the lower reaches of understanding. For Proclus, for instance, what is divine is ineffable in itself, though it may be apprehended through what participates in it.[2] Much earlier, Plato had repeatedly stressed how hard it is to grasp, and convey, the highest wisdom, but had also insisted that the philosopher must be able to give an account (*logon didonai*) of what he knows.[3]

Like the ancient Chinese, the Greeks were often suspicious of glib talk and warn against it, though there is a certain ambivalence about this. The fast-talking Athenians were sometimes stereotypically contrasted with the strong, silent Spartans, but some of those who criticised the former on that score were themselves fair examples of fast-talking Athenians (Cleon in Thucydides, for instance[4]).

The key difference, in this regard, between Greece and China, lies in the contexts in which you needed all the fluency you could muster. The Chinese developed skills in persuasion for use especially to win round those who really counted, rulers, or their ministers or advisers. *Hanfeizi* (12) in particular offers a brilliant analysis of how to play on the ruler's psychology and get round him, and especially how not to *seem* to be doing so, and indeed how not to seem to be too clever by half. But that was mainly for confrontations in private or in court. Greek political life, by contrast, generally demanded the *public* exercise of skills in argument. Public debate, which was often the medium of philosophical and scientific discussion too, called for skills in polemic, where nothing was to be gained by invoking the ineffability of the wisdom you claimed to possess.

My second preliminary point relates to esoteric, or deliberately obscure, language. One extreme type of case has been discussed by Fernandez, Boyer and others, under the rubric of 'empty concepts', illustrated by such examples as 'taboo' or 'mana', though let me take the less hackneyed, less naturalised, instance of *evur* among the Fang.[5] That is learnt not by being told *what* it is (no one can really say) but by observing what is claimed of its effects, 'witchcraft' (but then what does that mean?): you have to have encountered it to recognise it. Then you can say, with

---

[2] Proclus, *Elements of Theology*, propositions 121, 123, Dodds 1963, pp. 106f, 108f, cf. Plotinus, *Enneads* V 5, VI 9 4.

[3] Plato, *Republic* 534b. This comes a few pages after Socrates has said (at 505de) that he cannot say what the good itself is, but can only describe its offspring, which he proceeds to do in the images of the Sun, the Divided Line and the Cave.

[4] E.g. Thucydides III 37ff.   [5] Fernandez 1982, Boyer 1990 ch. 2, 1993.

everyone else around you 'Aha! *Evur*' (everyone else bar the witch, that is). Participation in performance, in other words, is the only path to understanding, for the elucidation of sense cannot proceed independently of such experience.

Neither the Chinese nor the Greeks have terms that are exactly equivalent to *evur*, though in both cases the language to express the numinous, the spiritual, the sacred, fulfils some of the criteria for empty concepts. But in other respects both societies illustrate how esoteric or exclusive vocabulary was used in particular contexts. In both Chinese and Greek alchemy, for example, many ordinary terms are redeployed in technical senses intelligible only to the initiated. The Chinese term *fu*[1], for instance, which normally means 'cause to submit' or 'subdue', is used for the treatment of a volatile substance so that it loses its volatility.[6]

In Greek alchemy, similarly, there is much talk of processes called conquering and dominating (along with taming, delighting, punishing) where the first is used of one substance imposing its properties on another and suppressing the other's, while the second – 'dominating' – implies that one substance stops another from acting and neutralises it.[7] To understand what is going on, the initiate will need the guidance of the master, and even then not all the practitioner needs to know will be conveyed in the texts used to instruct him or her. There are certain procedures the pupil can only learn by doing them, not by having them described in words. The obscurity of some texts, accordingly, may be due to esoteric, technical, language, but in others it is a matter of some of the key information being withheld, while in yet others it reflects the difficulty of any merely verbal description.

Alchemy was particularly secretive, for there were tricks to be learned – the dyeing of base metals to pass them off as gold – and at the more philosophical end of the art, where, for instance, the search was for the elixir of immortality, it was not that anyone who thought they were near discovering that would seek to broadcast their results. But some of the same features figure also far more generally in, for example, medicine.

There is, to be sure, wide variation in the degree of openness with which both Chinese and Greek practitioners were prepared to speak about what they claimed to know. But we find secretiveness in parts of both sets of traditions. The doctor Chunyu Yi is overjoyed when both of his teachers, in turn, say they will hand on their secret ('prohibited')

---

[6] See Sivin 1968, Needham and Sivin 1980, pp. 4ff, 250ff.
[7] See Mertens 1995, p. 168.

formulas, and he swears that he, for his part, will not divulge them to anyone else.[8]

In Greek medicine, too, the Hippocratic *Law* (ch. 5, *CMG* I 1, 8.15f) insists that 'holy things' (in this case medicine) 'are revealed only to holy persons: such things must not be made known to the profane until they are initiated into the mysteries of knowledge'. The application of rigorous rules of apprenticeship, oath-taking and so on, is one way of controlling access to specialist knowledge. But esoteric language is another. Some of the Hippocratic aphoristic works rival Heraclitus in that respect. Indeed *Nutriment* (ch. 45, *CMG* I 1, 84.3) quotes 'the way up and down is one' without any context or indication as to how, in medicine, that is meant to be taken. The next chapter (ch. 46, *CMG* I 1, 84.4) continues with another paradox: 'the power of nourishment is greater than its bulk: the bulk of nourishment is greater than its power'. Perhaps such dicta served as summaries of points that the teacher would have gone into with some care. But they may also function more as a warning of the difficulties of the subject than as an aid to overcoming them. Yet at the opposite end of the spectrum, another Hippocratic work, *On Ancient Medicine* (ch. 2, *CMG* I 1, 37.9ff), insists that the doctor should be intelligible to the lay person.

These preliminary points illustrate some of the possible tensions in the adaptation of language to the requirements of new inquiries as they develop. On the one hand, the vocabulary must be able to do justice to the complexities of the material under investigation. On the other, the more recherché the language – the more it relies on neologisms – the more obscure it will tend to become, though (as noted) some may positively seek obscurity and some inquiries may gain a certain cachet from a reputation as exclusive.

I shall take just two from among the gamut of possible subject-areas in order to explore the Greek and Chinese experience in them. The first is the terminology used to describe the human body (we should beware of equating this too straightforwardly with our 'anatomy' and 'physiology' for reasons that will become apparent), and the second the study of plants. In both cases there is a very considerable expansion of knowledge, as both Greek and Chinese thought developed. The pressures on language look at first sight broadly similar. But as we shall see, the study of just these two fields already reveals certain differences in the response those pressures evoked.

[8] Sima Qian, *Shiji* 105: 2796.7, 2815.11.

Three of the main sources for ideas about the insides of the body were surface observation, butchery and inference from therapeutic procedures, though they were supplemented, to a much greater extent in Greece than in Han China, by the practice of dissection[9] – first on animals, in a programme initiated by Aristotle in Greece with teleological interests in mind (he says the parts of animals are worth investigating because they reveal the beauty of nature), but then in Hellenistic Alexandria on humans, where we have an exceptional example of Greek state support for research. We are told that Herophilus and Erasistratus practised dissection and vivisection on human subjects 'obtained out of prison from the Kings'.[10] I shall be coming back to some of the issues that raises in my final chapter.

The techniques of investigation used do not, however, get to the fundamental point that concerns us here, namely what those investigations chose to focus on. In Greece the overriding concern was with structures, where indeed dissection led not just to many new discoveries but also to new problems. Once the valves of the heart were discovered, the Alexandrian anatomists faced the difficulty of explaining the flow of blood (and air) into and out of the two sides. But a whole new vocabulary of terms was needed to describe the structures that came to be revealed.[11] New coinages were generally based on analogies with objects outside the body. But two recurrent problems were first the use of different terms for the same structure, and secondly and conversely, the use of the same term for quite different parts. The treatise that Rufus of Ephesus devoted to the *Naming of Parts*, in the early second century CE, illustrates both difficulties.

Take the names for the membranes of the eye (see figure 25). What we call the retina (from Latin *rete*, net) had no less than four names. It was called the net-like membrane, *amphiblestroeides*, from *amphiblestron*, a casting-net. This was an analogy first drawn, we are told, by Herophilus. But it was also named the spider's-web-like one, *arachnoeides*, and the 'glass-like', *hualoeides*, from the vitreous humour it contained. One joint name for the cornea and sclera was *keratoeides*, the horn-like, another the 'first', another the 'bright' (*leukos*) though maybe that applied,

---

9 While *Huangdi neijing*, *lingshu* 12.2, suggests the possibility of dissection, the sole apparent extant record of an actual dissection being carried out is that ordered by Wang Mang, reported in his biography in the *Hanshu* 99B: 4145–6: see Yamada Keiji 1991, p. 39, Kuriyama 1995, 1999, pp. 155–60. On the development of dissection in ancient Greece, see Lloyd 1991, ch. 8.

10 The key evidence is in Celsus, *On Medicine* 1 Pref. 23f, *CML* 1, 21.13ff. The Kings in question certainly included the Ptolemies, and may be (and in my view were) limited to them.

11 I have discussed aspects of the development of Greek anatomical terminology in Lloyd 1983, part III ch. 4.

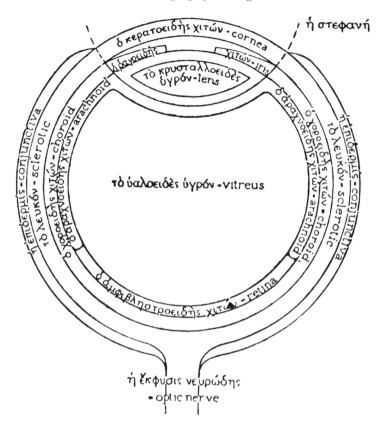

Fig. 25   The membranes of the eye and their names according to Rufus of Ephesus.

more strictly, to the opaque sclera. Again the choroid had four names, the 'grape-like' (*rhagoeides*), the 'after-birth-like' (*chorioeides*), the 'pierced' (*tetremenos*) and more simply, the second. Finally the capsular sheath of the crystalline lens was the 'lentil-like' (*phakoeides*), 'discus-like' (*diskoeides*) and 'ice-like' (*krustalloeides*).[12]

There was, to be sure, particular interest in the eye and its internal anatomy, going back to the Presocratic philosopher Empedocles who compared it with a lantern (Fr 84). But in the case of many other structures, too, a similar situation applies. Thus to give just a single example from the many that could be cited, Rufus gives three names for the uvula

---

[12] See *On the Naming of Parts* 154, cf. also the treatise entitled *Anatomy*, 170ff, though its attribution to Rufus is more doubtful.

at *On the Naming of Parts* (141.3ff), namely *kion*, *gargareon* and Aristotle's *staphulophoron*, to which we can add two others from the *Anatomy* (173.6ff), namely *kionis* and *staphule*, though Rufus himself says (141.5f) that the latter term should be reserved for the inflammation of the uvula, not for the uvula itself.

One type of confusion arose from the same structure having different names. But the converse kind of confusion was when a single term was used of quite different parts. Thus the term *aorta* ('hanger', 'suspender') was used not just for what we call the aorta, but also for the pulmonary artery and indeed for the bronchi.[13] More strikingly still, the term *neuron* – which was used, from Herophilus on, for both the sensory and motor nerves – continued to be applied, as in classical Greek it had been indiscriminately, to tendons, ligaments and sinews.[14] Although there is no doubt what Galen was referring to, in his experimental vivisections of the nerves in the spinal cord of a pig (described at length in *On Anatomical Procedures* IX chs. 13f), on many occasions in many texts both outside the medical literature and within it, the identification of the objects called *neura* remains problematic.

The lack of standardisation of Greek anatomical terminology stems in the main, I would argue, from the same centrifugal tendencies we have identified elsewhere, and not just in Greek medicine. The rivalry between individual theorists extended, in this instance, as far as the ambition to develop and impose their own coinages for the structures that their anatomical research revealed. At least that ambition seems often to have won out over any sense of the desirability of promoting a uniform terminology. It is true that both Rufus and Galen draw attention to certain shifts in the meaning and reference of particular terms.[15]

---

[13] See, for example, Aristotle, *History of Animals* 496a7, and in the Hippocratic Corpus, *Coan Prognoses*, xx 394, Littré v 672.5, *On the Heart* ch. 10, Littré IX 86.17ff, with the comments of Rufus, *On the Naming of Parts* 155.11 and 163.5ff. Cf. Irigoin 1980, pp. 252ff.

[14] See especially Staden 1989, pp. 159f, 250–9, and cf. Lloyd 1987, pp. 212–13. Galen, for instance, points out differences between the 'ancient' and his own use of the term *neuron*, and has many occasions to criticise the continuing errors of his own contemporaries in this area: *On Anatomical Procedures* VII ch. 8, Kühn II 612.2ff, 15ff, 613.1ff, *On the Use of Parts* I ch. 17, Helmreich I 33.26ff.

[15] Rufus, for example, has this to say about the change in the sense of *phlebes*. 'In ancient times they used to call the arteries *phlebes*. And when they say that the *phlebes* beat, they meant the arteries, for it is the function of the arteries to beat.' For good measure, he adds: 'And they also called them [the arteries] *aortai* ['suspenders'], *pneumatika angeia* ['pneumatic vessels'], *seranges* ['hollows'], *kenomata* ['vacancies'] and *neura* ['nerves/sinews']' (*On the Naming of Parts*, 163.3ff). Similarly Galen remarks (*On the Doctrines of Hippocrates and Plato* VI ch. 8, *CMG* V 4 1 2, 416.16–20) 'Now the earliest physicians and philosophers gave to vessels of this kind the name "vein", as they did to the other kind; but the rest call the pulsating vessel an artery, the pulseless a vein. The older usage has been pointed out by many before me, and by me elsewhere.'

But even after Galen had become, by the fourth century CE, the chief authority through whom medicine was taught, plenty of indeterminacy remained, reflecting the indeterminacy in Galen's own usage. Galen is, in fact, extraordinarily carefree about terminology, sometimes saying it does not matter what term you use – provided, that is, you know what it is you are talking about.[16]

In China the prime focus of attention was very different, not on structures, but on processes, the normal interactions to be expected within the body and the abnormal ones to be countered. On the one hand there was the normal flow of qi^{II}: on the other, the movements of so-called heteropathic (*xie*) qi^{II}. Already in the classical medical texts, eleven main visceral systems, cardiac, pulmonary, hepatic and so on, are identified, five *yin* ones, known as *zang*, and six *yang* ones, the fu^{II}.[17] In addition to these, there were the circulation tracts ($jing^{II}$) that provided, in Sivin's expression, a 'network through which the nutritive essences are distributed throughout the body'. These essences included not just qi^{II}, but also *xue* (blood), but any attempt to identify the tracts with either blood-vessels or nerves or some combination of both is misguided – for we should not assume that they are meant to correspond to anatomical structures in the first place. Rather, they enabled the idea of health as free flow, disease as obstruction in the body, to be represented, and therapeutic procedures to be accounted for.[18]

This basic set of concepts was pretty stable but underwent, at points, some detailed elaboration, partly under the pressure of the development of those procedures. In the Mawangdui texts, where acupuncture is not mentioned, the vessels (*mai*) are associated with cauterisation procedures. We may compare the way in which, in Greece, before the use of dissection, the paths of the blood-vessels were sometimes *inferred* from practices in venesection (see figure 26). Thus in Polybus' scheme, a first pair of blood-vessels runs from the back of the head through the neck past the backbone to the loins and so to the legs and on to the outer ankles and the feet. Then the text adds the tell-tale note: 'that is why they make venesections ... in the outer parts of the ankles to relieve pains in the back and loins'. He goes *from* the therapeutic procedure, assumed efficacious, *to*

[16] Barnes 1991, pp. 72ff, remarks on a number of similar cases where Galen shows an indifference to exactness in terminology, and not just in anatomy, and cf. Lloyd 1996c.
[17] See Sivin 1987, pp. 124ff, cf. Kuriyama 1999.
[18] The notion of the importance, for health, of free flow and proper communications within the body, is developed in the *Lüshi chunqiu*, 20, 5: 1373, as well as in classical medical texts such as *Huangdi neijing suwen* 8 1–2. See Sivin 1995b, I pp. 6ff and Lloyd and Sivin 2002, ch. 5.

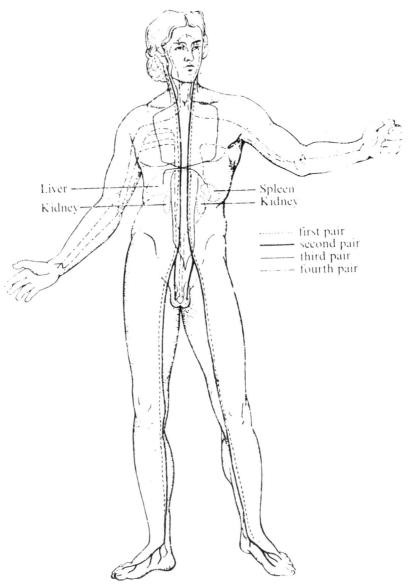

Fig. 26 Reconstruction of Polybus' scheme of the vessels in the body (after Aristotle
History of Animals, III, ch. 3 and *On the Nature of Man*, ch. 11).

the anatomical structure, not the other way round.[19] But in China, once acupuncture therapy came to be developed, that led to increasingly elaborate classifications of acupuncture points and tracts (figure 27). Although there was plenty of disagreement on points of detailed interpretation,[20] the eventual proliferation of terminology reflected the development of therapy and of correlative systematics, rather than the competing views of individuals attempting to promote their own coinages.[21]

In the study of plants, the second field I chose for examination, three main types of interest may be distinguished, first one in plant names and plant classification for its own sake, secondly an interest in plants as food-stuffs, and third in their medicinal uses. As knowledge of flora expands, the need for a similarly expanded vocabulary to convey that knowledge becomes obvious. But once again this happened, in certain respects, in rather different ways in China and in Greece.

In China, one of the first extant discussions of plants comes in the *Erya*,[22] an encyclopedic compilation dating principally from the third century BCE that contains glosses on a great variety of terms in different subject-areas. Here the primary interest is lexicographical, the interpretation and explanation of the uses of the terms themselves. This catered, in the main, for a learned audience, who needed to know the 'proper' names, as opposed to whatever popular ones might be in use. But in the process we also have detailed accounts of what each of the parts of a given plant should be called. There is, for example, a quite detailed description of the lotus (figure 28) which assigns names to eight different parts of the plant. It has special names for *its* leaves, stem, root, seed and so on. Needham (1986, p. 135) praised this account for its exactness, though he also noted what he called the 'scientific' drawback, namely that 'the rich array of names belonged only to this particular plant, and could not easily become generalised as technical terms more widely useful'. Indeed the interest here is not at all in taxonomy or in providing the

[19] The theory of Polybus is reported by Aristotle, *History of Animals* 512b12ff, and cf. *On the Nature of Man* ch. 11, *CMG* I 1 3, 192.15ff, cf. Lloyd 1991, p. 180.
[20] Thus the question of the interpretation of the *sanjiao* system (conventionally translated 'triple burner'), mentioned in a prominent text in the *Huangdi neijing suwen* 8 1–2: 28, was the subject of much commentary. One suggestion (Sivin 1987, pp. 124f) is that it was added to an original five *yang* visceral system (paralleling the five *yin* ones, see above at n. 17) to give a sixth and provide a connection, in turn, to the Six Warps (*liu jing*), setting out a regular sequence of interaction between three *yang* and three *yin* phases (Sivin 1987, pp. 8off). Again the *shanzhong* system, mentioned in the same passage in the *suwen*, appears to be named after the corresponding acupuncture point, and may come from a variant tradition, though some commentators, to get round the anomaly, identified it (quite arbitrarily, as Sivin 1987, p. 126 n. 14 notes) with the Cardiac Envelope Junction to bring it into line with the more regular view.
[21] See Sivin 1987, Harper 1998, Kuriyama 1999.
[22] See *Erya* 15–19 especially, Needham 1986, pp. 130ff, Bretschneider 1892, ch. 1, and cf. Bray 1988.

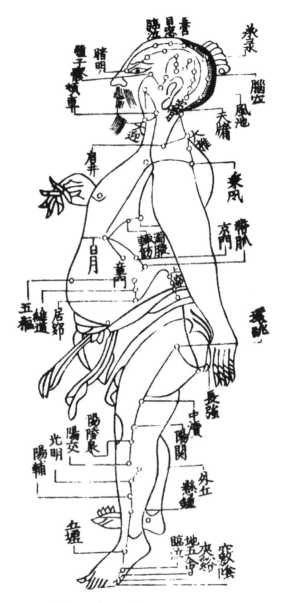

Fig. 27   Chart of acupuncture tracts.

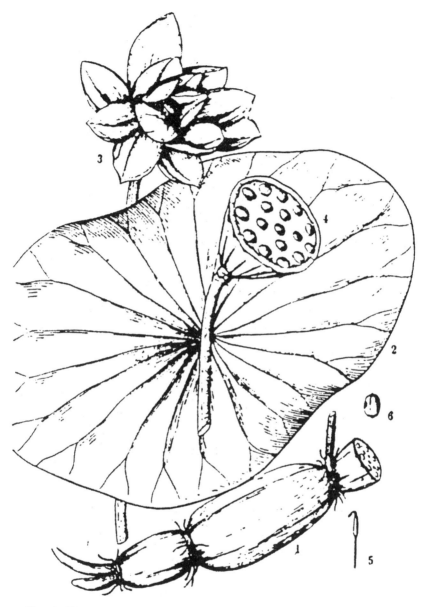

Fig. 28   The parts of the lotus, *Nelumba nucifera*, from a modern representation, identifying six of the parts named in the *Erya* description.

basis for generalising from one plant to another. Rather it is to establish a correct description and nomenclature for each of the parts of the lotus itself, many of them used as foodstuffs or as medicines, while the plant as a whole was one heavy with symbolic and literary associations.

A more severely practical orientation of interest is, however, displayed first in agricultural treatises dealing with different kinds of plant food-stuffs, including even what were called famine foods, and then in what came to be the voluminous *bencao* literature (which I also mentioned in the last chapter) dealing especially with the pharmacological properties of eventually huge numbers of plants.[23]

With the expansion of China's own territories, and its knowledge of foreign lands, came a considerable growth in the knowledge of plants and their uses. However, when a new species was discovered, it was not just up to the discoverer to name it. Rather the ultimate responsibility there rested with the Emperor – or at least with officials working on his behalf. There was, on occasion, considerable rivalry in attempts to gain their approval, or even their ear, but the system had the enormous advantage that, in principle at least, it ensured the standardisation of nomenclature. But such standardisation, when it occurred, came, as always in China, from the centre.

This becomes important when we compare the Greek experience, where, as we saw in Greek anatomical terminology, but for rather different reasons, confusion was widespread. Our first chief source, Theophrastus (in the fourth century BCE) repeatedly points out both that the same plant is given different names, and that the same name is used of quite different plants. Take the name *struchnos* or *struchnon*.[24] Here, for once, Liddell–Scott–Jones' dictionary starts off by resisting its usually well-developed positivist tendencies to give a determinate iden-tification. Often LSJ and Hort, the editor of the Loeb Theophrastus *Enquiry into Plants* – under the influence of the advice they received from an erstwhile director of Kew, Sir William Thiselton-Dyer – attempt full-blooded Linnaean binome classifications, but the vast majority of these are drastically misleading as John Raven pointed out in an excoriating J. H. Gray lecture in Cambridge in 1976. His denunciation of the damage done by Thiselton-Dyer to the study of Greek botany over many gen-erations was originally entitled 'poo to a polymath', but that was toned

[23] See Bray 1984, cf. Métailié 2001a and b. Bray 2001 discusses the relative transparency of the vocabulary used in agronomic treatises – compared, for example, with alchemy and geomancy – and the care with which technical terms, when introduced, were explained.
[24] See Theophrastus, *History of Plants* VII 15 4, IX 11 5f. I am grateful to Nicholas Jardine for discussions of this and other issues in Greek botanical nomenclature.

down to 'the unreliability of some of Thiselton-Dyer's identifications of Greek plant names', when the lectures were later first published.[25] In this instance, *struchnon*, LSJ cautiously begins by informing us, is a 'name of various plants'. But then it offers four proposals: *Physalis Alkekengi* (winter cherry), *Solanum nigrum* (hound's berry), *Datura Stramonium* (thorn apple) and *Withania somnifera* (sleepy nightshade).

Theophrastus, for his part, says it is used of three different plants, one edible and two with different, powerful, medicinal properties, one that induces sleep (hence partly the *Withania* identification). But the other causes madness, or in larger doses, death. This is called *manikos*, but it also has two other names, *thryoros* or *thryon* according to some editors (that just means reed) and *perittos*. The *manikos* is identified by Hort with the thorn apple (and that fits some of Theophrastus' description well enough, though hardly all of it: and it is strange that he makes no mention of the distinctive white or purple trumpet-shaped flowers if the thorn apple is indeed what he had in mind). But when *struchnos* is illustrated in the famous Vienna Dioscorides, that looks more like solanum nigrum (figure 29). The scope for possible confusion is, obviously, considerable.

Let me give just one more example: *diktamnon* ('dittany', LSJ *origanum dictamnus*) is used, Theophrastus tells us (*History of Plants* IX 16 1–3), first of true dittany, which is peculiar to Crete, then of 'false dittany' (*pseudodiktamnon*), though he shows some hesitation. LSJ, however, partly on the basis of Dioscorides, identify this as *ballota acetabulosa*. 'Some say', Theophrastus proceeds, IX 16 2, that this is the same plant and just an inferior variety produced by being grown on richer soil. Then there is a third plant called by the same name, but whose appearance and properties are quite different (this, according to Hort, is another of the *Labiatae*, *ballota pseudodictamnus*, though LSJ identify this too as *acetabulosa*) (see figure 30).

Faced with these signs of potential muddle, Theophrastus and Dioscorides after him (first century CE) attempt careful and often quite detailed descriptions of each plant, often recording the habitat, sometimes even the specific locations in the Greco-Roman world where it lives, mentioning its apparent varieties and sometimes puzzling over whether different varieties are in fact different species. As with many Chinese herbals, pictorial illustrations of the plants in question came to be an important aid to identification. In Greece this goes back to Crateuas in the first century BCE. But without the use of wood-blocks such as came to be used extensively in China, the degradation of illustrations as they

[25] Raven 2000 (original publication 1990).

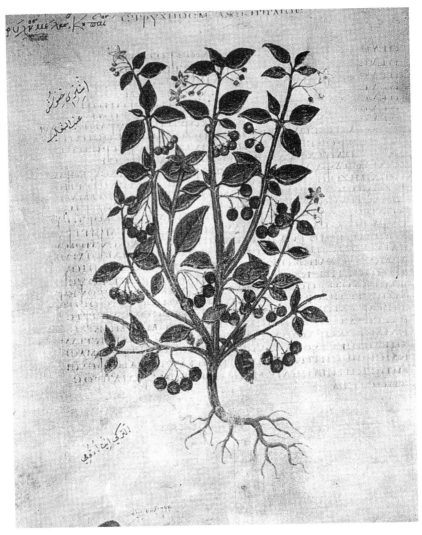

Fig. 29   Illustration of a plant named *struchnos* from the Vienna Dioscorides.

were copied from one text to another, took a heavy toll on their usefulness in the Greco-Roman tradition.[26]

The terminological variety registered in the texts of Theophrastus does not appear to represent the efforts of individual specialists seeking

[26] Crateuas is mentioned in Pliny, *Natural History* xxv 8. For a discussion of botanical illustration in China, see Haudricourt and Métailié 1994, who point out, for example, the problems that arose when old illustrations, when reused, came to be misapplied to the wrong plants.

Fig. 30   Illustration of *diktamnos* from the Vienna Dioscorides.

to promote their own coinages, as I suggested may be the case with Greek anatomy. The different names given to the same plant in many cases reflect existing local differences – as was true also in China. Yet a further factor in play in Greece relates to the gap that opens up between the interests of the botanical specialists on the one hand (who were primarily concerned with classification and with natural philosophy), and the doctors on the other (who focussed chiefly on the pharmaceutical properties of plants – one of the key principles used

in Dioscorides' organisation of his material). In China too the doctors
had different interests from the literati, for sure, but the latter were not
generally in business attempting natural philosophical orderings and
explanations.

A comparison between the terminology employed in Theophrastus
and in the pharmacological sections of approximately contemporary
Hippocratic treatises shows that the latter are, on the whole, much *less*
conscientious in specifying which, of several possible varieties of plants
with the same name, is the one to be used for a particular ailment or
in a particular recipe. In some cases, communicating with their medical colleagues, the medical writers may have felt that they did not need
to be specific – on the grounds that it would be well known to them
what the different varieties of *struchnos* (for instance) would be used for.[27]
Yet in other cases we may have our doubts. We find one Hippocratic
writer prescribing half a cotyle (that would come to about an eighth
of a litre or a quarter of a pint) of the juice of *struchnos* together with
some other ingredients as a pain-killer to be taken daily (*On Internal
Affections* ch. 27, Littré VII 238.3ff). If one took the wrong *struchnos*, it
would be more than just the pain that would be killed. There was obviously great scope for passing one drug off as another, or indeed un-
intentionally mistaking one for another. Although the point cannot be
quantified, the confusion over the identities of plants that in popular
belief had special powers or associations seems greater than with others
where that was not the case. (Mandragora would be one example: 'moly'
another).[28] Moreover in the absence of any agency, imperial or otherwise,
to impose uniformity, those confusions were more or less ineradicable,
and that despite the efforts of such as Theophrastus and Dioscorides
themselves.

[27] *struchnos* is mentioned in such texts as *Ulcers* ch. 11, Littré VI 410.16, *Fistulae* ch. 7, Littré VI 454.23,
On Diseases III ch. 1, *CMG* I 2 3, 70.15, *On the Nature of Women* ch. 29, Littré VII 344.14, ch. 34,
376.8, *On the Diseases of Women* I ch. 78, Littré VIII 196.11 and 18, as well as the passage from
On Internal Affections ch. 27 that I mention in my text, and on no occasion is the variety of *struchnos*
to be used discussed.
[28] As I document in some detail in Lloyd 1983, pp. 122–5, Theophrastus is sometimes in two
minds as to how to respond to the tales he says are told, by root-cutters, drug-sellers and others,
concerning the need to take particular precautions in collecting certain plants. On the one
hand he acknowledges that the 'powers of some plants are dangerous' (*History of Plants* IX 8
6: this relates to certain injunctions he has heard about concerning gathering roots at night or
standing to windward of the plant). On the other he dismisses other beliefs as 'adventitious and
far-fetched', as for instance the idea that if a person collects the fruit of the peony called *glukuside*
by day and a woodpecker sees him, he risks losing his sight, while if he is caught digging up the
root, he gets prolapse of the anus. It is notable that certain stories about collecting cinnamon
and cassia are rejected as sheer 'myth' (*muthos*), IX 5 2.

The needs of different technical fields, the nature of the new data they have to assimilate, how that needs to be processed, and for whose benefit, all vary far beyond anything I have thus far been able to suggest. But the two fields I have taken alert us to the possibility that cultural and institutional factors may play a role in the distinctive responses of the relevant Greek and Chinese specialists. However, in both societies there were also sophisticated general reflections on language use that have a bearing on the conduct of inquiries as a whole. The particular difficulty of this part of our study is to do justice to the very different aims and ambitions that underpin those reflections in either case.[29]

In Greece, to start with the easier, or at least the more familiar, case, one of the most important developments was the concerted bid, first by Plato and then more especially by Aristotle, to purify language of obscurity. In Aristotle's case the key move was the introduction of the contrast between terms used strictly, *kurios*, and those said 'by way of transfer', *kata metaphoran*, that is, very roughly speaking, between the literal and the metaphorical.[30]

Self-conscious reflections on language use go back, in Greece, much further than the fourth century. Already by the end of the sixth century the possibility of reading Homer allegorically had been proposed by Theagenes of Rhegium. In the fifth century, there are indications of an interest in the grammatical classification of words, in the elements of rhetorical style, in the distinctions between the meanings of near synonyms, and especially in the issue of whether names have a natural, or merely a conventional, relationship with what they signify. That last was the problem the Greeks called that of the correctness of names (*orthotes onomaton*) and, some time before Plato set out the main contending positions in the *Cratylus*, it had attracted attention from Democritus, as well as Antiphon, Protagoras and Prodicus.

Those debates came to be overshadowed by Plato's own analysis. His attack on the poets, in the *Republic*, is based primarily on moral grounds, on the content of what they teach, though also on how they teach it. But in a variety of contexts he criticises the use of images, *eikones*,

---

[29] The discussion that follows develops the line of argument that I already sketched out in my contribution to seminars run by George Boys-Stones at Oxford in 1997: see Boys-Stones forthcoming.

[30] At *Poetics* 1457b6ff Aristotle defines metaphor in terms of the application (*epiphora*) of a strange term, either from genus to species, or from species to species or by analogy.

likenesses, *homoiotetes* (as when he calls them a 'most slippery tribe' in the *Sophist*)[31] and myth (where *muthos* is used, to rejoin the themes of chapter 1, to contrast with *logos* in the sense of rational account, the kind that philosophy should be able to give).

Yet Plato nowhere proposed a literal/metaphorical dichotomy as such. That was the fateful step that Aristotle (as a first approximation) may be said to have taken. He repeatedly criticises specific *metaphorai* used by his predecessors as obscure.[32] He allows that such expressions have a use in poetry – indeed skill in their use, he says in the *Poetics*, 1459a6ff, is a mark of natural genius – and in rhetoric he even concedes that metaphor achieves perspicuity, pleasure and a foreign air (*Rhetoric* 1405a8–9). But metaphors will not do in philosophy. They certainly will not do in syllogistic, and so not in strict demonstration either, for the validity of a deduction is immediately compromised by any departure from univocity.

Quite how far Aristotle himself thought that he could apply, in practice, the strictest model of demonstration as set out in the *Posterior Analytics*, is another, interestingly complex, question.[33] It is evidently not the case that his own scientific and metaphysical investigations have been completely purged of the transferred use of terms. He recognises that some of his own basic metaphysical concepts, such as actuality and potentiality, cannot be given definitions in standard, *per genus et differentiam*, form. Rather, their elucidation proceeds by way of the apprehension of the analogical relationships between different items: or the analysis proceeds by way of the concept of 'focal meaning'. But while Aristotle's own practice often departs from his strictest ideals, that they were his ideals in the *Posterior Analytics* is clear. Even so, let me repeat the point about his remarkable ambivalence. Metaphor is a mark of the poet's natural skill: it is useful in rhetoric in adding vividness; yet it is no good for natural science (for explanation) and it is disastrous for logic. That extraordinary gradation of reactions testifies to Aristotle's acute sense of the boundaries

31 At *Sophist* 231a1–8 the Eleatic Stranger worries about whether the account he has given is appropriate to the sophists or assigns to them too honourable a rank. Theaetetus remarks 'and yet your description, just now, bears a resemblance to such a one'. To which the Stranger replies: 'But so too does the wolf to the dog, the one a most fierce, the other a most tame animal. But a careful person should always be on his guard against resemblances above all: for they are a most slippery tribe.' Cf. also *Phaedo* 92cd, *Phaedrus* 262a-c, *Theaetetus* 162c.

32 Thus Empedocles is criticised for his idea that the salt sea is the sweat of the earth (*Meteorology* 357a24ff) and Plato's characterisation of the Forms as models, *paradeigmata*, is rejected with the remark that to claim that and to say that other things 'share' in them is 'to speak nonsense and to use poetic metaphors' (*Metaphysics* 991a20ff).

33 I have discussed the relation between Aristotle's theories and practices in 1996b, especially ch. 1. Contrast, especially, Lennox 2001.

between different types of discourse – however hard they may be to maintain.

The bid to purify language of obscurity has, we may say, several complex strands. For the formal validity of arguments, terms have to be univocal, at least over the stretch of reasoning in question. The demand for strict definition may be a laudable response to fuzziness or just plain fudge. Yet there are obvious limits to the reasonableness of the demand for exactness in language. The bid to construct formal languages secures validity, but at the price of inapplicability to the world, unless translation protocols are in place to allow for conversion to natural languages, and then the price those protocols are likely to have to pay is the lack of the very precision that was the strength of the formal language in the first place.

The philosophical issue becomes the more acute as we turn, next, to evaluate Chinese reflections on language use. There in classical times, and down to the period of European influence indeed, there is – I would argue – no equivalent to the dichotomy between the literal and the metaphorical. I shall be discussing the chief classical text, from *Zhuangzi*, that has been cited in this context, in a moment. But the further question that has to be faced is: if indeed (as I claim) the Chinese lacked that dichotomy, is that to be taken as a sign of a basic weakness in their reflections on language use? To answer that, we shall need not just further philosophical analysis ourselves, but also an examination of how they got on without what I called the fateful dichotomy.

First, however, we should mention some other aspects of the Chinese evidence, to illustrate the range and nature of their interests in the analysis of language. We may begin with the discussions of *zhengming*.[34] This is conventionally translated the 'rectification of names', which appears, on the surface, similar to the Greek *orthotes onomaton*. That is, however, no more than a surface similarity. While *zhengming* covers a variety of doctrines, they relate principally to social roles and statuses. Generalising crudely, where the Greek correctness of names was a logical matter of the relationship between signifier and signified, the Chinese rectification was a matter of good order in the social and moral sense.

In a prominent text in the *Lunyu/Analects*, Confucius is asked what he would do if the Prince of Wei entrusted the government to him, and he replies 'rectify names'.[35] That advice, it is generally agreed, is specific to the Lord of Wei. But commentators differ on whether this is an oblique

[34] See especially Gassmann 1988, Vandermeersch 1993, Lackner 1993, Sivin 1995b 1 p. 3.
[35] *Lunyu* 13.3, on which see Vandermeersch 1993 and cf. Gassmann 1988, Lackner 1993.

criticism of his lack of filial piety (the Prince had been named Lord of Wei, but he should have renounced his position in favour of his exiled father) or whether Confucius is referring to a more general confusion between statuses, between master and servant, lord and minister, in the previous reign. However, it is clear from the sequel, where the rectification of names is said to be important for the due application of punishments, that it is to do with good conduct, not just language use in general.

Similarly, in the fullest discussion, in *Xunzi* 22, rectification is related to securing the proper social distinctions in the hierarchy of high and low.[36] Only by using the right names can the correct differences be maintained. Correct language is stressed as essential to avoid moral and political confusion. This has nothing to do with any transferred or metaphorical usage of terms. Rather it is, if anything, similar to Thucydides' famous denunciation of the warping of language that was a product of the moral degeneracy he diagnoses as the result of political *stasis* in the Peloponnesian war.[37]

Yet morality is not the sole concern expressed in Chinese reflections on language (of course). Elsewhere attention is paid to certain grammatical distinctions, for example between 'solid' or 'full' terms (*shi*[IV]) and 'empty' (*xu*) ones.[38] That corresponds roughly to a contrast between content words and particles (though I should add that the same dichotomy is also used in a very different way to dismiss 'empty' speech as dim or wrong-headed). Moreover – to get closer to an interest in metaphor – comparison figures prominently in Chinese analyses of poetic discourse. In a famous passage in the Great Preface to the Mao edition of the *Odes* (*Shi*[V]), various types of poetry are distinguished, where *bi*, the comparative/analogical is contrasted, for instance, with *fu*[III] (descriptive/expository) and *xing* (elevated/evocative). The interpretation

---

36 *Xunzi* 22: 10ff. 'Should a True King appear, he would certainly retain some old names but he would also have to invent new names. That being so, it is indispensable that he investigate the purpose for having names, together with the basis for distinguishing the similar from the different, and the crucial considerations for instituting names.' When arbitrary names are introduced, 'then the connection between the name and the object is obscure, what is noble and what is base is unclear, and things that are alike and things that are different are not distinguished'. There is then a real danger that the ruler's intentions will not be properly understood 'and the execution of a person's duties will certainly be hampered and obstructed' (trans. based on Knoblock 1988–94, III pp. 128–9).

37 Thucydides III 82. 'Unreasoning rashness', for instance, came to be judged as 'courage favouring partisans', while 'delay that was inspired by forethought' was considered 'cowardice under a specious name'. This too, for sure, is not a matter of metaphor, but of what Thucydides judges to be the perverse use of language.

38 See Harbsmeier 1981, 1998, pp. 130ff, Graham 1989, p. 222 and Appendix 2, pp. 389ff, Lloyd and Sivin 2002, ch. 5.

of these categories occupied an extensive commentary tradition.[39] But while that tradition accepted that comparison marks out poetry of a particular type, there was no suggestion that this type – let alone poetry in general – thereby exploited a non-strict or deviant use of language. No criticism is made or implied of the use of comparison in poetry: on the contrary, it is a virtue to be cultivated in one style of poetic composition. Here, for once, there is a resonance between a Chinese and an Aristotelian appreciation, though Aristotle did not mark out one type of poetry as (especially) comparative/analogical – and we have seen the barrier he erects between poetry in general and philosophy.

But what of the chief text that has been held to indicate a Chinese recognition of the category of the metaphorical as such? This is ch. 27 in the *Zhuangzi* compilation, which distinguishes between three types of sayings (*yan*), including one, *yu yan*, that has often been cited as equivalent to metaphor and in some translations is actually rendered 'metaphor'.[40] Yet this has to be said to be radically misleading.

Zhuangzi's three types are *yu yan*, *zhong yan* and *zhi yan*, that is, to adapt Graham's translations, 'lodge sayings', 'weighty sayings' and 'spill-over sayings'.[41] 'Saying from a lodging-place', we are told at the outset, 'works nine times out of ten, weighty saying works seven times out of ten. Spill-over saying is new every day, smooth it out on the whetstone of heaven.' There is much, evidently, in this that is obscure. Weighty sayings are, perhaps, the easiest of the three types to understand. They are said to be what you say on your own authority – the aphorism with the weight of the speaker's experience behind it, to follow Graham's lead again. 'Spill-over sayings' take their name, it seems, from a kind of vessel that is designed to tip and right itself when filled too near the brim. 'Use it to go by', the text says, 'and let the stream find its own channels: this is the way to last out your years', which Graham glossed – with some optimism it has to be said – as 'the speech proper to the intelligent spontaneity of Taoist behaviour in general, a fluid language which keeps its equilibrium through changing meanings and viewpoints'.

'Saying from a lodging-place', the type we are chiefly concerned with, is said in the text to be a matter of 'borrowing a standpoint outside to sort the matter out'. The traditional view took this to refer primarily to

[39] *Shijing daxu, shimaoshi* 1 1, on which see Liu 1975, pp. 109ff, F. Cheng 1979, Jullien 1985, pp. 67ff, 175ff, Yu 1987, pp. 57ff, 168ff.
[40] *Zhuangzi* 27: 1–5. For the translation 'metaphor' see Legge 1891 part II p. 142, Mair 1994.
[41] Graham 1989, pp. 200f. The interpretation of the object Zhuangzi has in mind when talking about 'spill-over' sayings is discussed by Lau 1968.

the expression of ideas through imaginary conversations, but Graham argued that the lodging-place is rather the standpoint of the other party in debate. You temporarily 'lodge' at the other person's standpoint in order to win him over. Zhuangzi, on this interpretation, 'seems to be referring to persuasion by *argumentum ad hominem*, the only kind of victory in debate that would have any point for him'.

Though the interpretation of this whole text is fraught with difficulty, certain points at least are clear. First, saying from a lodging-place is some way away from the root idea of the metaphorical in Greek, as the transfer of a term from a primary context to a secondary, derivative one. Secondly, it is certainly not as if the other two categories between them yield anything that can be taken remotely to correspond to the antonym of the metaphorical, namely the strict or literal use of terms. Third, while Zhuangzi is indeed interested in evaluating the appropriateness of different types of sayings in different contexts, it is not that he makes any attempt to restrict discourse to any particular, privileged, type, even within a given context. He certainly did not need to do so, as Aristotle did, for the sake of a formal analysis of the conditions of valid deduction – given that there was no Chinese interest in formal logic as such at all, and Zhuangzi is obviously not concerned with any such analysis.

We have clear evidence in ancient Chinese texts before the end of the Han of a range of interests in language and in language use. But to see any of those interests as concerned with anything like the literal/metaphorical dichotomy is a gross example of the violence done to Chinese thought by imposing Western categories on it.

Yet there are those who might agree that the ancient Chinese did not develop a contrast between the literal and the metaphorical, but who might then argue that that just shows up shortcomings in their philosophy of language. There would be those who would claim that the literal/metaphorical dichotomy is fundamental to any analysis of language and suggest that *we* can still diagnose *their* metaphors, even if they did not have a word for them. So I turn back, now, to the question of what they might have needed any such category for and to the philosophical issue of whether indeed the dichotomy is indispensable.

With regard to definition, to the fixing of clear meanings and the avoidance of misunderstandings, it might be thought that the lack of a contrast between the literal and the metaphorical might carry certain disadvantages. To be sure, having such a dichotomy available is going to be no guarantee of transparency in communication. But its absence might be taken to be a potential handicap. To test whether it was, in ancient China, we may turn to the field where this might be thought to be most likely to be the case, namely mathematics.[42]

The Chinese certainly did not engage in definition *per genus et differentiam*, in mathematics or anywhere else. Nor did they aim to secure definitions as one type of self-evident primary premises along the lines of Aristotle's analysis of axiomatic-deductive demonstration in the *Posterior Analytics*. But they were perfectly capable of being precise about the way in which certain terms are to be understood. Take the introduction of particular terms for particular procedures in Liu Hui's commentary on the first section of the *Nine Chapters of the Mathematical Art*, where the problem tackled is that of the addition of fractions.[43] Liu Hui shows that $a/b + c/d = (ad + bc)/bd$ is correct. But he first gives names to the two procedures involved, first the multiplying of denominators by numerators that do not correspond to them (as in ad and bc in the equation just set out) and secondly the multiplication of the denominators by one another (as in the new denominator bd on the right hand side of that equation). To quote his text: 'Every time denominators multiply a numerator that does not correspond to them, we call this homogenise (qi^{III}). Multiplying with one another the set of denominators, we call this equalise (*tong*).'

The terms introduced here are both ones that otherwise have a range of general uses. Thus qi^{III} means even, level, uniform. *Tong* is used of similarity, sameness, as well as equality, and further of sharing, association, together. Yet they are now used, by Liu Hui, as the names of certain well-defined mathematical procedures (ones that provide some of the unifying principles of mathematics to which – as I said in chapter 3 – he attaches such importance). He marks his new usage clearly with the expression *wei* (we call this: or call this).[44] He does not attempt to coin a brand new term on these occasions (as is sometimes required, for instance, for complex mathematical figures). Rather he redeploys existing terms. If we choose to puzzle over whether or how far this introduces figurative or even 'metaphorical' uses, that should not blind us to the more important point that there is absolutely no unclarity nor imprecision in the new acceptance. The sense, in any event, is given by the two explanations,

---

[42] I draw here on the Cambridge PhD by O'Brien 1995.

[43] Liu Hui's text appears at Qian Baocong 1963, 96.1: cf. Chemla 1992, 1994, and Chemla and Guo, forthcoming.

[44] This use of *wei* is common in every field of Chinese thought, not just in mathematics, but also in philosophy, medicine and technology as well as elsewhere. So too *yue*, 'it is said', is used to explain terms, notably in such texts as *Sunzi* 10 of the six different types of terrain the commander may experience, and *Sun Bin* 22 of the five different 'postures', or the tactical attitudes to be adopted in the face of different types of enemy, similarly.

where there is a mutual dependence of the senses of the terms explained and those of the terms doing the explaining.

Indeed, there is more to this text than has yet emerged. I chose it to show Liu Hui at work, building up a more or less technical vocabulary in this case for the validation of an algorithm. But he does not do this out of nothing, of course. In the translation of the two sentences that give the meanings of qi^{III} and *tong*, I used the terms 'denominator' and 'numerator'. But the terms so translated are *mu* and *zi*, and *mu* ordinarily means 'mother' and *zi* 'son'. But so familiar and well understood are their uses, in context, of the denominator and numerator of fractions that Liu Hui does not bother to explain them.

One can go further. The term for 'multiply', *cheng*, means: ride, mount, avail oneself, and that too causes not a moment's pause.[45] Nor are we dealing here with a peculiarity of Chinese, to be sure. Plenty of examples of Greek terms, too, can be given that start life with concrete meanings related to physical objects, and are then given derivative, but precise, mathematical ones. Euclid's circle is not a band or ring, nor any other of the three-dimensional objects of which *kuklos* is used. His *sphaira* is not one that Nausicaa could have played with. Thus to apply the hard-line Aristotelian dichotomy to the text of Liu Hui leads to bizarre results. None of the chief terms is used *kurios* (strictly). 'Every time mothers avail themselves of sons reciprocally (*hu*) we call this level. When the crowd of mothers avails itself of each other (*xiang*) we call this equal.' But if Liu Hui redeploys ordinary language for mathematical purposes, he still secures the degree of precision that is adequate for his task. I say 'degree of precision' to avoid any suggestion that there is some ultimate goal of complete precision to be aimed at, let alone attained. Moreover the complex associations of the terms he uses are not simply to be dismissed, for the resonances of highly polyvalent words may always be important, and not just in poetry. But it is one thing to diagnose polyvalence, another to claim there is unclarity in the use of a particular term in a particular context.

One point at which the Aristotelian dichotomy is open to criticism is in its normative aspects, associating the strict with the ideal, the transferred

---

[45] I am not suggesting, of course, that there are no terminological problems in Chinese mathematics, no possible room for confusion. Right at the start of his commentary on the area of the rectangular field, Liu Hui says (93.5) that the product (*ji*) – that is, of length times breadth – is called (*wei*) the area (*mi*) of the field. But a later commentator, Li Chunfeng, immediately complains that 'product' and 'area' do not have the same sense (*yi*[II]). The product is the result of two quantities multiplied together, while area refers to the dimension of the field, determined, in rectangular ones, by length times breadth.

with what is in some sense inferior, if not deviant. But a second, more fundamental weakness lies in its being, precisely, a dichotomy. The literal and the metaphorical are taken as mutually exclusive and exhaustive alternatives. So presented, the alternatives allow, indeed force, issues to be pressed. If a term is not used literally, the challenge is to state what the metaphor is a metaphor for.

Yet it is not as if the Aristotelian dichotomy, or those derived from it, represent our only option. Porzig's notion of semantic stretch presents a different analysis with two main advantages.[46] First it allows the differences we recognise to be ones of degree, rather than exclusive alternatives. Secondly, it allows that every term has *some* stretch, even, at the limit, those terms deemed to be univocal.

This is not to say that there is a metaphorical element in the use of every term, nor to collapse the literal into the metaphorical by treating the former as a null class. Rather it is to overhaul the terms in which the issue is presented, to reject the alternatives of *either* literal *or* metaphorical, *either* strict *or* derived.

If those arguments are accepted, the status of Chinese reflections on language use may be assessed in a different light. So far from commiserating with the ancient Chinese, for failing to develop and use the literal/metaphorical dichotomy or some equivalent, and for allegedly running into some confusion in both their practice and analysis of language as a consequence, we may rather say that there was a positive advantage in their *not* proceeding down the Aristotelian route. We cannot exactly congratulate them for avoiding a pitfall they were evidently entirely unaware existed. Nor of course did they arrive at their reflections on language by pondering on the problems that stem from the literal/metaphorical dichotomy. But we may recognise first that in the test-case of the elucidation of terms in mathematics, their non-use of that dichotomy proved no handicap. Secondly, the reflections on language use that we find in *Zhuangzi*, in particular, allow for a pluralism that suits the non-exclusivity of their appreciation of others' points of view very well. *Yu yan* works: but so too does *zhong yan*, and as for *zhi yan*, 'let the stream find its own channels: this is the way to last out your years'. All three thus have their place. None states, but all allow for, what I call semantic stretch, while incorporating also some recognition of the pragmatics of any communication situation.

[46] See Porzig 1934, cf. Lloyd 1987, ch. 4.

I may now attempt briefly to survey our findings in this chapter. Inquiry, as it develops, sooner or later puts pressure upon ordinary language, in some cases even before language itself becomes an object of inquiry. We have found evidence of such pressures in particular domains both among the ancient Greeks and the Chinese. Both develop extended vocabularies to talk about the body, about plants, about mathematics and so on, both by means of new coinages and by the new applications of existing terms.

Yet in certain respects the Chinese and the Greek experience differ, notably in the comparative success in achieving a uniform or standard-ised vocabulary in certain areas. We cited the terminological confusion in Greek anatomy and botany, for instance. One factor that seems to con-tribute to that comparative lack of success, in Greece, was, I suggested, the rivalry between competing would-be experts, all keen to demon-strate their own originality. Chinese experts too certainly vied with one another on many issues, but generally did so within limits that stopped short of challenging the shared framework of discourse. In the context of the memorial to the throne, particularly, there was usually not much to be gained by attempting a radical revision of the very terminology in which the problems were customarily stated.

The difference between the Greek and Chinese experience is far greater where explicit reflections on language itself are concerned. The Greeks, in the person first of Plato and then of Aristotle, especially, show a highly developed sense of the desire to impose norms, and to proscribe anomalous, inferior or deviant uses, those that relied on images or myths, for instance, or were based on metaphor. They might be acceptable, un-der certain conditions, in poetry or rhetoric, but they were disastrous for philosophy and science in the highest modes.

The Chinese too had their prescriptive tendencies, stressing the need for the 'rectification of names', but that was chiefly a matter, we said, of maintaining good order in social roles. In their reflections on language, in other contexts, they were far less inclined – indeed not inclined at all – to lay down general rules that had the effect of downgrading whole types of language use, whether in poetry or in prose.

The apparent paradox is that while the Greeks produce some ar-ticulate spokesmen for clarity and precision in discourse, their actual technical terminology in certain areas at least (though not in all) suffered from considerable confusion, verging on anarchy. Yet in reality that may not be quite the paradox that it at first appears, for we may suggest that one factor that is at work in both cases – *both* in the demand for clarity *and* in the lack of success in attaining it – is precisely the same. Both, it may be thought, bear the hallmarks of that competitiveness we have found so often elsewhere in Greek intellectual life. One consideration that certainly weighed with Plato and Aristotle was a concern to promote their own views of the search for truth and its expression in genuine philosophy, but one way they did so was by disqualifying the modes of discourse of rivals – 'sophists', poets, even other philosophers – as a whole. But a similar competitiveness, the rejection of others' views in advancing one's own, also contributed to the actual terminological instability that we find in at least some of the specific subject-areas where technical vocabulary was developed.

CHAPTER SIX

Individuals and institutions

The major topic that I have left until the end of this book concerns the different types of institutional framework within which ancient investigators worked and the effect these had on the investigations they undertook. Those different frameworks include not just well-established official organisations such as bureaux and academies, but also institutions in a wider sense, such as those provided by the custom of the memorial to the throne, the public lecture, the public debate. How did investigators make a living? How were they employed and recruited? To what extent or in what ways were programmes of inquiry circumscribed or influenced by state sanctioned institutions? If so, how were innovations possible? But if innovators worked outside such institutions, what chance did their ideas have of being accepted or diffused? What, in other words, can institutional frameworks tell us about the factors that stimulated or inhibited systematic inquiry?

The potential double-bind is obvious. On the one hand, investigators need the institution for employment or as a forum for the presentation of ideas. Research is unlikely to be initiated if it does not in some way fit a niche in the values of the society in question. The efforts of researchers must be seen to be directed towards some useful, if not practical, end, even though (as we have seen in chapter 4) both usefulness and practicality are open to wide interpretation.

On the other hand, the more that research is institutionalised, the less room the individual may have for genuinely innovative ideas. The more the programme of research enjoys the blessings and approval of the authorities, the greater the pressure to conform to it. The obvious danger then is that the programme 'degenerates' (though not necessarily in the Lakatosian sense), with individuals finding it increasingly difficult to introduce new ideas, let alone to suggest new directions for the programme itself. Yet individuals who decide to go it alone, for the sake of independence, risk having no job, no audience, no hope, even, of their ideas surviving.

That last remark points to a particular difficulty in our sources, over and above the general ones we have faced all along. What has come down to us is what has been selected for transmission – in some cases several times over, for example Greek materials first by late ancient pagan scribes and commentators, then by Christian ones. True, it was not always chosen because it represented orthodoxy: for ideas can be preserved precisely in order to be criticised and refuted. But in those circumstances, those who did the preserving are not swayed by any great desire to make sure that the ideas in question are given the fullest and fairest hearing possible.

Yet evidently what later generations considered the more acceptable elements of ancient ideas had a greater chance of survival. The Mohists in China, and atomists of various persuasions in Greece, are far less well represented than more orthodox members of the literate elite – the '*ru*' (the term that is usually translated 'Confucian', though it need not imply any particular allegiance to what passed for his ideas) – or those Greek writers who favoured teleology. Maverick individuals are particularly vulnerable to the vagaries – or rather to the all too predictable prejudices – of the fortunes of transmission. The best hope, there, for preservation, may have been some kind of *succès de scandale* – a point relevant to what is ascribed to a thinker such as Gongsun Long (in the third century BCE, famous for the paradox that a white horse is not a horse) or to Heraclitus. But for many others the price of individualism was oblivion. We have then to bear in mind that while the institutions are, on the whole, identifiable, independent-minded individuals may have existed in far greater numbers than we can now recover.

That said, let me begin with the official institutions, and other modes of livelihood, concentrating, as usual, on Greece and China, where I shall draw on the detailed analyses in Lloyd and Sivin 2002 chapters 2 and 3, but picking up some points also from my earlier discussion of Mesopotamian astronomy.

Various types of 'scholars' figure in our Babylonian sources. Those who were chiefly responsible for the study of the heavens, the ṭupšarru were based either in courts or more often later in temples, such as those at Babylon and Uruk. Temples figure elsewhere too among the institutions relevant to our analysis, not so much in China as in Greece. In China, the Emperor's worshipping in temples was, indeed, of cosmological significance, but did not otherwise bear on inquiry. In Greece, however, one of the most popular and successful traditions of medical practice was that carried on in shrines dedicated to healing gods or heroes – Apollo or Heracles or, especially, Asclepius. Their wealth is obvious from the imposing remains of the shrines of Asclepius at Epidaurus and Pergamum, and we know from Aelius Aristides that their clientèle, still in the second century CE, included some of the most distinguished members of the literate elite.

My next category, officially established state bureaux, is especially important in China, at least from Han times onwards. The role of the Astronomical Bureau, and its responsibility for the study of the heavens over more than 2,000 years, have been mentioned before. The key point was that the due regulation of the calendar and the interpretation of celestial signs were not just essential for civic order: they were crucial concerns of the Emperor himself, as the bearer of the mandate of heaven.

Nor was the Astronomical Bureau by any means the only such state institution set up to oversee important fields of activity. Ministries, as we may think of them, of public works, war, law, eventually agriculture, were founded, in some cases already before the unification of China. Although there was no imperial bureau for medicine in Han times, some of the attendant physicians of Kings or nobles were given such titles as *taiyi*[II] or *taiyi ling*, 'Grand Physician'. While some official posts were hereditary (Sima Qian duly succeeded his father Sima Tan as *taishi*), access to others came to be by recommendation or by merit, or at least through success in what became from the seventh century on the increasingly complex civil service examinations.[1]

Yet eligibility to enter for the higher exams depended in some cases on birth or rank, while what was tested was, first and foremost, knowledge of the great literary classics, far less often a command of more technical subjects. The canon of the five classics, *Odes* (*Shi*[V]), *Documents* (*Shu*[III]), *Changes* (*Yi*[III]), *Springs and Autumns* (*Chunqiu*) and *Rites* (*Li*[II]), was already standardised as the basis for the education of government officials by edict of the Emperor in 136 BCE (see Nylan 2001).

The bureaucratisation of many aspects of Chinese society from Han times is well known. But how far were there any analogous state institutions or official positions in Greco-Roman antiquity? The haul of examples, by comparison, is meagre indeed.

---

[1] Cf. Sivin 1995a III on access to the bureaucracy in the eleventh century in connection with the career of Shen Gua. Cf. Elman 1984, 2000, Elman and Woodside 1994.

The institutions founded by the Ptolemies at Alexandria, the Museum and the Library, are the chief exception (see Fraser 1972). The post of Librarian was stipendiary, and while most of those who held it were literary scholars in the first instance, Eratosthenes for one was a polymath with a range of mathematical and scientific interests, and I mentioned in chapter 5 a different way in which the Ptolemies sponsored research (other than via the Library and the Museum) namely by making available human subjects for the anatomical investigations of Herophilus and Erasistratus. We shall be discussing teachers later, but should note, at this stage, that there came to be salaried positions for a very limited number of those who taught Platonic, and other, philosophies at Athens (that is, basically the heads of the various schools). That was, however, only under the Roman empire, on the initiative especially of Marcus Aurelius. Originally all the philosophical schools depended, for their upkeep, on the wealth of their members and the fees of pupils.

In medicine I mentioned before that, already in the fifth century BCE, there were a few posts to be had as public doctors appointed by certain Greek city-states, and later, in the Hellenistic period, certain privileges, notably tax-exemption, attached to those appointed as *archiatroi*, 'chief doctors'.[2] Those public doctors were sometimes appointed in the classical period, so we are told, not by other experts, but by the citizen body in the Assembly, no less. The *archiatroi*, by contrast, had at least on occasion to pass a scrutiny conducted by other doctors who were responsible for electing up to a certain quota (the *numerus*) for any given district. The pressures on candidates in the two sets of circumstances would be quite different, though in both verbal dexterity would be at a premium – and different again, for sure, from those associated with the written tests of the Chinese civil service examinations.

In addition to the official posts so far considered, other less formal associations with rich and powerful patrons provided, in both China and Greece, other sources of support. That depended, of course, on remaining in favour with the patron in question, while, from his point of view, the main role of courtiers or clients was often just a matter of the prestige they brought.

In China, maybe from as early as around 400 BCE, there were rulers who prided themselves on the gentleman-retainers (*shi*[VI]) and 'guests' (*ke*) they collected around them (see Lloyd and Sivin 2002, ch. 2, and cf. Lewis 1999, ch. 2). What has often been thought the most significant group,

---

[2] See especially Nutton 1977, and cf. Kudlien 1979. On the public doctors of the classical period, see Cohn-Haft 1956.

for the development of philosophical patronage, was that assembled by King Xuan of Qi, 'below the Ji' gate, that is *Jixia*, of his capital, in the last decades of the fourth century. That has sometimes been dubbed the *Jixia* 'Academy', but that, as Sivin has shown, is something of a misnomer.[3] Even though the *Shiji* records the presence there, at various times, of Zou Yan, Xunzi and others, there is nothing in our early evidence to suggest that they were engaged in any educational programme. They were there among the 'literary scholars' (*wenxue*) and 'itinerant advisers' (*youshui*).

The *Shiji* also refers to a number of third-century lords – those of Xinling of Wei, Chunshen of Chu, Pingyuan in Zhao, Mengchang of Qi – who tried to outdo one another, collecting 'retainers' and 'guests' around them. The lord of Mengchang was one of several who boasted of feeding 3,000 of these.[4] They were, however, a very mixed bag, for they included entertainers, jesters, burglars, mercenaries and assassins, as well as scholars and advisers. However, courts such as these may have provided the model for the group assembled by Lü Buwei, responsible for one of the first great syntheses of knowledge, the *Lüshi chunqiu*, that I have cited several times before in this book, some time before 237 BCE.

The key point here is that from the perspective of the philosophers, finding a worthy ruler to advise was the regular ambition of Confucius, Mozi, Mencius, Xunzi, Hanfeizi and many others. After the unification, too, the pattern continues (as we can see from Dong Zhongshu for instance), even though by then as a source of patronage, and as the person you needed to persuade, the Emperor was supreme.

Some of these features can be paralleled also in the Greek world, though with this important difference, that in the city-state period, at least, Greek political pluralism was not just a matter of there being different independent states, but also of differing political ideologies, not just monarchies and tyrannies, but also democracies and oligarchies exhibiting a variety of constitutional arrangements. But in Greece, too, the courts of 'tyrants' attracted poets, musicians, artists and craftsmen, as well as philosophers. In the rather special case of Plato's visits to Sicily, his aim, so the *Seventh Letter* tells us, was to educate Dionysius II, though if he really thought he could make a philosopher-King out of him, he was strangely naive.[5]

---

3 See Sivin 1995b IV on the evidence in *Shiji* 46: 1895.1 ff and 74: 2344.1 ff and 2346.1 ff especially.
4 See *Shiji* 75: 2359.7 and 85: 2510.3ff.
5 See the Platonic *Seventh Letter* 327d–329b and the discussion of the problems in Lloyd 1990b. Isocrates' attempts to win round Philip of Macedon and others to his pan-Hellenic policy of conquest of the East were not much more successful.

Again, the entourages of Hellenistic Kings and then of Roman Emperors could provide supportive, if risky, environments for intellectuals (one thinks of Vitruvius, Seneca, Galen[6]). Yet even after the effective political autonomy of the city-states had been crushed, first by Macedon and then by Rome, they still enjoyed a measure of prestige as centres of intellectual life. Philosophers still thought of Athens as the prime seat of philosophical activity, and their own peers there as the people on whom their reputation depended. Greek philosophers did not, as a matter of course, see finding a patron as their most pressing need, and if that reflects their sense of the values of independence, it has also to be said to reflect the fewer opportunities for patronage that were available.

Temples, state bureaux and the courts of Kings all offered, in different ways in different ancient societies, possible 'career options'. But if you had a skill or provided a service that others besides the great and powerful were prepared to pay for, you could, to that extent, be independent. Among such skills were those of the doctor, the architect, the engineer, the astrologer and the teacher. Each of these poses distinct problems of interpretation, not least concerning how those activities were perceived. But I shall focus here on the most important of these, namely teaching.

First we should distinguish between teaching as a supplement to the practice of what is taught, and teaching as the prime occupation. In many fields, medicine for instance, those with skills handed them on to pupils – and sometimes to others – who might pay a fee, or otherwise serve, their teachers. But then there were those for whom teaching was the prime activity. Getting clear about them has been bedevilled first by the stridently negative reactions to the 'sophists' in many Greek writers, notably Plato, and secondly because of the disastrous export of that category to the Chinese context.[7] There it is used of Hui Shi (fourth century) and of Gongsun Long, whom I have already mentioned, both of whom displayed an interest in paradox and gained something of a reputation for disputatiousness in that connection. Yet they did not specialise in teaching rhetoric (as many Greek sophists did), nor was the context of their teaching the public lecture or public debate. As with most Chinese philosophers, they offered teaching and counsel. But the people they

[6] Vitruvius dedicated his *On Architecture* to his patron Augustus; Seneca taught and then was minister to Nero, who, however, forced him to take his own life; and Galen was physician to the imperial household under Marcus Aurelius. In the early Hellenistic period, the Ptolemies attempted to attract prominent philosophers from Athens to Alexandria, and succeeded, for a time, with Strato, although their invitation to Theophrastus was rebuffed (Diogenes Laertius v 37 and 58).
[7] Reding 1985 is very aware of the problems, yet still uses the term 'sophist' in the Chinese context.

aimed to offer it to were rulers and nobles, in the first instance, not just any individual who was prepared to pay a fee.

The Greek sophists, by contrast, were prepared to teach anything anyone was ready to pay for. That was one of the grounds on which Plato criticised them: Socrates, his hero, did not accept payment for teaching, although, as is well known, for Aristophanes, Socrates passed as a sophist, and as noted Plato's Academy came to take fees from its pupils. It was shocking, Plato thought, to teach skills in public speaking irrespective of how they were to be used, but it was obvious that such skills were very much in demand, not, as the accusation was, to 'make the worse cause seem the better', but for success in the wide variety of political and legal contexts in which even ordinary citizens in the classical period would be involved in trying to win their cases.[8]

Moreover many of the sophists not only taught rhetoric, but also practised it. The format of much of their instruction was the lecture or debate, and these were often conducted in public, in part in order to attract pupils, who, if sufficiently impressed, would sign up to take the more elaborate and expensive advanced courses. Plato makes Socrates say that he does not know much about the correctness of names since he only heard the one drachma lecture by Prodicus, not the 50-drachma course (*Cratylus* 384bc). The sophists' own reputations, and to that extent their livelihood, depended on their skills in such performances. We shall come back, in a minute, to the implications of these practices for teacher–pupil relationships.

But the reaction first of Plato and then of Aristotle to all of this was not just moral disapproval, but a determination to break away from the patterns of argument that the orators practised and the sophists taught. Plato insisted on the contrast between (mere) persuasion and demonstration, which Aristotle duly defined as proceeding from self-evident (indemonstrable) primary premisses, via valid deductions, to in-controvertible conclusions.[9] That model, as I have explained before, had

---

[8] As Antiphon's extant *Tetralogies* show, the sophists offered training in developing arguments on either side of any given question. That by itself is, however, far from justifying the accusations of immoralism that we find, for example, in Aristophanes *Clouds* 882ff.

[9] For Plato see especially *Gorgias* 471e, 475e ff, *Phaedo* 85e, *Theaetetus* 162e ff. Aristotle's definition of demonstration is set out in the opening chapters of his *Posterior Analytics*. Thus at 71b20 ff he says that demonstrative understanding necessarily depends on premisses that are true, primary, immediate, better known than, prior to and explanatory of, the conclusion. At 72b7ff he argues against those who claimed that knowledge is impossible on the grounds of the unknowability of *ta prota*, the primary premisses or principles. The knowledge of those first premisses is not secured by demonstration, to be sure (for they are the primary premisses from which other things are demonstrated) but they can be known nevertheless. If that were not the case, then we would only

widespread repercussions, not just in philosophy and (especially) mathematics, but in many other areas of Greek science and even medicine, where proof in the 'geometrical manner', *more geometrico* (as it was said) came to be the ideal – at least for some (see above chapter 3 at n. 44).

But that whole development was not just the result of admittedly acute intellectual analysis. In part the stimulus came from that negative reaction to the exceptional circumstances of the teaching and practice of Greek political and forensic rhetoric. Of course Plato would not have seen himself as in direct competition with the sophists, of whom he disapproved so much. But as teachers they were, in fact, rivals, competing for influence and prestige, in the final analysis for pupils, even though Plato certainly did not need pupils for the *income* that they might provide. He was certainly wealthy enough not to have to follow the patterns established by the sophists in that regard. True, the question of when precisely fees were charged in the Academy is controversial, and, as noted, Plato certainly made it an important point about Socrates' teaching that he did not charge for it. Then a further respect in which Plato's position differed from that of most sophists was that, after the founding of the Academy, he operated from a well-established base. Even so, we should bear in mind that this was a *private* foundation, not one instituted by, and serving, the state, and as we shall see in a minute, neither it nor the other philosophical schools that took it as a model commanded or could command the lifelong allegiances of their members.

Further differences between Greece and China come to light when we consider how pupils were instructed and what was expected of them. In China, the first task was often to master, in the first instance to memorise, the relevant canon, *jing*[II]. These were handed on within lineages (the Eastern Han term was *jia*, which could just mean 'families'),[10] induction into which was often a matter of some solemnity, oath-taking, even initiation. The prestige of the official classics, was immense, but there were *jing*[II] with considerable status also in medicine, astronomy and mathematics, the various recensions of the *Huangdi neijing*, the *Zhoubi suanjing* and the *Jiuzhang suanshu*. Education, in that context, was preservation, interpretation, appreciation: more than that, it became, as I said, a means of access to official positions, when the imperial examination

---

know things hypothetically. *How* we can get to know the first principles is discussed cursorily at *Posterior Analytics* II ch. 19, 99b15ff, but *that* we can do so is assumed throughout the work.

[10] Intensive studies have recently been carried out, both on the Han usage of the term *jia* and on its antecedents: see Petersen 1995, K. Smith forthcoming, Csikszentmihalyi and Nylan forthcoming; the results are taken into account in Lloyd and Sivin 2002, ch. 2.

system was based on the literary classics. The premium was on repro-
ducing, so far as possible, the master's grasp of the text, not of going
beyond it, let alone of striving to outdo him.

But in Greece, the loyalty of pupils, whether taught by itinerant
sophists or in well-established schools, might well last only for as long as
the reputations of their teachers did. True, for those who belonged to
either a philosophical or a medical school, some allegiance to what the
founder stood for was expected. Yet with the exception of the Epicureans,
there was usually plenty of open disagreement about what precisely the
founder's teaching amounted to, even among those who saw themselves
as his followers. Moreover the record contains many examples, from both
philosophy and medicine, of defections, of pupils leaving one teacher or
school for another. Criticism of your own teacher – rare, if not quite
unknown in China – was common in Greece, sometimes as a prelude to
the pupil setting up a rival school of his own. The case of Aristotle is just
the most famous of many that can be cited.[11]

To be sure, the role of text-books in Greece eventually came to be
considerable, even though none, not even Euclid's *Elements*, achieved
quite the cachet of a Chinese major canon, at least not in Greco-Roman
antiquity. Of course, on the Chinese side, not all instruction was mediated
through such texts. In the *Lunyu*, Confucius, for instance, is described in
dialogue with his pupils in an open situation that might seem reminiscent
of the fictional conversations of Socrates in Plato. Yet two differences
remain: first Confucius' authority is never challenged by his pupils in the
way Socrates is contradicted by some of his interlocutors (however much
Plato stacks the cards in Socrates' favour in their eventual refutation).
Secondly, Confucius' pupils were not his sole, nor maybe even prime,
preoccupation, which was rather, we said, to find a ruler worthy to advise.

The variety of institutions and of livelihoods that we have identified
already suggests a certain room for manoeuvre that interested individuals
could exploit. It was not necessary to bid to become a court doctor in
order to practise medicine – in China, Greece or anywhere else. True,
the grander the patron you served, the more substantial the financial
rewards and the greater the prestige, even if also the higher the risks if
you fell from favour. Chunyu Yi (the doctor I discussed in chapter 2 in

---

[11] Zeno of Citium, for example, was taught by Crates the Cynic, Stilpo the Megarian and Polemo, head of the Academy, before he broke away from all of them to found his own school, the Stoa. In medicine, one may cite the similar departure of the person who became the founder of the Empiricist sect, Philinus, from his earlier associations with Herophilus. Among the far rarer examples from China, two of Xunzi's pupils certainly came to dissent from his views, namely Hanfeizi and Lisi (though the latter's career was as a statesman rather than as a teacher himself).

connection with pulse prognosis) testified to the problems that might be encountered with the authorities even by someone who did his best to avoid them. He was denounced for some unstated offence to the Emperor and thrown into prison, to be rescued from the mutilation to which he had been condemned only by a famous intervention on the part of his youngest daughter who offered herself as a public slave in order to save him. That's one of the main reasons we hear about Chunyu Yi in the first place: the daughter's self-denial was more famous than his medical work. As for those who played for the highest stakes, Galen records the intense rivalry between himself and others to secure the privilege of acting as physician to the Roman Emperor and his household.

By contrast, in several other areas of inquiry the room for manoeuvre was minimal, and you were lucky to have anyone much to teach, indeed anyone much to communicate with on equal terms. We sense the isolation Archimedes felt from the remarks he makes to the addressees of his treatises: after the death of Conon, he laments the lack of mathematicians competent to carry on research in certain areas, when he sends his next work to his new addressee, Dositheus.[12] When Liu Hui too speaks (Qian Baocong 1963, 91.10) of the lack of those who could appreciate the *Nine Chapters*, that was not *just* a conventional topos of the decline from past wisdom.

To sum up: the most important aspects of the institutional framework in China are, first, the existence of considerable numbers of official posts; second, the sense that it was the ruler or his ministers that were the prime audience; third, the acceptance of the authority of the canons. In Greece, with far fewer established positions available, far more depended on the skill that individuals showed in the cut and thrust of open debate – whether within a school or group, or between them, or just among individuals. It was success in argument with rivals that secured a reputation, essential not least if you were to make a living as a teacher. In these respects, the tradition of debate itself stands out as the key institution (of a different kind from those of bureaux or courts) in the situation within which most Greek intellectuals operated.

The principal questions for which I have undertaken this rapid survey must now be faced. What difference did the institutional framework make to the nature of the inquiries undertaken, the ways they were defined, how they were carried out, how their results were assimilated

---

[12] See the Prefaces to *On Spirals* HS II 2.2ff, and *On the Quadrature of the Parabola* I, HS II 262.3ff. See Netz 1999, pp. 277ff on the total numbers of Greek mathematicians in the extant records.

and evaluated? Let me focus on what I take to be the key issues, first with examples from the study of the heavens, then from cosmology and then far more briefly from medicine. We might expect, in general, that the greater the role of state institutions, or of state intervention, the more conservative, the less innovative, an inquiry would be. But we shall find that that certainly will not hold as a universal rule.

One exception I shall mention straight away is that of the Ptolemies' support for the anatomical investigations of humans in Alexandria. That certainly did not lead to the end of innovation nor of disagreement – rather quite the reverse, the opening up of new areas of inquiry. The trouble there was that that support did not last for long: and there is the further difference, that the Kings did not *need* the results that Herophilus and Erasistratus were getting in the way that the Chinese Emperors needed the information provided by the Astronomical Bureau on the calendar and in the matter of eclipse prediction. The Ptolemies were just in it for the prestige, as I said. It may initially seem paradoxical, but it should come as no surprise, that when researchers were supported for the sheer renown that the brilliance of their work brought with it, they had more room for manoeuvre than if their sponsorship depended on delivering results on a predetermined agenda.

The divergences we found in the study of the heavens are especially instructive. According to the Letters and Reports sent by the ṭupšarru, the neo-Assyrian Kings they served were hard taskmasters, constantly demanding information both about what was about to happen and as to whether the predicted outcome had occurred. But, as we noted, from some time in the seventh century BCE the ṭupšarru acquired a clear understanding of the regularities of certain phenomena – planetary phases and eclipses, for instance – that gave them the confidence to predict them. Here was what we may certainly describe as a research programme, under the highest auspices, carried on by state employees with politico-religious functions, a programme that was anything but static, but 'took off' in unforeseen directions with remarkable results.

There are both analogies and disanalogies in China. There the Astronomical Bureau similarly reported to the throne, and it had (as I said) both observational and theoretical successes to its credit. Yet in its more than 2,000 years' history there were periods when, as Chinese sources themselves say, the bureau was staffed by incompetents. The reaction to that, however, was not to close it down, but to expand it to incorporate some of those who had mounted the criticisms. The institution showed its capacity to survive, but not to change.

Greece had neither the benefits of state support for astronomy, nor the problems that it could bring. Greek astronomers could decide their own programmes, though find their results (as in calendar studies) were largely ignored. Moreover in their observational work they had to make do without teams of officials paid for by the state, though some of the indifferent performance of the Greeks there (their largely missing supernovae, for instance) reflects the assumptions they brought to bear on their work as much as any other factor.

The dominant tradition of Greek astronomical theorising sought geometrical models, linked explicitly by Ptolemy (as we saw) to the ambition to give demonstrations.[13] While he brought considerations to bear to show (as he hoped) that the earth is at rest in the centre, other counterintuitive suggestions were also proposed: that the centre is occupied by an invisible central fire (as in some Pythagorean views) or by the sun (Aristarchus), even if all but geocentricity proved stillborn.[14] What is so striking is the Greek readiness to try out wild conjectures even while the ostensible goal was to deliver demonstrable results.

What largely kept Greek astronomy going was astrology – for that was the way that most of the astronomers made a living. Not that it was uncontroversial. I mentioned before the foundational disputes that led to its being contrasted with astronomy, but also observed that it was not just astrology, but astronomy as well, whose status was challenged, the latter by Epicureans and Sceptics on the grounds that it was just speculative. In this controversy there were interested parties whose livelihoods were at stake, but insofar as that came (as it mainly did) from private practice, if the practitioners lost an argument with one group, they would not lack other possible audiences, another public, whom they might hope to persuade, if not by their abstract justification of astrology, then by what they claimed as their results.

The second area I chose for comment was 'cosmology', that is, systems of belief about the fundamental principles that govern change and coming-to-be and about the way things are, including the place of humans and human society in the dispensation of the whole. The histories of early Chinese and Greek thought on these topics exhibit rather different

[13] Ptolemy, *Syntaxis* I ch. 1, I 6.17–21: 'Only mathematics, if one attacks it critically, provides for those who practise it sure and unswerving knowledge, since the demonstration comes about through incontrovertible means, by arithmetic and geometry.' By mathematics, here, Ptolemy means, or at least includes, the astronomical study to which the *Syntaxis* is devoted.

[14] See Ptolemy, *Syntaxis* I ch. 5, I 16–20. Aristotle reports the Pythagorean view at *On the Heavens* II ch. 13, 293a20 ff. Archimedes *Sandreckoner* HS II 218.7ff is our chief source for Aristarchus' heliocentric theory.

patterns. How far do these seem to be associated with the institutional frameworks we have discussed? The suggestion I shall explore is that they are a factor contributing to the search for a consensus in China and to the diverging centrifugal tendencies that are strongly marked in Greece.[15]

First we must repeat that Chinese thought in this area was a long time in the formation. Sivin's studies have now transformed our understanding of the early stages, of how *yin* and *yang*, the shady and sunny sides of the hill, came to be transfigured into *yinyang*, a cosmic principle of interaction. The mature synthesis, combining *yinyang* and the doctrine of the five phases, *wuxing* (see above chapter 3), is prominent in two texts put together in the last decades of the millennium, the *Huangdi neijing* and the *Tai Xuan Jing* of Yang Xiong. But it is three earlier writings that contribute to the development of thought on microcosm–macrocosm relations that are of particular interest to my discussion here, namely the *Lüshi chunqiu*, *Huainanzi* and *Chunqiu fanlu*. I mentioned all three in chapter 1. Let me recapitulate first the key points about their authors or compilers. Lü Buwei, the compiler of the first, was chief minister to the man who became the first Qin Emperor, Qin Shi Huang Di. Liu An, responsible for the second compilation, was Prince of Huainan, and offered his work to his nephew, the Han Emperor, Wu Di, while Dong Zhongshu, responsible for parts at least of the *Chunqiu fanlu* as well as for some notable memorials to the throne, held office under that same Emperor.

Each of those texts develops a cosmology in which a key feature is the interdependence of the macrocosm of the heavens and the microcosms of the state and body. These are no mere analogies: heaven and earth, the state and the human body, all exhibit the *same* reciprocal processes and are parts of a single whole. Moreover the ruler has the crucial role of mediating between heaven and earth and ensuring the harmony between them. Thus far we might conclude that all three Chinese cosmologies just happen to agree on the main lines of the overall view they put forward. But there is more to it than that. As Sivin already showed in pioneering papers in the mid 1990s (1995b I and IV, 1995c, 1995d) there seems to be not merely a convergence of ideas among the authors/compilers, but also a convergence of interests between them and the rulers to whom their texts were (primarily) addressed.

On the one hand, these cosmologies underpin, even legitimate, the position of the ruler/Emperor, as the figure responsible for the welfare of

---

[15] I draw once again on the arguments of Lloyd and Sivin 2002, applying them here more particularly to the issue of the factors that stimulated or inhibited systematic inquiry.

'all under heaven'. At the tail end of the Warring States, with the authority of the Zhou dynasty in tatters, quite who could claim a right to the 'mandate from heaven' was a delicate issue – not that success in staking such a claim owed as much to marshalling cosmological arguments as to the force of arms, weaponry, in a word to conquest. As for the intellectuals themselves, they too faced a crisis well into the Han, a matter not just of the notorious episode of the 'burning of the books' (though that no doubt contributed to the sense of a need to preserve and hand on the canons for which they were responsible), but also of the extermination of many members of the literate elite (underlining the importance, to the survivors, of securing, as far as possible, their own positions).

On the other hand, the message the cosmologists conveyed as to how the ruler should conduct himself – precisely in order to ensure that welfare – put the emphasis on harmony, on interdependence, on complementarity: and complementarity, translated into political terms, meant the need for the ruler to rely on his ministers and advisers – including the individuals who were offering him that basis for the legitimacy of his rule.

Convergence of views and interests did not mean total uniformity, nor lead to the construction of a single rigid orthodoxy. Nor can we say that the authors were particularly successful in persuading their masters of their own indispensability. Lü Buwei was dismissed and forced to take his own life – as indeed also was Liu An. Even Dong Zhongshu was far from always in favour with Wu Di; indeed, he was sometimes treated with contempt.[16] Moreover while all three cosmologies have a guiding macrocosm–microcosm thread, there are (as I noted in chapter 3) plenty of divergences in the detail. Once five-phase correspondences get to be proposed, covering everything from star palaces to parts of the body, to colours, to ministries, there is still a good deal of variation as between one schema and another. There was, of course, far more to early Chinese cosmological thought than my brief remarks here suggest. However, they serve to illustrate one possible connection between the ambitions of advisers and the contents of the cosmological ideas they sought to have accepted.

The contrast with Greece is twofold. First there are points to do with the positions of the chief Greek cosmologists, then with those of the ideas they proposed. On the first point, we noted that some Greek

---

[16] For instance, while grand master of the palace, he was charged with the crime of 'immorality' and sentenced to death, though he was then pardoned by the Emperor and reinstated. Queen 1996, ch. 2, documents the varying fortunes of the political career of Dong Zhongshu.

intellectuals frequented the courts of tyrants. But many of the early Greek cosmologists had no ambitions to persuade the rulers of states – and no opportunities to do so. Rulers and philosophers occasionally interacted, in the classical and again in the Hellenistic and Roman periods, but unlike under the Han they had no sense that they systematically needed one another.[17]

Then so far as the cosmological theories go, the Greek offerings present the picture of a veritable free-for-all. Compared with China, one of the most striking features of Greek cosmological writing was the lack of anything remotely approaching the basis for a consensus.[18] For every theorist who argued that the cosmos is eternal, another insisted it was created. Against those who asserted that there is just one world, others believed in many, sometimes an infinite number, separated from this one in space or time or both. Space and time themselves were construed by some as continua, but by others as constituted by indivisible units. Equally on the question of the ultimate constitution of matter itself, continuum theorists were opposed by atomists of different types. In what was often the dominant view, the world manifests order, beauty, even providentiality – and that certainly suited those who were for stressing the need for order in human society as well. But that did not prevent anti-teleologists from explaining the regularities in nature as the outcome of purely physical interactions, and of what their opponents, and sometimes they themselves, called (mere) 'chance'.

It would be absurd to claim that it was solely the dialectical situation that was responsible for this whole congeries of views. But the way in which, on one topic after another, thesis is matched – sooner or later, or immediately – by antithesis, surely reflects the rivalries endemic in Greek intellectual life. While they were a response to different kinds of pressures, they include those that stem from a lack of stable, official posts and the need to make a reputation as a teacher or lecturer. Whatever might seem obvious – for example, that change occurs, or again that not everything is in constant change – might be denied (as the first was by Parmenides, the second by Heraclitus). While this meant that a far greater range of theoretical possibilities was explored than was generally countenanced in China, it just as surely inhibited the formation of anything like an

[17] However, among the philosophers who were involved in political affairs in the Hellenistic period, both Carneades and Posidonius acted as ambassadors for their home states (Athens and Rhodes). Later still, Seneca, as noted, was minister under Nero, and Marcus Aurelius was not just a considerable philosopher, but Emperor.

[18] I have examined the evidence for the controversies in question in 1996a ch. 10, pp. 223ff.

agreed framework for further inquiry. By late antiquity, those ongoing fundamental disagreements were cited by some Christians as evidence of the futility of pagan curiosity *in toto*. The paradox here was that one (recurrent) reaction of those pagan investigators themselves to the lack of common ground was to demand that theories be not just possible or plausible, but certain. But the trouble was that no sooner was a claim made to have given incontrovertible demonstrations than that claim was itself controverted. The Christian reaction, in some quarters, was that the whole ambition to inquire was misplaced. We have no need for curiosity after Jesus Christ, as Tertullian famously wrote (*On Prescriptions against Heretics*, ch. 7), nor for research after the gospel. I am conscious that on that basis there would have been nothing for my investigation in this book to have been about.

Some of the same features recur also in our third field, medicine, which offers the possibility of a direct comparison when, under the Roman empire, Greek doctors had the opportunity to seek appointments as court physicians much like those available to their Chinese counterparts. The evidence we considered from Chunyu Yi confirms what in any case we would expect, namely that Chinese doctors often disagreed about both diagnosis and treatment. Yet when we compare his practice, or what is contained in the Mawangdui texts, with what we find in the *Huangdi neijing*, the points where that classic departs from earlier traditions are not openly paraded.[19] In the context of the construction of a medical canon, at least, the Chinese doctors presented a united front, even when below the surface there had been and continued to be disagreements.

Almost the exact converse, one might say, is true of Greek medicine. At least Galen reports (*On Sects for Beginners* chs. 5–6, 12.3–18) that two of the chief medical sects, those he calls Dogmatists and Empiricists, agreed, generally, about therapies, but quarrelled about their justification and explanation. More strikingly, Galen also indicates that Greek doctors kept up their polemic even when in competition to serve the Roman imperial household. There Galen's own chief rivals were the Methodists, who claimed that the whole of medicine could be taught in a matter of six months – a challenge Galen evidently felt he could not afford to ignore.

[19] See Harper 1998, especially pp. 92–5. It is possible that the exchanges between the Yellow Emperor and his interlocutors in the *Huangdi neijing* mask certain differences in view-point, with the Yellow Emperor's more old-fashioned opinions being tactfully updated in the replies he is given. But if that is the case, it is done with great discretion, and not at all in the manner of overt polemic cultivated so often in Greek medical writings from the Hippocratics to Galen. On the different strata within the *Huangdi neijing* recensions, see, for example, Yamada Keiji 1979, Keegan 1988.

True, Galen tried to rally Greek medicine behind 'Hippocrates' – and, for later generations, he more or less succeeded in doing so. Yet in his own day he tells us himself about the rival views ascribed to Hippocrates by those who nevertheless styled themselves Hippocrateans (see Lloyd 1991, ch. 17). If what Hippocrates eventually came to stand for down through the long centuries until modern times was very much what Galen made him stand for, that was because Galen survived while those other Hippocrateans – with their images of Hippocrates – did not.

Overt competitiveness, whether for pupils or for patients, extended to every tradition of Greek medicine, although the modes of persuasion differed with the context and the audience. Moreover this whole controversy, which began in the classical period, was too deep-rooted by Roman times for Greek doctors to be able to present a united front, even if they had wished to do so, even in front of Emperors. The Hippocratics may have polemicised against those who believed that gods intervene in disease and cure. But some of the advocates of temple medicine criticised some of the drastic remedies favoured by some of the Hippocratics.[20] Galen himself sought wherever possible to capture the high ground by way of geometrical-style demonstrations, however hard it was to come by *axioms* in medicine. But others adopted a different tactic, rejecting theory as a whole as just so much dogmatic speculation, and taking their stand by what they claimed experience had shown to be effective.[21]

Our inquiry into inquiry has tackled such a wide range of problems that brief and snappy conclusions are out of the question. There was already too much reductionism in the discourse on the origins of science that my discourse on inquiry has been seeking to replace. On various

[20] Already in the inscriptions set up at the shrine of Asclepius at Epidaurus we find an instance where the god recommends *not* following a procedure commonly used in Hippocratic medicine (namely cautery, case 48, Herzog 1931, p. 28, cf. Lloyd 1979, p. 46) and much later, in the second century CE, Aelius Aristides, in praising the treatment he received at the hand of the 'god' (Asclepius), repeatedly has him contradicting the recommendations made by merely mortal doctors (e.g. *Sacred Tales* XLVII 62–3).

[21] The Empiricists, for instance, are quoted by Celsus (*On Medicine* Proem to book 1, paras. 38–9, *CML* I 23.16–27) as arguing that the only thing that matters in medicine is producing cures, not theorising about how they come about or about the physiological processes in the body. 'It does not matter what produces the disease but what relieves it. Nor does it matter how digestion takes place, but what is best digested . . . We have no need to inquire in what way we breathe, but what relieves laboured breathing . . . All this is to be learnt through experiences. In all theorising about a subject it is possible to argue on either side, and so cleverness and fluency may get the best of it. However it is not by eloquence, but by remedies, that diseases are treated. A man of few words who learns by practice to discern well would make an altogether better practitioner than he who, unpractised, overcultivates his tongue.'

occasions, in the former, everything has been held to depend on getting rid of the gods (Farrington 1961), or on the exercise of criticism in an open society (Popper 1962), or, if you were an internalist, on mathematisation, or the application of other features of an ideal scientific method. Yet none of these hypotheses will do individually, nor even will they do in combination. I shall not elaborate the obvious criticisms here, except to pause for a moment to remark the exceptional strangeness of the secularisation argument. The Babylonians, the Chinese and most Greeks (including the foremost Greek astronomers, such as Ptolemy), all held that the sun, moon, planets and stars are divine: but that never stopped them investigating their movements with energy and success.

I have been focussing especially on China and Greece and to a lesser extent Babylonia, all three societies that had developed economies, technology, literacy. Evidently the first two are vital, if corps of investigators, or even individuals, are to be supported. Evidently, too, the sustained study of the heavens, as well as the investigation of the past more generally, depends on written records. Not that literacy by itself can be held accountable for the growth of inquiry, for as we also noted, it could stimulate not just ruminative reflection, but also closure and control, when a text is accorded not just canonical status, but sacred authority. Such general features of societies, whether of the Axial Age (Eisenstadt 1986) or later, do not get to grips with the specificities of the phenomena we have been dealing with.

Historiography, prediction, numbering, finding practical uses, naming – we have been discussing highly disparate manifestations of curiosity. But certain patterns may be said to recur. Let me mention three, the unpredictability of outcomes, the momentum effect (as I shall call it) and the extrapolation trap. We have found a variety of instances of the first, of which the most striking was the Babylonian programme to interpret signs sent by heaven to rulers that established reliable regularities, not in those messages themselves, but in the sequences of celestial phenomena that were investigated to reveal them. It was not that those Babylonians failed to find what they were looking for – after all they continued to believe in those messages. But they found regularities that they had not foreseen in addition.

Inquiry, thus, I remarked, has an inherently destabilising potential, even when initiated by state authorities for purposes they specify and with an agenda they set out. Those authorities may seek to control – many are indeed largely successful in controlling – who is allowed to predict the future, or interpret the past, or even to name things. But what was there for inquiry to discover, that no one could ultimately control, however much the results were subject to systematic reinterpretation and manipulation and however much what was presented as discovery was often just invention.

Closely connected with that unpredictability – as the Babylonian study of the heavens also illustrates – is the momentum effect. Once an inquiry was held to deliver results, it could gather its own momentum, not only undergoing internal elaboration, but also generating new inquiries into new problems that came to light as spin-offs from the initial investigations. The casting of horoscopes exemplifies the internal elaboration effect. But Greek anatomical inquiry illustrates the growth through spin-offs. Initiated originally to show the beauties of nature, it came to be grappling with such problems as those generated by the discovery of the valves of the heart: if there are one-way valves controlling entry to and exit from the right and left sides of the heart, how do the two sides communicate with one another, or are they indeed two separate systems with quite distinct contents? Those problems reverberated, of course, down to Harvey.

Third, and again connectedly, there is the extrapolation trap. A result obtained in one context is invoked as the model to resolve other problems, or it is assumed that a technique that is effective in one domain can deliver success in others. Simple numbers yield the secret of concords: therefore they must do so for colours, or flavours, or pulses also. Greek axiomatic-deductive proof, originating in logic and mathematics, is a model applied also in medicine and in theology.[22] Chinese fivefold correspondences were subject to almost indefinite extension.

So we come back to the key question, of the interaction of different institutional and ideological frameworks with the different types of inquiry they frame – the chief topic I have been discussing in this chapter. I offer three concluding observations on that score. First we have found considerable *inter*action, the ideologies influencing the inquiries, and conversely the inquiries, in certain cases at least, helping to create the ideology. We saw that Chinese *yinyang* cosmological speculation not only responded to the need for an ideology legitimating imperial rule, but also helped to create it. Again while the pluralism of Greek political ideals fed directly into cosmology there by way of alternative models of cosmic order, conversely the Greek readiness to contemplate even the most counterintuitive physical theories had an influence on their

----

[22] Proclus' *Elements of Theology*, as its title already suggests, takes Euclid's *Elements* as its model, however different the styles of argument it actually deploys.

readiness also to *theorise* about political arrangements too, to the point of *theorising* even about the non-naturalness of slavery. In the *Politics* book 1, 1254a13ff, Aristotle reports the debate over whether or not there are natural slaves – not that the arguments made any difference in practice, for they certainly did not generate any policy to abolish slavery.

Secondly, more than one type of institutional and ideological framework allowed, even encouraged, inquiries to develop. Radical criticism in face-to-face confrontation, in the Greek manner, stimulated debates in cosmology and medicine where commonsense assumptions, indeed every basic foundational belief, were challenged. That, we said, was the way you made a name for yourself in Greece, where in the competition for prestige and for pupils you needed not just to do better than your rivals, but to be seen to do so.

Yet we found other styles of inquiry successfully developed in China, for example, in the absence of such an adversarial manner, and in the absence of any strong sense of a pluralism of political ideals. Autocratic regimes (and not just in China) may positively favour inquiry and not just into weapons technology (the Ptolemies supported that, but also anatomical research). Such was the perceived importance of order in the heavens to the political authorities in China and in Babylonia, their study received more sustained support than was ever available to Greek astronomers. The bureaucratic structures that channelled that support provided stable employment for generation after generation of workers, with undoubted advantages in terms of continuity, even if also disadvantages when the jobs got treated as sinecures.

That last remark takes me to my third (and final) observation, the way in which, in certain important respects, the advantages and disadvantages of the two main types of institutional framework tend to be mirror images of one another. Chinese historians, astronomers and others held official positions, and beyond them, the aim of many intellectuals who studied the classics was a secure job in the civil service. Such appointments carried their disadvantages, their dangers even. The support of the imperial authorities was a boon (in applied technology I argued that it was crucial in delivering results). Yet when they fell out of favour, many a talented individual came to a sticky end.

The Greeks we have been dealing with could set their own agenda, but had to do without stable official positions. The need to make an independent career as a teacher contributed greatly to the development of those combative styles of argument we have discussed, where there was a payoff in the radical critique of assumptions, but just as surely a downside in the way such styles inhibited the formation of a common framework for research.

That picture is, as we have seen, subject to substantial qualifications. Some Greeks were sponsored by Kings or tyrants, and ran the same risks as their Chinese counterparts. Some Chinese individuals operated outside the circles of court patronage or official employment, though the price they might have to pay was oblivion.

Our studies show that there was no simple institutional or ideological framework for success across the board – as it might be to increase bureaucratic support, or to decrease it, or again to maximise the radical scrutiny of foundations, or to minimise that. Insofar as the ideal environment for research comprises elements that are, in the final analysis, incompatible with one another – state support and total freedom – it is hardly surprising that it never existed in ancient Greece or China. The individuals and groups in our story all had to reach their own accommodation within the varied situations they faced. Whether or not there were authorities to please, there was always an audience to hold – where impressing a general public, or your own peers, could be as demanding, in its own way, as persuading a ruler to listen to you.

Besides, what counted as success was often as much a matter of the claims the practitioners themselves made, as of the judgements of outsiders, even those for whose benefit the inquiry was supposedly undertaken. In some cases there was little doubt about an outcome: the patient died, or the battle was lost. But then there was always the question, why? Was the system of prognosis at fault, or just the practitioner? In the matter of concrete results, several of the engineering feats I talked about left enduring legacies. Li Bing's division of the river Min still waters Sichuan: one or two Roman aqueducts functioned until quite recently. But where the influence of ideas is concerned, the judgement of your contemporaries was one thing, that of the future another. The more idiosyncratic the talent, the greater the chance of its being ignored or sidelined – especially so perhaps in China, given the premium on consensus and cooperation there. But even when not totally ignored, vindication could be very slow in coming – not that a *final* verdict is ever in.

In some cases the admiration expressed, by the ancients, for a hero of inquiry, was not matched by any clear sense of the need to take his work further: Archimedes would be one example. In others, incorporation into the educational curriculum, canonisation in that sense, ensured survival, but could inhibit further development. Again, on the question of whether an inquiry was seen as *not* getting anywhere, much depended not just on how clear-cut the results were, but on how well established the practitioners were, how immune to criticism, how clever at producing excuses for apparent failure. The rhetorical skills used to suggest that an inquiry might be worth pursuing were often redeployed to mitigate what might seem a poor performance. An inquiry needed to get established to ensure a continuity of effort to get results. But once entrenched, it could devote more energy to defending itself than to getting those results.

Some of the problems I have spoken of, the tension between freedom and beholdenness, certainly, continue to affect science as we know it today. But before the modern scientific juggernaut began to roll, the vulnerability of ancient inquiries was acute. On the one side, state institutionalisation posed the threat of stagnation. On the other, without it, what could ensure continuity? The Chinese only intermittently overcame the first problem. The Greeks in late antiquity, faced with the alternative goals that Christianity offered, succumbed, rather, to the second. Both societies, I have suggested, developed basic human capacities for curiosity in intriguing and ingenious ways. But in both, the ambitions of curiosity were often just that, just ambitions. But what ambitions: for in one context after another, they held out the hope of understanding what had never been understood before.

Glossary of Chinese and Greek terms

CHINESE

bencao	本草	herbals
bi	比	compare, analogical poetry
bu	卜	turtle shell divination
cheng	乘	ride, mount, avail, multiply
chunqiu	春秋	springs and autumns
danongcheng	大農丞	minister for agriculture
dashi	大史	scribe/historian
dao	道	way, guide, tell
dao ke dao fei chang dao	道可道非常道	the way that can be told is not the constant way
fu[I]	伏	cause to submit
fu[II]	腑	*yang* organs
fu[III]	賦	descriptive/expository poetry
gangji	綱紀	essential points
hu	互	reciprocal
ji	積	product
jia	家	family, lineage
jing[I]	靜	calm (type of pulse)
jing[II]	經	canon, circulation tract
junzi	君子	'gentleman'
ke	客	guests
lei	類	categories
li[I]	里	league (measure of distance)
li[II]	禮	propriety, rites
li[III]	利	profit
lifa	曆法	calendar studies
lü	律	pitch pipes
mai	脈	vessels (in body)

mi	冪	area
mu	母	mother, denominator
qi[I]	其	may (modal operator)
qi[II]	氣	breath, energy
qi[III]	**齊**	uniform, homogenise
ren	仁	humanity, humaneness
ru	儒	literatus, 'Confucian'
se	色	colour, expression
shang	上	above, superior generation of notes
shenhua	神話	spirit talk, 'myth'
shi[I]	史	scribe
shi[II]	筮	divine by milfoil
shi[III]	勢	propensity
shi[IV]	實	'full' terms
shi[V]	詩	songs, odes
shi[VI]	士	official: gentleman retainer
shu[I]	數	number
shu[II]	術	art, method
shu[III]	書	documents
shushu	術數	art/method of numbers
shuxue	數學	number-learning, mathematics
sinongsi	司農司	bureau of agriculture
suanshu	算數	study of numbers, mathematics
taishi	太史	grand scribe
taishi gong	太史公	honorific title for grand scribe
taishi ling	太史令	grand scribe
taiyi[I]	太一	'grand one' (in heavens)
taiyi[II]	太醫	grand physician
taiyi ling	太醫令	grand physician
tianwen	天文	(study of) celestial patterns
tong	同	equalise
wei	謂	call, name
wenxue	文學	literary scholars
wu	巫	mediums
wuxing	五行	five phases
xia	下	below, inferior generation of notes
xiang	相	each other
xie	邪	heteropathic *qi*
xin	信	trustworthiness
xing	興	elevated (poetry)

xiu	宿	lunar lodges
xu	虛	'empty' terms
xue	血	blood
yi[I]	義	righteousness
yi[II]	意	meaning
yi[III]	易	changes
yinyang	陰陽	shady/sunny, negative/positive
youshui	游説	itinerant advisers
yu yan	寓言	'lodge sayings'
yue	曰	say: it is said
yueling	月令	monthly ordinances
zang	臟	*yin* organs
zhengming	正名	rectification of names
zhi	知	knowledge
zhi yan	卮言	'spill-over sayings'
zhong shu ling	中書令	secretariat director
zhong yan	重言	'weighty sayings'
zhuan	傳	traditions
zhuo	濁	'muddy' (type of pulse)
zi	子	son, numerator

GREEK

agonisma	ἀγώνισμα	contest
alethes	ἀληθής	true
amphiblestroeides	ἀμφιβληστροειδής	'net-like': name for retina
andreia	ἀνδρεία	'manhood', courage
anexelegktos	ἀνεξέλεγκτος	incontrovertible
aorte	ἀορτή	'hanger' 'suspender': name used for aorta, pulmonary artery and bronchi
apodeixis	ἀπόδειξις	'showing forth': proof
arachnoeides	ἀραχνοειδής	'spider's-web-like': name for retina
archiatroi	ἀρχιατροί	'chief doctors'
aristeia	ἀριστεία	excellence, prowess
arithmos	ἀριθμός	positive integer greater than one
chorioeides	χοριοειδής	'afterbirth-like': name for choroid membrane of eye

deisidaimonie	δεισιδαιμονίη	superstition
dikasteria	δικαστήρια	law-courts
diktamnon	δίκταμνον	'dittany'
diskoeides	δισκοειδής	'discus-like': name for crystalline lens of eye
dunamis	δύναμις	power, capacity
eikones	εἰκόνες	images
epiphora	ἐπιφορά	transport, transfer
exochon sophismaton	ἔξοχον σοφισμάτων	supreme among devices
gargareon	γαργαρεών	uvula
genos	γένος	family, race
glukuside	γλυκυσίδη	peony
historia, historie	ἱστορία, ἱστορίη	inquiry or knowledge based on it
homoiotetes	ὁμοιότητες	similarities
hualoeides	ὑαλοειδής	'glass-like': name for vitreous humour and the retina as including it
isonomia	ἰσονομία	equality of sights
kata metaphoran	κατὰ μεταφοράν	'by way of transfer'
kenomata	κενώματα	'vacancies': name used for arteries
keratoeides	κερατοειδής	'horn-like': cornea
kion	κίων	pillar: name for uvula
kionis	κιονίς	uvula or its inflammation
krustalloeides	κρυσταλλοειδής	'ice-like': name for crystalline lens of eye
kuklos	κύκλος	hoop, ring, circle
kurios	κυρίως	strictly (of how terms may be used)
leukos	λευκός	bright/white: name for sclera
logographos	λογογράφος	writer of *logoi*
logon didonai	λόγον διδόναι	give an account
logopoiein logopoios	λογοποιεῖν λογοποιός	writer or maker of *logoi*, sometimes used of rumour-mongering
logos	λόγος	word, speech, account, argument, reason

magos	μάγος	mage, magician
mathema,	μάθημα,	learning, study: to learn
manthanein	μανθάνειν	
mathematike	μαθηματική	mathematics
mathematikos	μαθηματικός	mathematician, astronomer
manikos	μανικός	'causing madness': used of a kind of *struchnon*
mantike	μαντική	art of prophecy
metaphora	μεταφορά	transferred use of terms, 'metaphor'
muthos	μῦθος	account, story, fiction, myth
neuron	νεῦρον	term used for sinews, ligaments, tendons, nerves
orthotes onomaton	ὀρθότης ὀνομάτων	correctness of names
paradeigmata	παραδείγματα	paradigms, models
peri	περί	concerning, about
perittos	περιττός	odd, exceptional: name used for a kind of *struchnon*
phakoeides	φακοειδής	'lentil-like': name for crystalline lens of eye
phlebes	φλέβες	arteries, veins
phusis	φύσις	nature
pneumatika angeia	πνευματικὰ ἀγγεῖα	'pneumatic vessels': name for arteries
poliorketika	πολιορκητικά	'for beseiging': name for a military treatise
pseudodiktamnon	ψευδοδίκταμνον	'false dittany'
rhagoeides	ῥαγοειδής	'grape-like': name for choroid membrane of eye
seranges	σήραγγες	'hollows': name for arteries
staphule	σταφυλή	bunch of grapes: name for uvula, or its inflammation
staphulophoron	σταφυλοφόρον	grape-bearing: name for uvula
stasis	στάσις	faction, civil strife
struchnon, struchnos	στρύχνον, στρύχνος	plant-name (may include *solanum nigrum*)
sustoichia	συστοιχία	table of opposites
sphaira	σφαῖρα	ball, sphere

ta prota	τα πρῶτα	primary premises, principles
techne	τέχνη	art, skill
tetremenos	τετρημένος	pierced: name for choroid membrane of eye
thruon, thruoron	θρύον, θρύορον	reed, name for kind of *struchnon*

Bibliography

Allan, S. (1991) *The Shape of the Turtle: Myth, Art, and Cosmos in Early China* (Albany)

Ames, R. T. (1993) *Sun-tzu: The Art of Warfare* (New York)

Anderson, B. R. O'G. (1991) *Imagined Communities*, revised edn (orig. 1983) (London)

Arbuckle, G. (1989) 'A Note on the Authenticity of the *Chunqiu fanlu*', *T'oung pao* 75: 226–34

    (1991) 'Restoring Dong Zhongshu (BCE 195–115)' (unpublished PhD dissertation, University of British Columbia)

Baldini Moscadi, L. (1998) 'Conoscere il futuro', in *I Greci*, ed. S. Settis *et al.*, vol II.3, Turin, pp. 1245–59

Barker, A. (1978) '*hoi kaloumenoi harmonikoi*: The Predecessors of Aristoxenus', *Proceedings of the Cambridge Philological Society* n.s. 24: 1–21

    (1981) 'Methods and Aims in the Euclidean *Sectio Canonis*', *Journal of Hellenic Studies* 101: 1–16

    (1989) *Greek Musical Writings*: vol. II, *Harmonic and Acoustic Theory* (Cambridge)

    (2000) *Scientific Method in Ptolemy's* Harmonics (Cambridge)

Barnes, J. (1991) 'Galen on Logic and Therapy', in *Galen's Method of Healing*, ed. F. Kudlien and R. J. Durling (Leiden), pp. 50–102

Barnes, J., Brunschwig, J., Burnyeat, M. and Schofield, M. eds. (1982) *Science and Speculation* (Cambridge)

Barton, T. S. (1994) *Ancient Astrology* (London)

Bascom, W. (1969) *Ifa Divination* (Bloomington)

Bates, D. ed. (1995) *Knowledge and the Scholarly Medical Traditions* (Cambridge)

Beard, M. (1986) 'Cicero and Divination: The Formation of a Latin Discourse', *Journal of Roman Studies* 76: 33–46

Beasley, W. G. and Pulleyblank, E. G. eds. (1961) *Historians of China and Japan* (Oxford)

Berryman, S. (1998) 'Euclid and the Sceptic: A Paper on Vision, Doubt, Geometry, Light and Drunkenness', *Phronesis* 43: 176–96

Bielenstein, H. (1980) *The Bureaucracy of Han Times* (Cambridge)

Bodde, D. (1981) 'Harmony and Conflict in Chinese Philosophy', in *Essays in Chinese Civilization*, ed. C. LeBlanc and D. V. Borei (Princeton) pp. 237–98

    (1991) *Chinese Thought, Society and Science* (Honolulu)

Bottéro, J. (1974) 'Symptômes, signes, écritures en Mésopotamie ancienne', in Vernant ed. (1974) pp. 70–197

    (1992) *Mesopotamia: Writing, Reasoning and the Gods* (trans. Z. Bahrani and M. van de Mieroop of *Mésopotamie: l'écriture, la raison et les dieux*, Paris 1987) (Chicago)

Bottéro, J., Herrenschmidt, C. and Vernant, J.-P. (1996) *L'Orient ancien et nous: l'écriture, la raison, les dieux* (Paris)

Bouché-Leclercq, A. (1879–82) *Histoire de la divination dans l'antiquité*, 4 vols. (Paris)

Bowen, A. C. and Goldstein, B. R. (1989) 'Meton of Athens and Astronomy in the Late Fifth Century B.C.', in *A Scientific Humanist: Studies in Honor of Abraham Sachs*, ed. E. Leichty, M. de J. Ellis and P. Gerardi (Philadelphia) pp. 39–81

Bowman, A. K. and Woolf, G. eds. (1994) *Literacy and Power in the Ancient World* (Cambridge)

Boyer, P. (1986) 'The "Empty" Concepts of Traditional Thinking', *Man* n.s. 21: 50–64

    (1990) *Tradition as Truth and Communication* (Cambridge)

    (1993) 'Pseudo-natural Kinds', in *Cognitive Aspects of Religious Symbolism*, ed. P. Boyer (Cambridge) pp. 121–41

Boys-Stones, G. ed. (forthcoming) *Metaphor, Allegory and the Classical Tradition* (Oxford)

Bray, F. (1984) *Science and Civilisation in China*, vol. VI part 2, *Agriculture* (Cambridge)

    (1988) 'Essence et utilité: la classification des plantes cultivées en Chine', *Extrême-Orient Extrême-Occident* 10: 13–26

    (2001) 'L'Agricoltura', in Chemla ed. (2001), ch. 17, pp. 204–19

Bretschneider, E. (1892) *Botanicon Sinicum* part 2, *The Botany of the Chinese Classics* (Shanghai)

Bridgman, R. F. (1955) 'La Médecine dans la Chine antique', *Mélanges chinois et bouddhiques* 10: 1–213

Brooks, E. B. (1994) 'The Present State and Future Prospects of Pre-Han Text Studies', *Sino-Platonic Papers* 46: 1–74

Brooks, E. B. and Brooks, A. T. (1998) *The Original Analects* (New York)

Brown, D. (2000) *Mesopotamian Planetary Astronomy-Astrology* (Groningen)

Brownson, C. D. (1981) 'Euclid's Optics and its Compatibility with Linear Perspective', *Archive for History of Exact Sciences* 24: 165–94

Burkert, W. (1959) 'ΣΤΟΙΧΕΙΟΝ. Eine semasiologische Studie', *Philologus* 103: 167–97

    (1972) *Lore and Science in Ancient Pythagoreanism* (revised trans. E. L. Minar of *Weisheit und Wissenschaft*, Nuremberg, 1962) (Cambridge, MA)

Burnyeat, M. F. (1982) 'The Origins of Non-Deductive Inference', in Barnes *et al.* eds. (1982) pp. 193–238

    (2000) 'Plato on Why Mathematics is Good for the Soul', in *Mathematics and Necessity*, ed. T. Smiley (Oxford) pp. 1–81

Butler, K. D. (1966) 'The textual evolution of the *Heike Monogatari*', *Harvard Journal of Asiatic Studies* 26: 5–51

Calame, C. (1996) *Mythe et histoire dans l'antiquité grecque* (Lausanne)

(1999) 'The Rhetoric of *Muthos* and *Logos*. Forms of Figurative Discourse', in *From Myth to Reason?*, ed R. Buxton (Oxford) pp. 119–43

Calame, C. ed. (1988) *Métamorphoses du mythe en Grèce antique* (Geneva)

Cartledge, P. (1995) ' "We Are All Greeks"? Ancient (especially Herodotean) and Modern Contestations of Hellenism', *Bulletin of the Institute of Classical Studies* 40: 75–82

Cartledge, P., Cohen, E. and Foxhall, L. eds. (2001) *Money, Labour and Land* (London)

Charles, D. (2000) *Aristotle on Meaning and Essence* (Oxford)

Chavannes, E. (1898) *Les Mémoires historiques de Se-Ma Ts'ien*, vol. III. (Paris)

Chemla, K. (1992) 'Résonances entre démonstration et procédure', *Extrême-Orient Extrême-Occident* 14: 91–129

(1994) 'Nombre et opération, chaîne et trame du réel mathématique', *Extrême-Orient Extrême-Occident* 16: 43–70

Chemla, K. ed. (2001) *Storia della scienza*, vol. II, Sezione 1 *La Scienza in Cina* (Rome)

Chemla, K. and Guo Shuchun (forthcoming) *Les neuf chapitres sur les procédures mathématiques* (Paris)

Chen, Cheng-Yih (1987) 'The Generation of Chromatic Scales in the Chinese Bronze Set-Bells of the −5th Century', in *Science and Technology in Chinese Civilization*, ed. Cheng-Yih Chen (Singapore) pp. 155–97

Cheng, A. (1993) 'Ch'un ch'iu, Kung yang, Ku liang and Tsu chuan', in Loewe ed. (1993) pp. 67–76

Cheng, F. (1979) 'Bi et xing', *Cahiers de linguistique asie orientale* 6: 63–74

Clark, D. H. and Stephenson, F. R. (1977) *The Historical Supernovae* (Oxford)

Cohn-Haft, L. (1956) *The Public Physicians of Ancient Greece* (Smith College Studies in History 42, Northampton, MA)

Connor, W. R. (1993) 'The *Histor* in History', in *Nomodeiktes: Greek Studies in Honor of Martin Ostwald*, ed. R. M. Rosen and J. Farrell (Ann Arbor) pp. 3–15

Cook, C. (1995) 'Scribes, Cooks, and Artisans: Breaking Zhou Tradition', *Early China* 20: 241–77

Csikszentmihalyi, M. (1997) 'Chia I's "Techniques of the Tao" and the Han Confucian Appropriation of Technical Discourse', *Asia Major* 10: 49–67

Csikszentmihalyi, M. and Nylan, M. (forthcoming) 'Constructing Lineages and Inventing Traditions in the *Shiji* '

Cullen, C. (1980–1) 'Some Further Points of the *Shih*', *Early China* 6: 31–46

(1993) 'A Chinese Eratosthenes of the Flat Earth: A Study of a Fragment of Cosmology in *Huainanzi* ' (originally *Bulletin of the School of Oriental and African Studies* 39 (1976) 106–27) revised in Major (1993) pp. 269–90

(1996) *Astronomy and Mathematics in Ancient China: The Zhou bi suan jing* (Cambridge)

(2000) 'Seeing the Appearances: Ecliptic and Equator in the Eastern Han', *Studies in the History of Natural Sciences* 19: 352–82

Cuomo, S. (2001) *Ancient Mathematics* (London)

Daston, L. and Park, K. (1998) *Wonders and the Order of Nature* (New York)

Dawson, R. (1994) *Sima Qian: Historical Records* (Oxford)

Denyer, N. (1985) 'The Case against Divination: An Examination of Cicero's *De Divinatione*', *Proceedings of the Cambridge Philological Society* n.s. 31: 1–10

Detienne, M. (1996) *The Masters of Truth in Archaic Greece* (trans. J. Lloyd of *Les Maîtres de vérité dans la Grèce archaique*, Paris 1967) (New York)

Detienne, M. ed. (1988) *Les Savoirs de l'écriture en Grèce ancienne* (Lille)

Detienne, M. ed. (1994) *Transcrire les mythologies* (Paris)

DeWoskin, K. J. (1981) 'A Source Guide to the Lives and Techniques of Han and Six Dynasties *fang-shih*', *Society for the Study of Chinese Religions, Bulletin* 9: 79–105

(1982) *A Song for One or Two. Music and the Concept of Art in Early China* (Michigan Papers in Chinese Studies 42, Ann Arbor)

(1983) *Doctors, Diviners, and Magicians of Ancient China* (New York)

Djamouri, R. (1993) 'Théorie de la "rectification des dénominations" et réflexion linguistique chez Xunzi', *Extrême-Orient Extrême-Occident* 15: 55–74

(1999) 'Écriture et divination sous les Shang', *Extrême-Orient Extrême-Occident* 21: 11–35

Dodds, E. R. (1951) *The Greeks and the Irrational* (Berkeley)

(1963) *Proclus: The Elements of Theology* (1st edn 1933) 2nd edn (Oxford)

Drachmann, A. G. (1963) *The Mechanical Technology of Greek and Roman Antiquity* (Copenhagen)

Durkheim, E. (1915) *The Elementary Forms of the Religious Life* (trans. J. W. Swain of *Les Formes élémentaires de la vie religieuse*, Paris, 1912) (London)

Durrant, S. (1995) *The Cloudy Mirror: Tension and Conflict in the Writings of Sima Qian* (Albany)

Egan, R. C. (1977) 'Narratives in the Tso Chuan', *Harvard Journal of Asiatic Studies* 37: 323–52

Eijk, P. van der (2000–1) *Diocles of Carystus*, 2 vols. (Leiden)

Eisenstadt, S. N. ed. (1986) *The Origins and Diversity of Axial Age Civilizations* (New York)

Elman, B. (1984) *From Philosophy to Philology* (Harvard East Asian Monographs 110, Cambridge, MA)

(2000) *A Cultural History of Civil Examinations in Late Imperial China* (Berkeley)

Elman, B. and Woodside, A. eds. (1994) *Education and Society in Late Imperial China 1600–1900* (Berkeley)

Eno, R. (1990) *The Confucian Creation of Heaven* (Albany)

Evans-Pritchard, E. E. (1937) *Witchcraft, Oracles and Magic among the Azande* (Oxford)

Farquhar, J. (1994) *Knowing Practice* (Boulder, CO)

(1996) ' "Medicine and the Changes are One": An Essay on Divination Healing with Commentary', *Chinese Science* 13: 107–34

Farrington, B. (1961) *Greek Science* (1st edn 2 vols. 1944, 1949) revised edn (Harmondsworth)

Fernandez, J. W. (1982) *Bwiti: An Ethnography of the Religious Imagination in Africa* (Princeton)

Finkelstein, J. J. (1963) 'Mesopotamian Historiography', *Proceedings of the American Philosophical Society* 107.6: 461–72

Finley, M. I. (1965) 'Technical Innovation and Economic Progress in the Ancient World', *Economic History Review* 2nd ser. 18: 29–45

 (1983) *Politics in the Ancient World* (Cambridge)

Fraser, P. M. (1972) *Ptolemaic Alexandria* 3 vols. (Oxford)

 (1994) 'The World of Theophrastus' in Hornblower ed. (1994) pp. 167–91

Frede, M. (1985) *Galen: Three Treatises on the Nature of Science* (Indianapolis)

 (1987) *Essays in Ancient Philosophy* (Minneapolis)

Fritz, K. von (1952) 'Der gemeinsame Ursprung der Geschichtsschreibung und der exakten Wissenschaften bei den Griechen', *Philosophia naturalis* 2.2: 200–23

Galter, W. D. ed. (1993) *Die Rolle der Astronomie in den Kulturen Mesopotamiens* (Grazer morgenländische Studien, Graz)

Garlan, Y. (1972) *La Guerre dans l'antiquité* (Paris)

 (1974) *Recherches de poliorcétique grecque* (Paris)

Gassmann, R. H. (1988) *Cheng ming. Richtigstellung der Bezeichnungen. Zu den Quellen eines Philosophems im antiken China. Ein Beitrag zur Konfuzius-Forschung* (Etudes asiatiques suisses 7, Berne)

Gentili, B. and Paioni, P. eds. (1985) *Oralità: cultura, letteratura, discorso* (Rome)

Gernet, J. (1974) 'Petits écarts et grands écarts', in Vernant ed. (1974) pp. 52–69

Goldstein, B. R. and Bowen, A. C. (1983) 'A New View of Early Greek Astronomy', *Isis* 74: 330–40

Goody, J. (1972) *The Myth of the Bagre* (Oxford)

 (1977) *The Domestication of the Savage Mind* (Cambridge)

 (1986) *The Logic of Writing and the Organization of Society* (Cambridge)

 (1987) *The Interface between the Written and the Oral* (Cambridge)

 (1997) *Representations and Contradictions* (Oxford)

Goody, J. and Gandah, S. W. D. K. (1981) *Une Récitation du Bagré* (Classiques africains 20, Paris)

Goody, J. and Watt, I. P. (1962–3) 'The Consequences of Literacy', *Comparative Studies in Society and History* 5: 304–45 (repr. in J. Goody, ed., *Literacy in Traditional Societies*, Cambridge, 1968, pp. 27–68)

Graham, A. C. (1978) *Later Mohist Logic, Ethics and Science* (London)

 (1981) *Chuang-tzu: The Seven Inner Chapters* (London)

 (1989) *Disputers of the Tao* (La Salle, IL)

Graham, A. C. and Sivin, N. (1973) 'A Systematic Approach to the Mohist Optical Propositions', in *Chinese Science*, ed. S. Nakayama and N. Sivin (Cambridge, MA) pp. 105–52

Hankinson, R. J. (1991) 'Galen on the Foundations of Science', in *Galeno: Obra, Pensamiento e Influencia*, ed. J. A. López Férez (Madrid) pp. 15–29

Harbsmeier, C. (1981) *Aspects of Classical Chinese Syntax* (London)

 (1989) 'Marginalia Sino-logica', in *Understanding the Chinese Mind*, ed. R. E. Allinson (Oxford) pp. 125–66

(1998) *Science and Civilisation in China*, vol. VII part 1, *Language and Logic* (Cambridge)

Hardy, G. (1999) *Worlds of Bronze and Bamboo: Sima Qian's Conquest of History* (New York)

Harper, D. J. (1978–9) 'The Han Cosmic Board (*shih*)', *Early China* 4: 1–10

(1980–1) 'The Han Cosmic Board: A Response to Christopher Cullen', *Early China* 6: 47–56

(1998) *Early Chinese Medical Literature: the Mawangdui Medical Manuscripts* (London)

(1999a) 'Warring States Natural Philosophy and Occult Thought', in Loewe and Shaughnessy eds. (1999) ch. 12, pp. 813–84

(1999b) 'Physicians and Diviners: The Relation of Divination to the Medicine of the *Huangdi neijing* (Inner Canon of the Yellow Thearch)', *Extrême-Orient Extrême-Occident* 21: 91–110

(2001a) 'Iatromancy, Diagnosis, and Prognosis in Early Chinese Medicine' in Hsu ed. (2001) pp. 99–120

(2001b) 'La Nascita della medicina' in Chemla ed. (2001), ch. 18, pp. 219–27

Harris, W. V. (1989) *Ancient Literacy* (Cambridge, MA)

Hartog, F. (1988) *The Mirror of Herodotus* (trans J. Lloyd of *Le Miroir d'Hérodote*, Paris, 1980) (Berkeley)

Haudricourt, A. G. and Métailié, G. (1994) 'De l'illustration botanique en Chine', *Etudes chinoises* 13: 381–416

Havelock, E. A. (1963) *Preface to Plato* (Oxford)

(1982) *The Literate Revolution in Greece and its Cultural Consequences* (Princeton)

Heessel, N. P. (2000) *Babylonisch-assyrische Diagnostik* (Alter Orient und Altes Testament 43, Münster)

Henderson, J. B. (1984) *The Development and Decline of Chinese Cosmology* (New York)

(1991) *Scripture, Canon and Commentary* (Princeton)

Herrenschmidt, C. (1996) 'L'écriture entre mondes visible et invisible en Iran, en Israël et en Grèce', in Bottéro, Herrenschmidt and Vernant (1996) pp. 95–188

Herzog, R. (1931) *Die Wunderheilungen von Epidauros* (Philologus Suppl. Bd 22,3, Leipzig)

Ho, Peng-Yoke (1991) 'Chinese Science: The Traditional Chinese View', *Bulletin of the School of Oriental and African Studies* 54: 506–19

(forthcoming) *Chinese Mathematical Astrology: Reaching Out to the Stars* (London)

Hollis, M. and Lukes, S. eds. (1982) *Rationality and Relativism* (Oxford)

Hornblower, S. ed. (1994) *Greek Historiography* (Oxford)

Hsu, E. (2001) 'Pulse Diagnostics in the Western Han', in Hsu ed. (2001) pp. 51–91

(forthcoming) *Canggongzhuan*

Hsu, E. ed. (2001) *Innovation in Chinese Medicine* (Cambridge)

Huang Yi-long (1990) 'A Study of Five-planet Conjunctions in Chinese History', *Early China* 15: 97–112

(1991) 'Court Divination and Christianity in the K'ang Hsi Era', *Chinese Science* 10:1–20

(2001) 'Astronomia e astrologia', in Chemla ed. (2001) ch. 13, part 4, pp. 167–70

Huang Yi-long and Chang Chih-Ch'eng (1996) 'The Evolution and Decline of the Ancient Chinese Practice of Watching for the Ethers', *Chinese Science* 13: 82–106

Huang Yi-long and Moriarty-Schieven, G. H. (1987) 'A Revisit to the Guest Star of A.D. 185', *Science* 235: 59–60

Hucker, C. O. (1985) *A Dictionary of Official Titles in Imperial China* (Stanford)

Huffman, C. A. (1993) *Philolaus of Croton* (Cambridge)

Hulsewé, A. F. P. (1955) *Remnants of Han Law*, vol. 1: *Introductory Studies* (Leiden)
   (1961) 'Notes on the Historiography of the Han Period', in Beasley and Pulleyblank eds. (1961) pp. 31–43
   (1986) 'Ch'in and Han Law', in Twitchett and Loewe eds. (1986) ch. 9, pp. 520–44
   (1993) 'Shih chi', in Loewe ed. (1993) pp. 405–14

Hunger, H. (1992) *Astrological Reports to Assyrian Kings* (State Archives of Assyria 8, Helsinki)

Hunger, H. and Pingree, D. (1989) *MUL.APIN. An Astronomical Compendium in Cuneiform* (Archiv für Orientforschung, Beiheft 24, Horn)
   (1999) *Astral Sciences in Mesopotamia* (Leiden)

Immerwahr, H. R. (1960) '*Ergon*: History as a Monument in Herodotus and Thucydides', *American Journal of Philology* 81: 261–90

Irigoin, J. (1980) 'La Formation du vocabulaire de l'anatomie en grec: Du mycénien aux principaux traités de la Collection hippocratique', in *Hippocratica*, ed. M. D. Grmek (Paris) pp. 247–56

Jameson, M. H. ed. (1985) *The Greek Historians: Literature and History. Papers Presented to A. E. Raubitschek* (Stanford)

Jones, A. (1994) 'Peripatetic and Euclidean Theories of the Visual Ray', *Physis* 31: 47–76

Jones, H. S. and Powell, J. E. (1900) *Thucydides* (revised Oxford Classical text) vol. 1

Jullien, F. (1985) *La Valeur allusive. Des catégories originales de l'interprétation poétique dans la tradition chinoise* (Paris)
   (1993) *Figures de l'immanence: Pour une lecture philosophique du Yi King* (Paris)
   (1995) *The Propensity of things* (trans. J. Lloyd of *La Propension des choses*, Paris, 1992) (New York)

Kalinowski, M. (1991) *Cosmologie et divination dans la Chine antique* (Ecole française d'extrême Orient, Paris)
   (1999) 'La rhétorique oraculaire dans les chroniques anciennes de la Chine. Une étude des discours prédictifs dans le *Zuozhuan*', *Extrême-Orient Extrême-Occident* 21: 37–65
   (forthcoming) in *Storia della Scienza*, vol. III (Rome)

Kaltenmark, M. and Ngo Van Xuyet (1968) 'La Divination dans la Chine ancienne', in *La Divination*, ed. A Caquot and M. Leibovici, 2 vols., vol. 1 (Paris) pp. 333–56

Keegan, D. J. (1988) 'The "Huang-ti nei-ching": The Structure of the Compilation, the Significance of the Structure' (unpublished PhD dissertation University of California, Berkeley)

Keightley, D. N. (1979–80) 'The Shang State as Seen in the Oracle-Bone Inscriptions', *Early China* 5: 25–34

  (1984) 'Late Shang Divination: The Magico-Religious Legacy', in *Explorations in Early Chinese Cosmology* (JAAR Thematic Studies 50.2), ed. H. Rosemont (Chico, CA) pp. 11–34

  (1988) 'Shang Divination and Metaphysics', *Philosophy East and West* 38: 367–97

  (1999) 'Theology and the Writing of History: Truth and the Ancestors in the Wu Ding Divination Records', *Journal of East Asian Archaeology* 1: 207–30

Kern, M. (2000) *The Stele Inscriptions of Ch'in Shih-huang* (American Oriental Series 85, New Haven)

Kiechle, F. (1969) *Sklavenarbeit und technischer Fortschritt im römischen Reich* (Wiesbaden)

Kienast, H. J. (1995) *Samos XIX: Die Wasserleitung des Eupalinos auf Samos* (Deutsche archäologisches Institut, Bonn)

Kim Yung-Sik and Bray, F. eds. (1999) *Current Perspectives in the History of Science in East Asia* (Seoul)

Knoblock, J. (1988–94) *Xunzi. A Translation and Study of the Complete Works*, 3 vols. (Stanford)

Knoblock, J. and Riegel, J. (2000) *The Annals of Lü Buwei* (Stanford)

Knorr, W. R. (1975) *The Evolution of the Euclidean Elements* (Dordrecht)

Koch-Westenholz, U. (1995) *Mesopotamian Astrology. An Introduction to Babylonian and Assyrian Celestial Divination* (Copenhagen)

Kollesch, J. (1965) 'Galen und seine ärztlichen Kollegen', *Das Altertum* 11: 47–53

Kudlien, F. (1979) *Der griechische Arzt im Zeitalter des Hellenismus* (Akademie der Wissenschaften und der Literatur, Mainz, Abhandlungen der geistes- und sozialwissenschaftlichen Kl., Jahrgang 1979, 6, Wiesbaden)

Kuhn, T. S. (1977) *The Essential Tension* (Chicago)

Kullmann, W. and Althoff, J. eds. (1993) *Vermittlung und Tradierung von Wissen in der griechischen Kultur* (ScriptOralia 61, Tübingen)

Kuriyama, S. (1995) 'Visual Knowledge in Classical Chinese Medicine', in Bates ed. (1995), pp. 205–34

  (1999) *The Expressiveness of the Body and the Divergence of Greek and Chinese Medicine* (New York)

Labat, R. (1951) *Traité Akkadien de diagnostics et pronostics médicaux* (Paris)

Lackner, M. (1993) 'La portée des événements: Réflexions néo-confucéennes sur la "rectification des noms" (*Entretiens* 13.3)', *Extrême-Orient Extrême-Occident* 15: 75–87

Lakatos, I. (1978) *The Methodology of Scientific Research Programmes, Philosophical Papers*, vol. 1, ed. J. Worrall and G. Currie (Cambridge)

Landels, J. G. (1978) *Engineering in the Ancient World* (London)

Lasserre, F. (1976) 'L'historiographie grecque à l'époque archaïque', *Quaderni di storia* 2.4: 113–42

Lateiner, D. (1989) *The Historical Method of Herodotus* (Toronto)

Lau, D. C. (1968) 'On the Term ch'ih ying and the Story Concerning the So-called Tilting Vessel', *Symposium on Chinese Studies commemorating the Golden Jubilee of the University of Hong Kong*, vol. III (University of Hong Kong) pp. 18–33

Lau, D. C. and Ames, R. T. (1996) *Sun Pin: The Art of Warfare* (New York)

Leach, E. R. (1961) *Rethinking Anthropology* (London)

Lear, J. (1982) 'Aristotle's Philosophy of Mathematics', *Philosophical Review* 91: 161–92

Legge, J. (1891) *The Texts of Taoism*, vol. II (vol XL of *The Sacred Books of the East*, London)

Lennox, J. G. (2001) *Aristotle's Philosophy of Biology* (Cambridge)

Levi, J. (1993) 'Quelques aspects de la rectification des noms dans la pensée et la pratique politiques de la Chine ancienne', *Extrême-Orient Extrême-Occident* 15: 23–53

Lévi-Strauss, C. (1966) *The Savage Mind* (trans. of *La Pensée sauvage*, Paris, 1962) (London)

(1967) 'The Story of Asdiwal' (trans. N. Mann of 'La Geste d'Asdiwal', *Ecole Pratique des Hautes Etudes, Section des Sciences Religieuses*, 1958–9, pp. 3–43) in *The Structural Study of Myth and Totemism*, ed. E. Leach (London) pp. 1–47

(1968) *Structural Anthropology* (trans. C. Jacobson and B. G. Schoepf of *Anthropologie structurale*, Paris, 1958) (London)

(1973) *Tristes Tropiques* (trans. J. and D. Weightman of *Tristes Tropiques*, Paris, 1955) (London)

Lewis, M. E. (1990) *Sanctioned Violence in Early China* (Albany)

(1999) *Writing and Authority in Early China* (Albany)

Li Qibin (1988) 'A Recent Study on the Historical Novae and Supernovae', in *Second Workshop in High Energy Astrophysics*, ed. G. Borner (Berlin) pp. 2–25

Li Yan and Du Shiran (1987) *Chinese Mathematics: A Concise History* (trans. J. N. Crossley and A. W.-C. Lun) (Oxford)

Lin Shuen-fu (1994) 'The Language of the "Inner Chapters" of the *Chuang Tzu*', in *The Power of Culture*, ed. W. J. Peterson, A. M. Plaks and Ying-shih Yü (Hong Kong) pp. 47–69

Liu, J. J. Y. (1975) *Chinese Theories of Literature* (Chicago)

Lloyd, G. E. R. (1979) *Magic, Reason and Experience* (Cambridge)

(1983) *Science, Folklore and Ideology* (Cambridge)

(1987) *The Revolutions of Wisdom* (Berkeley)

(1990a) *Demystifying Mentalities* (Cambridge)

(1990b) 'Plato and Archytas in the Seventh Letter', *Phronesis* 35: 159–74

(1991) *Methods and Problems in Greek Science* (Cambridge)

(1996a) *Adversaries and Authorities* (Cambridge)

(1996b) *Aristotelian Explorations* (Cambridge)

(1996c) 'Theories and Practices of Demonstration in Galen', in *Rationality in Greek Thought*, ed. M. Frede and G. Striker (Oxford) pp. 255–77

Lloyd, G. E. R. ed. (2001) *Storia della scienza*, vol. 1, sez 4 *La Scienza Greco-romana* (Rome)

Lloyd, G. E. R. and Sivin, N. (2002) *The Way and the Word* (New Haven)

Loewe, M. A. N. (1974) *Crisis and Conflict in Han China* (London)

(1994) *Divination, Mythology and Monarchy in Han China* (Cambridge)

Loewe, M. A. N. ed. (1993) *Early Chinese Texts: A Bibliographical Guide* (Early China Special Monograph Series 2, Berkeley)

Loewe, M. A. N. and Shaughnessy, E. L. eds. (1999) *The Cambridge History of Ancient China. From the Origins of Civilization to 221 B.C.* (Cambridge)

Long, A. A. (1982) 'Astrology: Arguments Pro and Contra', in Barnes *et al.* eds. (1982) pp. 165–92

Mair, V. H. (1994) *Wandering on the Way* (Honolulu)

Major, J. S. (1993) *Heaven and Earth in Early Han Thought* (Albany)

Mansfeld, J. (1990) *Studies in the Historiography of Greek Philosophy* (Assen)

(1998) *Prolegomena Mathematica. From Apollonius of Perga to Late Neo-Platonism* (Philosophia Antiqua 80, Leiden)

Marincola, J. (1997) *Authority and Tradition in Ancient Historiography* (Cambridge)

Marsden, E. W. (1969) *Greek and Roman Artillery. Historical Development* (Oxford)

(1971) *Greek and Roman Artillery. Technical Treatises* (Oxford)

Martzloff, J.-C. (1997) *A History of Chinese Mathematics* (trans. S. L. Wilson of *Histoire des mathématiques chinoises*, Paris, 1988) (Berlin)

Matilal, B. K. (1971) *Epistemology, Logic and Grammar in Indian Philosophical Analysis* (Janua linguarum series minor III) (The Hague)

(1985) *Logic, Language and Reality* (Delhi)

Mendell, H. (1998a) 'Reflections on Eudoxus, Callippus and their Curves: Hippopedes and Callippopedes', *Centaurus* 40: 177–275

(1998b) 'Making Sense of Aristotelian Demonstration', *Oxford Studies in Ancient Philosophy* 16: 161–225

(2000) 'The Trouble with Eudoxus', in *Ancient and Medieval Traditions in the Exact Sciences: Essays in Memory of Wilbur Knorr*, ed. P. Suppes, J. Moravcsik and H. Mendell (Stanford) pp. 59–138

Meritt, B. D. (1961) *The Athenian Year* (Berkeley)

Mertens, M. (1995) *Les Alchimistes grecs*, vol. IV, part 1 (Paris)

Métailié, G. (1988) 'Des mots et des plantes dans le *Bencao gangmu* de Li Shizhen', *Extrême-Orient Extrême-Occident* 10: 27–43

(1992) 'Des mots, des animaux, et des plantes', *Extrême-Orient Extrême-Occident* 14: 169–83

(2001a) 'Uno sguardo sul mondo naturale' in Chemla ed. (2001), ch. 20, pp. 255–63

(2001b) 'Uno sguardo sul mondo naturale' in Chemla ed. (2001), ch. 48, pp. 536–48

Momigliano, A. (1985) 'History between Medicine and Rhetoric', *Annali della scuola normale superiore di Pisa, classe di lettere e filosofia* ser 3, 15.3, 767–80

(1990) *Classical Foundations of Modern Historiography* (Berkeley)

Moore, O. K. (1957) 'Divination – A New Perspective', *American Anthropologist* 59: 69–74

Moritz, L. A. (1958) *Grain-Mills and Flour in Classical Antiquity* (Oxford)
Mueller, I. (1981) *Philosophy of Mathematics and Deductive Structure in Euclid's Elements* (Cambridge, MA)
Murray, O. (2000) 'History', in *Greek Thought* ed. J. Brunschwig and G. E. R. Lloyd (trans. of *La Pensée grecque*, Paris, 1996) (Cambridge, MA) pp. 328–37
Needham, J. (1956) *Science and Civilisation in China*, vol. II, *History of Scientific Thought* (Cambridge)
    (1959) *Science and Civilisation in China*, vol. III, *Mathematics and the Sciences of the Heavens and the Earth* (Cambridge)
    (1965) *Science and Civilisation in China*, vol. IV part 2, *Mechanical Engineering* (Cambridge)
    (1971) *Science and Civilisation in China*, vol. IV part 3, *Civil Engineering and Nautics* (Cambridge)
    (1986) *Science and Civilisation in China*, vol. VI part 1, *Botany* (Cambridge)
Needham, J. and Robinson, K. G. (1962) *Science and Civilisation in China*, vol. IV part 1, *Physics* (Cambridge)
Needham, J. and Sivin, N. (1980) *Science and Civilisation in China*, vol. V part 4, *Spagyrical Discovery and Invention* (Cambridge)
Needham, J. and Yates, R. D. S. (1994) *Science and Civilisation in China*, vol. V part 6, *Military Technology: Missiles and Sieges* (Cambridge)
Netz, R. (1999) *The Shaping of Deduction in Greek Mathematics* (Cambridge)
Neugebauer, O. (1975) *A History of Ancient Mathematical Astronomy*, 3 vols. (Berlin)
Neugebauer, O. and Sachs, A. (1945) *Mathematical Cuneiform Texts* (American Oriental Series 29, New Haven)
Ngo Van Xuyet (1976) *Divination, magie et politique dans la Chine ancienne* (Paris)
Nienhauser, W. H. ed. (1994a) *The Grand Scribe's Records*, vol. I (Bloomington)
    (1994b) *The Grand Scribe's Records*, vol. VII (Bloomington)
Nutton, V. (1977) '*Archiatri* and the Medical Profession in Antiquity', *Papers of the British School at Rome* 45: 191–226 (repr. in *From Democedes to Harvey*, London 1988)
Nylan, M. (1992) *The Shifting Center. The Original 'Great Plan' and Later Readings* (Monumenta Serica Monograph series 24, Nettetal)
    (1993) *The Canon of Supreme Mystery* (Albany)
    (1994) 'The *chin wen/ku wen* Controversy in Han Times', *T'oung Pao* 80: 83–145
    (1998–9) 'Sima Qian: A True Historian?', *Early China* 23–4: 203–46
    (2001) *The Five 'Confucian' Classics* (New Haven)
Nylan, M. and Sivin, N. (1995) 'The First Neo-Confucianism. An Introduction to Yang Hsiung's "Canon of Supreme Mystery" (*T'ai hsuan ching*, ca. 4 B.C.)' (originally in *Chinese Ideas about Nature and Society*, ed. C. LeBlanc and S. Blader, Hong Kong, 1987, pp. 41–99), revised version in Sivin 1995b, ch. III
Ober, J. (1998) *Political Dissent in Democratic Athens* (Princeton)
O'Brien, D. (1995) 'Mathematical Definition in Selected Greek and Chinese Texts' (unpublished PhD dissertation, University of Cambridge)
Oleson, J. P. (1984) *Greek and Roman Mechanical Water-Lifting Devices* (Toronto)

Oppenheim, A. Leo (1962) 'Mesopotamian Medicine', *Bulletin of the History of Medicine* 36: 97–108

Osborne, R. and Hornblower, S. eds. (1994) *Ritual, Finance, Politics. Athenian Democratic Accounts presented to David Lewis* (Oxford)

Park, G. K. (1963) 'Divination and its Social Contexts', *Journal of the Royal Anthropological Institute* 93: 195–209

Parpola, S. (1970) *Letters from Assyrian Scholars to the Kings Esarhaddon and Assurbanipal*, part 1, *Texts* (Alter Orient und Altes Testament, 5,1, Neukirchen)

  (1983) *Letters from Assyrian Scholars to the Kings Esarhaddon and Assurbanipal*, part 2, *Commentary and Appendices* (Alter Orient und Altes Testament, 5,2, Neukirchen)

  (1993) *Letters from Assyrian and Babylonian Scholars* (State Archives of Assyria, 10, Helsinki)

Parry, J. P. (1985) 'The Brahmanical Tradition and the Technology of the Intellect', in *Reason and Morality*, ed. J. Overing (London), pp. 200–25

Petersen, J. O. (1995) 'Which Books did the First Emperor of Ch'in Burn? On the Meaning of *pai-chia* in Early Chinese sources', *Monumenta Serica* 43: 1–52

Peterson, W. J. (1994) 'Ssu-ma Ch'ien as Cultural Historian', in *The Power of Culture*, ed. W. J. Peterson, A. H. Plaks and Ying-shih Yü (Hong Kong) pp. 70–9

Phillips, N. (1981) *Sijobang. Sung narrative poetry of West Sumatra* (Cambridge)

Picken, L. E. R. (1957) 'The Music of Far Eastern Asia, I China', in *New Oxford History of Music*, vol. 1, pp. 83–114

Pines, Y. (1997) 'Intellectual Change in the Chunqiu period: the Reliability of the Speeches in the *Zuo Zhuan* as Sources of Chunqiu Intellectual History', *Early China* 22: 77–132

Pleket, H. W. (1973) 'Technology in the Greco-Roman world: a general report', *Talanta* (Proceedings of the Dutch Archaeological and Historical Society) 5: 6–47

Popper, K. R. (1962) *The Open Society and its Enemies*, 2 vols. (1st edn 1945) 4th edn (London)

Porkert, M. (1974) *The Theoretical Foundations of Chinese Medicine* (Cambridge, MA)

Porzig, W. (1934) 'Wesenhafte Bedeutungsbeziehungen', *Beiträge zur Geschichte der deutschen Sprache und Literatur* 58: 70–97

Press, G. A. (1982) *The Development of the Idea of History in Antiquity* (Kingston)

Pritchett, W. K. and Neugebauer, O. (1947) *The Calendars of Athens* (Cambridge, MA)

Qian Baocong (1963) *Suanjing shishu* (Beijing)

Queen, S. (1996) *From Chronicle to Canon* (Cambridge)

Raven, J. E. (2000) *Plants and Plant Lore in Ancient Greece* (original publication *Annales Musei Goulandris* (1990) 8: 129–80) (Oxford)

Reding, J.-P. (1985) *Les Fondements philosophiques de la rhétorique chez les sophistes grecs et chez les sophistes chinois* (Berne)

Reece, D. W. (1969) 'Technological Weakness of the Ancient World', *Greece and Rome* 16: 32–47

Reiner, E. (1999) 'Babylonian Celestial Divination', in Swerdlow ed. (1999) pp. 21–37

Reiner, E. and Pingree, D. (1975) *Babylonian Planetary Omens, part 1, the Venus Tablet of Ammiṣaduqa* (Bibliotheca Mesopotamica 2,1, Malibu)

(1981) *Babylonian Planetary Omens, part 2, Enūma Anu Enlil Tablets 50–51* (Bibliotheca Mesopotamica 2,2, Malibu)

Riddle, J. M. (1985) *Dioscorides on Pharmacy and Medicine* (Austin, TX)

Rochberg, F. (1988) *Aspects of Babylonian Celestial Divination* (Archiv für Orientforschung, Beiheft 22, Horn)

(1999) 'Empiricism in Babylonian Omen Texts and the Classification of Mesopotamian Divination as Science', *Journal of the American Oriental Society* 119: 559–69

(2000) 'Scribes and Scholars: The *ṭupšar Enūma Anu Enlil*', in *Assyriologica et semitica* (Alter Orient und Altes Testament, 252, Münster)

(2001) 'La divinazione mesopotamica. I presagi spontanei', in *Storia della scienza*, vol. 1 sezione 3, ed. M. Liverani, (Rome) pp. 249–66

Rutherford, R. B. (1994) 'Learning from History: Categories and Case-Histories', in Osborne and Hornblower eds. (1994) pp. 53–68

Saller, R. P. (1982) *Personal Patronage under the Early Empire* (Cambridge)

Schaberg, D. (1997) 'Remonstrance in Early Zhou Historiography', *Early China* 22: 133–79

Scheidel, W. (1994) *Grundpacht und Lohnarbeit in der Landwirtschaft des römischen Italien* (Frankfurt)

Schneider, H. (1992) *Einführung in die antike Technikgeschichte* (Darmstadt)

Schofield, M. (1986) 'Cicero For and Against Divination', *Journal of Roman Studies* 76: 47–65

Schürmann, A. (1991) *Griechische Mechanik und antike Gesellschaft* (Stuttgart)

Scribner, S. and Cole, M. (1981) *The Psychology of Literacy* (Cambridge, MA)

Sedley, D. N. (1982) 'On Signs', in Barnes *et al.* eds. (1982) pp. 239–72

Shankman, S. and Durrant, S. (2000) *The Siren and the Sage* (London)

Shapiro, A. E. (1975) 'Archimedes's Measurement of the Sun's Apparent Diameter', *Journal for the History of Astronomy* 6: 75–83

Shaughnessy, E. L. (1988) 'Historical Perspectives on the Introduction of the Chariot into China', *Harvard Journal of Asiatic Studies* 48: 189–237

(1996) *I Ching. The Classic of Changes* (New York)

Shaughnessy, E. L. ed. (1997) *New Sources of Early Chinese History* (Early China Special Monograph Series, 3, Berkeley)

Sigurdarson, E. S. (2002) 'Studies in *Historia*' (unpublished PhD dissertation, University of Cambridge.)

Siu, M.-K. and Volkov, A. (1999) 'Official Curriculum in Traditional Chinese Mathematics: How Did Candidates Pass the Examinations?', *Historia Scientiarum* 9: 87–99

Sivin, N. (1968) *Chinese Alchemy: Preliminary Studies* (Harvard Monographs in the History of Science 1, Cambridge, MA)

(1969) 'Cosmos and Computation in Early Chinese Mathematical Astronomy', *T'oung Pao* 55: 1–73 (revised version repr. in Sivin 1995a, ch. II)

(1987) *Traditional Medicine in Contemporary China* (Ann Arbor)

(1995a) *Science in Ancient China: Researches and Reflections*, vol. I (Aldershot)

(1995b) *Medicine, Philosophy and Religion in Ancient China: Researches and Reflections*, vol. II (Aldershot)

(1995c) 'Text and Experience in Classical Chinese Medicine', in Bates ed. (1995) pp. 177–204

(1995d) 'State, Cosmos, and Body in the Last Three centuries B.C.', *Harvard Journal of Asiatic Studies* 55: 5–37

Sleeswyk, A. W. and Sivin, N. (1983) 'Dragons and Toads. The Chinese seismoscope of A.D. 132', *Chinese Science* 6: 1–19

Smith, A. M. (1981) 'Saving the Appearances of the Appearances: The Foundations of Classical Geometrical Optics', *Archive for History of Exact Sciences* 24: 73–99

(1996) *Ptolemy's Theory of Visual Perception* (Transactions of the American Philosophical Society, 86.2, Philadelphia)

Smith, K. (forthcoming) 'Sima Tan and the Invention of Daoism "Legalism" etc.', *Journal of the Asiatic Society*

Smith, R. J. (1991) *Fortune-Tellers and Philosophers: Divination in Traditional Chinese Society* (Boulder, CO)

Smith, W. D. (1973) 'Galen on Coans versus Cnidians', *Bulletin of the History of Medicine* 47: 569–85

Staden, H. von (1982) 'Hairesis and Heresy: The case of the *haireseis iatrikai*', in *Jewish and Christian Self-Definition*, vol. III, ed. B. F. Meyer and E. P. Sanders (London) pp. 76–100, 199–206

(1989) *Herophilus: The Art of Medicine in Early Alexandria* (Cambridge)

(1995) 'Anatomy as Rhetoric: Galen on Dissection and Persuasion', *Journal of the History of Medicine and Allied Sciences* 50: 47–66

(2001) 'La Medicina nel mondo ellenistico-romano', in Lloyd ed. (2001) ch. 13, pp. 708–35

Steele, J. M. (1998) 'Predictions of Eclipse Times Recorded in Chinese History', *Journal for the History of Astronomy* 29: 275–85

Stephenson, F. R. (1997) *Historical Eclipses and Earth's Rotation* (Cambridge)

Stephenson, F. R. and Clark, D. C. (1978) *Applications of Early Astronomical Records* (Bristol)

Stol, M. (1993) 'Diagnosis and Therapy in Babylonian Medicine', *Journal of the Ancient Near Eastern Society: Ex Oriente Lux* (1991–2, Leiden 1993) 32: 42–65

Street, B. V. (1993) ed. *Cross-cultural Approaches to Literacy* (Cambridge)

(1997) 'Orality and Literacy as Ideological Constructions: Some Problems in Cross-cultural Studies', *Culture and History* 2: 7–30

Swerdlow, N. M. (1998) *The Babylonian Theory of the Planets* (Princeton)

Swerdlow, N. M. ed. (1999) *Ancient Astronomy and Celestial Divination* (Cambridge, MA)

Teng, S. Y. (1961) 'Herodotus and Ssu-ma Ch'ien: Two Fathers of History', *East and West* 12.4: 233–40

Thapar, R. (1996) *Time as a Metaphor of History in Early India* (Oxford)

Thomas, K. (1971) *Religion and the Decline of Magic* (London)

Thomas, R. (1994) 'Literacy and the City-state in Archaic and Classical Greece', in Bowman and Woolf eds. (1994) pp. 33–50

    (2000) *Herodotus in Context: Ethnography, Science and the Art of Persuasion* (Cambridge)

Todd, S. (1990) 'The Purpose of Evidence in Athenian Courts', in *Nomos*, ed. P. Cartledge, P. Millett and S. Todd (Cambridge) pp. 19–39

Twitchett, D. C. (1961) 'Chinese Biographical Writing', in Beasley and Pulleyblank eds. (1961) pp. 95–114

Twitchett, D. C. and Loewe, M. A. N. eds. (1986) *The Cambridge History of China*, vol. I, *The Ch'in and Han Empires* 221 BC–AD 220 (Cambridge)

Unschuld, P. U. (1985) *Medicine in China: A History of Ideas* (Berkeley)

Vandermeersch, L. (1977–80) *Wangdao ou la voie royale*, 2 vols. (Paris)

    (1993) 'Rectification des noms et langue graphique chinoises', *Extrême-Orient Extrême-Occident* 15: 11–21

    (1994) 'L'imaginaire divinatoire dans l'histoire en Chine', in Detienne ed. (1994) pp. 103–13

Vansina, J. (1965) *Oral Tradition* (trans. H. M. Wright of *De la tradition orale*, Tervuren, 1961) (London)

    (1985) *Oral Tradition as History* (Princeton)

Vegetti, M. (1981) 'Modelli di medicina in Galeno', in *Galen, Problems and Prospects*, ed. V. Nutton (London) pp. 47–63

    (1994) 'L'utilità della divinazione. Un argomento stoico in Tolomeo, *Tetrabiblos* I 3.5', *Elenchos* 15.2: 219–28

Vernant, J.-P. (1983) *Myth and Thought among the Greeks* (trans. of *Mythe et pensée chez les grecs*, 2nd edn, Paris, 1965) (London)

    (1996) 'Ecriture et religion civique en Grèce', in Bottéro, Herrenschmidt and Vernant (1996) pp. 191–223

Vernant, J.-P. ed. (1974) *Divination et rationalité* (Paris)

Vernant, J. P. and Gernet, J. (1983) 'Social History and the Evolution of Ideas in China and Greece from the Sixth to the Second Centuries BC', in *Myth and Society in Ancient Greece* (trans. J. Lloyd of *Mythe et société en Grèce ancienne*, Paris, 1974) (New York) pp. 79–100

Vidal-Naquet, P. (1986) *The Black Hunter* (trans. A Szegedy-Maszak of *Le Chasseur noir*, Paris, 1981) (Baltimore)

Vlastos, G. (1953) 'Isonomia', *American Journal of Philology* 74: 337–66

    (1973) *Platonic Studies* (Princeton)

    (1975) *Plato's Universe* (Oxford)

Volkov, A. (1994) 'Large Numbers and Counting Rods', *Extrême-Orient Extrême-Occident* 16: 71–92

    (1996–7) 'The Mathematical Work of Zhao Youqin: Remote Surveying and the Computation of π', *Taiwanese Journal for Philosophy and History of Science*, 5.1 (1996–7), 129–89

    (1997) 'Zhao Youqin and his Calculation of π', *Historia Mathematica* 24: 301–31

Waerden, B. L. van der (1960) 'Greek Astronomical Calendars and Their Relation to the Athenian Civil Calendar', *Journal of Hellenic Studies* 80: 168–80

Wang, Aihe (2000) *Cosmology and Political Culture in Early China* (Cambridge)

Watson, Burton (1958) *Ssu-ma Ch'ien: Grand Historian of China* (New York)

(1961) *Records of the Grand Historian of China*, 2 vols. (New York)

White, K. D. (1984) *Greek and Roman Technology* (London)

Whitehead, D. (1990) *Aineias the Tactician: How to Survive under Siege* (Oxford)

Wikander, O. ed. (2000) *Handbook of Ancient Water Technology* (Leiden)

Xi Zezong (1981) 'Chinese Studies in the History of Astronomy 1949–1979', *Isis* 72: 456–70

Xi Zezong and Po Shujen (1966) 'Ancient Oriental Records of Novae and Supernovae', *Science* 154: 597–603

Yamada Keiji (1979) 'The Formation of the *Huang-ti nei-ching*', *Acta Asiatica* 36: 67–89

(1991) 'Anatometrics in Ancient China', *Chinese Science* 10: 39–52

Yates, R. D. S. (1980) 'The Mohists on Warfare: Technology, Technique and Justification', *Journal of the American Academy of Religion* Thematic Studies Supplement 47,3: 549–603

(1988) 'New Light on Ancient Chinese Military Texts: Notes on their Nature and Evolution, and the Development of Military Specialization in Warring States China', *T'oung Pao* 74: 211–48

(1997) *Five Lost Classics* (New York)

Yavetz, I. (1998) 'On the Homocentric Spheres of Eudoxus', *Archive for History of Exact Sciences* 52: 221–78

Yu, P. (1987) *The Reading of Imagery in the Chinese Poetic Tradition* (Princeton)

Yunis, H. ed. (forthcoming) *Writing into Culture: Written Text and the Rise of Literate Culture in Ancient Greece* (Cambridge)

Zimmermann, F. (1992) 'Remarques comparatives sur la place de l'exemple dans l'argumentation (en Inde)', *Extrême-Orient Extrême-Occident* 14: 199–204

Index

IDEAS IN CONTEXT

Edited by QUENTIN SKINNER (*General Editor*),
LORRAINE DASTON, DOROTHY ROSS and JAMES TULLY

11 TERENCE BALL, JAMES FARR and RUSSELL L. HANSON (eds.)
    Political Innovation and Conceptual Change
    pb: 0 521 35978 3

12 GERD GIGERENZER *et al.*
    The Empire of Chance
    How probability changed science and everyday life
    pb: 0 521 39838 X

13 PETER NOVICK
    That Noble Dream
    The 'objectivity question' and the American historical profession
    pb: 0 521 35745 4

14 DAVID LIEBERMAN
    The Province of Legislation Determined
    Legal theory in eighteenth-century Britain
    hb: 0 521 24592 3

15 DANIEL PICK
    Faces of Degeneration
    A European disorder, c. 1848–c. 1918
    pb: 0 521 45753 X

16 KEITH BAKER
    Inventing the French Revolution
    Essays on French political culture in the eighteenth century
    pb: 0 521 38578 4

17 IAN HACKING
    The Taming of Chance
    pb: 0 521 38884 8

18 GISELA BOCK, QUENTIN SKINNER and MAURIZIO VIROLI (eds.)
    Machiavelli and Republicanism
    pb: 0 521 43589 7

19 DOROTHY ROSS
    The Origins of American Social Science
    hb: 0 521 42836 X

20 KLAUS CHRISTIAN KOHNKE
    The Rise of Neo-Kantianism
    German Academic Philosophy between Idealism and Positivism
    hb: 0 521 37336 0

21 IAN MACLEAN
    Interpretation and Meaning in the Renaissance
    The Case of Law
    hb: 0 521 41546 2